Rilke:
The
Last
Inward
Man

LESLEY CHAMBERLAIN is a British writer and critic who has written extensively on German and Russian literature and published three novels. Her books include *The Philosophy Steamer: Lenin and the Exile of the Intelligentsia*, *The Secret Artist: A Close Reading of Sigmund Freud* and *Motherland: A Philosophical History of Russia*. *Nietzsche in Turin* is also available from Pushkin Press.

Rilke: The Last Inward Man

—

Lesley Chamberlain

Pushkin Press

Pushkin Press
Somerset House, Strand
London WC2R 1LA

Copyright © 2022 Lesley Chamberlain

Rilke: The Last Inward Man was first published by Pushkin Press in 2022
This edition published 2023

1 3 5 7 9 8 6 4 2

ISBN 13: 978-1-78227-721-7

Designed and typeset by Tetragon, London
Printed and bound by Clays Ltd, Elcograf S.p.A.

www.pushkinpress.com

Contents

ONE

How to Read Rilke Today

It can only be symbolic to call one of the greatest European poets of the twentieth century the *last* inward man. Some of us, perhaps at different stages in our lives, will always be attracted to the mystical and the metaphysical. On the other hand, the age of inwardness, the flowering of cultures in the West that were individualistic and reflective, has passed. Rilke himself experienced a great shift in attitude, as more organized forms of religious worship, and faith itself, dwindled in his lifetime. He was never a believer in God. But still the idea, or, rather, the *feeling* of God, meant a great deal to him. This is one clue to what makes him not only a great poet but an important figure historically. His reputation was at its height, early in the twentieth century, when the cultural momentum was suddenly intensely secular and political. The politically engaged future challenged what art should be. Rilke's 'angels' and 'roses' suddenly seemed absurdly irrelevant. Yet it seems to me Rilke's achievement, and his standing, are all the more poignant, viewed from this crossroads in time.

In 1926, when he died aged only fifty-one, 'everyone' was reading Rainer Maria Rilke, if by everyone we can mean the English novelist Virginia Woolf and, say, the future American art critic Meyer Schapiro, who made his first trip to Europe carrying Rilke in his pocket. The Austrian modernist novelist Robert Musil was another huge admirer, while in France André Gide, a delicate novelist caught between religious inwardness and Nietzschean amoralism, and Paul Valéry, a modernist poet of comparable complexity, had both met Rilke and held him in high artistic esteem.

Musil hailed the richness of Rilke's language in a lengthy memorial address in 1927. But then, just ten years later in German-speaking circles, and just a little later in Britain, with the outbreak of war, Rilke was no longer relevant. The German critical avant-garde favoured the imagination of Kafka, a poet writing a new kind of prose; and Brecht, a poet who wanted to change the world by revolutionizing the dramatic stage.

It's easy to see why. Rilke was too refined. He appealed to an educated minority. Brecht by contrast was about to transform the lyric poem, and the very concept of theatre, in the hope of addressing the mass of people. His task was to welcome them—and *their* experience, and *their* language, rougher and hungrier and more spontaneous—into the cultural mainstream. Kafka's parables of the mysterious ways of authority meanwhile tapped a new kind of political experience. This was how the confused ordinary man found himself up against menacing 'higher' authorities. The pressure of authority was constantly there yet so hard to grasp that it went without a name. Political references back to Kafka would abound throughout the totalitarian twentieth century, whereas it was said that Rilke was not political at all. And that was true, though not, as we shall see, the whole story. Meanwhile, I wonder if any account of a great artist read in many countries, absorbed into diverse cultures, can ever be the whole story. Germany–Austria, France, Britain and the United States all had their particular Rilke timelines in the last century. Within that comparison American readers seemed to have loved Rilke uninterruptedly, because he gifted them a moving critique of the pace and style of industrial life, which otherwise they could often not bear. Rilke gave, and still gives, a function for poetry to help any and all of us withstand the materialist–technological onslaught. He is a secular bulwark, spiritual but not religious, something these days increasingly rare.[1]

The European timeline reflected the way that spiritual influence became old-fashioned so quickly, with the Continent wracked by war and in political crisis. Poetry modernized itself radically and became more social in the politically charged 1930s, in Germany especially, after defeat against England, and hyperinflation, and the rise of nationalism and organized labour power. England itself followed, but more spasmodically, and at a decade's remove, and never with quite the same relentlessness. Still, all this, and the speed of change, was a revolution, and, from our point of view here, a revolution in sensibility—a revolution in the way things were felt and evaluated. This new revolution had everything to do with what 'modern' and 'modernism' in literature meant. Those cultural phenomena—for they were more phenomenal than consciously organized—had in their turn other causes too.

Two or three decades earlier, above all, there had been an aesthetic revolution, of which Oscar Wilde and Henry James caught the outside edge, and Rilke was touched by it too. Indeed he was closer to the hub of the wheel. He was driving the change. It was there in the way he wrote. He was subjective. He wanted to tell the world about his inner feelings and how hard he found it to place himself in the world. Some of that difficulty had to do with the early years of the twentieth century, and the very way he recorded his inwardness reflected the need to find a new way to say how anxious he was. And yet, at the same time, he didn't entirely leave the nineteenth century and its calmness—and in German literature its regionalism—behind.

I will often talk about 'art' in this book. I don't like 'the arts' because that is already a commercial concept and a commodity. It's the way art goes because artists have to live, and because people who can afford it, and many who can't, want art in their lives and find a way to buy or borrow or steal it. But there, I'm saying what they want—what I want—is art, not 'the arts'. It's a great need. At the same time the word, somehow misleading in English, doesn't just mean painting. As I use the word 'art' I mean everything encompassed by the German word *die Kunst*. That includes music, sculpture, poetry and drama. (Film would be there, except it's too early in Rilke's lifetime, and his particular experience, for film.) The idea of art binds all these creative activities together in a refined, deeply worked response to what is human. Nature may be inimitably beautiful, dramatic, portentous and sublime. We can read many messages into nature. But it can never produce, of itself, what art and artists give us, namely, a record of how the life around us collides with, and stimulates, our imagination.

Take music. Classical music offers a fabulous example of what was happening to art in Rilke's Austria and Germany in the early twentieth century. Though audiences protested, already Schoenberg's atonal music seemed to express the modern technology-driven condition. It was exciting, bewildering, but also repetitive and seemingly forever unfinished. The sentimental human heart suddenly didn't know where to take refuge—and nowhere was probably the implicit answer. Face up to modernity, that is, to a certain new kind of bleakness and rawness, exposed by the age of the machine. Don't hide away.

The neo-Romantic style of composition which preceded Schoenberg was quite different. Schoenberg himself caught the tail end of the fashion, which is why many Romantic listeners prefer the richly textured, but still tonal, early work. Personally

I love to embed myself in the First String Quartet in D Minor, op. 7. I can find a home there—the kind of 'spiritual' home Rilke would often allude to, and meaning a home in the imagination. The neo-Romantics were composers like late Brahms and the searingly emotive Hugo Wolf. Their emotionally laden and discordant harmonies pointed ways out of the nineteenth century. But they did not compel the abiding Western tradition to reinvent itself, as Schoenberg did, perhaps regrettably, but necessarily, after he left that op. 7 behind.

Early Schoenberg was in-between, and in-between is roughly where I think we should place Rilke too, between these two moments in music, that is, the last notes of romanticism and the first signs of rupture. Rilke's intensely individually felt lyrics and his so-called 'thing-poems', his elegies and his sonnets were new and unique, and yet they could be absorbed into what went before—even centuries before. And so on their evidence Rilke seems, like the earliest Schoenberg, not yet 'modern' enough.

But to call Rilke conservative and exclusively aesthetic-minded diverts attention precisely from what made him new. The world he addressed was losing its spirituality, and just as Schoenberg felt music needed a new language, so Rilke toyed with whether the old language could continue: what it could refer to, and mean, as references like God and the soul lost credibility.

Rilke worked with a limited range of physical experiences. His life had a narrow focus. But his poems grew into huge questions. Born in Prague, in 1875, and living in Munich, he travelled to Italy just before the nineteenth century ended. In Rome and Florence he began to test his secular faith in the great humanist tradition. He went to Russia, spent a year in the north-German countryside, and moved, in 1902, to Paris. Confined to Munich during the Great War he was only modestly peripatetic thereafter, and gratefully accepted a Swiss bolthole purchased in his name for his last five years. When he died in 1926, of leukaemia, having struggled with terrible pain for the last two of those years, his poetry was dazzlingly new to his ever-increasing number of readers—and yet still covering ground that preoccupied him as a young man.

And so we go, back and forth, sideways into the new age. What made Rilke creative was how he responded to his limited series of environments. He relished nature and works of art everywhere, and lived among animals, birds and trees, under dark and light skies. The wind and the stars and the soil were strong presences, but people were relatively scarce. He saw them as strangers, mostly, from a distance, although there were a few people he knew well, and studied, and remembered, in a handful of special poems. Meanwhile he loved, and noticed, colours, cathedrals, Greek sculptures and children's merry-go-rounds, and flowers. Two of his most famous short poems evoked the hydrangea and the rose, and, like Van Gogh, he was fascinated by once-beautiful forms of life—blossoms, most notably—in decline. But then not only flowers. He spent months of sponsored solitude in some of the minor family houses where the entire European aristocracy— German, Danish, Bohemian—was declining. Whether we read him in the original German, or whether we come to him as the English Rilke, or the French Rilke, of the Japanese Rilke, or read him in Braille, he is a great poet, for the music of his language, and preoccupations like this, that link him to other artists, and to his times.

What made him great though, for it surely wasn't just some kind of relevance? To repeat the question and anticipate the answer this book gives, I would say he was trying to find a new sensibility for the twentieth century, at a time when a certain style of philosophy had not yet made 'the meaning of life' a naive question. His poems concern our gender and sexuality, our sense of what we ought to be doing with our lives, the possibility of the existence of God, the charmed kinship with animals which brings us such happiness, the importance of childhood, the attraction of the physical objects we make and buy and choose to live among, the landscapes we respond to, the books we read and the paintings in whose company we live. There is no object under Rilke's gaze that resists transformation into a feature of a marvellous universe that envelops us in a world that might otherwise leave us restless and afraid.

Human existential identity was the conundrum. Rilke searched not for a definition but for places and seasons that would allow him to speak of it. So it is a marvellous experience to follow daily life with his eyes, through the park and along the street, and occasionally into a more exotic landscape. The search was not for a vantage point but for a metaphor. The metaphor once found, he could transform anything. He doesn't need clichéd Romantic inspiration to enchant his readers. In his tenth Duino Elegy, for instance, he lists the kinds of places humans frequent: '*Stelle, Siedlung, Lager, Boden, Wohnort*', and we can immediately feel something significant about ourselves in that thesaurus-like list. Each of those five German words is an approximation or an aspect of something that actually we feel every day. Since they can all roughly mean 'place to live' the question is: where are we? Where do we dwell? Where do we call home, and for what reason? More questions follow. For instance, in what place do we flower and bear fruit before, like flowers, we too fade and drop? Where do we plant ourselves and where do we flourish? Ripeness is one of Rilke's preoccupations too, just as much as decline.

How to translate that string of places varies. It's 'place and dwelling, camp and ground and home' for Vita and Edward Sackville-West, the very first translators of the *Elegies*; 'place and settlement, foundation and soil and home' for the outstanding contemporary translator Stephen Mitchell; 'soil, place, village, storehouse, home' for the eccentric but sometimes illuminating Rilke pilgrim William Gass. (Notes on where to find the various translations are given at the end of this book.) The point though, however more or less successfully the nuances of the original are rendered, is that all kinds of places matter to us: our geographical location, the place we have settled with others, the place we have chosen to rest; where we were born; what is our present address. Add landscapes: mountains, valleys, meadows, streams, the river Nile, the bridge at Ronda, an ancient volcano. And townscapes: marketplaces, post offices. All these 'locations' bring out features of our human existence to help us speculate on what we are doing here, on this earth, in what Rilke indirectly called our *Weltraum*, literally the space our world occupies, though also conventionally the universe.[2] For me the right translation of the word, or, more often, evocation of the thought, will sometimes be 'space and time'.

By 1899, as he came of age amidst the most important love affair of his life, and scored his first great literary success, Rilke was well aware of the pressures falling on an idealized conception of humanity. The task of his still nominally Christian generation was crucially to respond to Darwin. Reflecting that challenge of an evolved rather than a divinely created humanity, Rilke occasionally expressed a wish to have studied biology. He did take a class in Munich just as the century turned. But mostly he read a little and improvised.[3] The point is that he was caught up in the great onslaught of the secular that followed the collapse of a Biblical version of the past. The avalanche was set in motion by persuasive evidence that it was not a force called God that created the world, according to some divine plan whose alleged goodness and higher rationality had long troubled the critical and the suffering. Evolution—though it could be made to include God, by some—was more plausible. And so Rilke, never in so many words, registered the death of God. But like Nietzsche he was radically engaged in seeking 'superabundant substitutes' for discredited metaphysical consolations, enjoying them even as they faded. Nietzsche's spirit was one of bold independence of mentality and phrase, and, likewise, Rilke sought out those substitutes in his own stunningly rich German language—a language not 'faded' at all but rather intensely vibrant.

For much of my life I've felt drawn to Rilke precisely because in his presence art can still stand in for a dying capacity for spiritual contemplation. But I've learnt to approach him now with some reservation. Theodor Adorno, the critic who in 1936 insisted the future was Kafka and not Rilke, branded Rilke's inner life a pernicious escapism, discouraging political awareness. Adorno was also the critic who not fifteen years later declared that 'to write poetry after Auschwitz is barbaric'.[4] Yet it seems obvious that the greatest poet of the Holocaust, Paul Celan, like Rilke another Germanophone writer from another corner of the lately defunct Austrian Empire, was deeply influenced by Rilke's evocation of the materiality of all things human.[5] For Celan, in the light of human evil the only moral building material left *was* language woven about earthly stuff. Moreover, from where did a German-Jewish poet in the post-war years learn that craft of language, and find a vision of equal power, but from Rilke? Both poets understood: if there is some power of goodness which shows up in the making of works of art, it is what compels us to go on reaching for the right words in the right order to give that goodness some flimsy hold on life.[6]

Take another critic of Rilke's 'inwardness' in his own time: the philosopher Ludwig Wittgenstein said Rilke was poisonous.[7] Yet we need dig only a little into Wittgenstein's own private life to find that he too was wrestling with his own introspective and depressive nature, and, surely in some way both unconscious and profound, did not want to be reminded of it in the poetry he read. Consciously Wittgenstein was as dependent on his philosophical gift for the sense of his life as Rilke was on the poetic, and had a comparable fear of loss. On the one hand Wittgenstein was deeply immersed in inwardness through his love of music; only the philosophical value was problematic because it couldn't be articulated; and then in the later work he insisted the inner life lacked value.[8]

Rilke—and I'm not the first to think this—was possibly given to us to help us withstand Wittgenstein.

Wittgenstein's particular focus was how we use language to make claims about truth and to communicate with each other. It helps me to imagine that for Wittgenstein language was a factory, like all the new factories around him in his time, and what it manufactured was meaning, pleasure and the possibility of agreement, alongside a great deal of confusion. Rilke meanwhile dwelt in a world of cities and of nature, of post offices and parklands and merry-go-rounds, and what he did was watch how human beings craft and fabricate the world they use. The disagreement with Rilke never came to a head between the two men. They never met. But had they done, and had a critic been present as a mediator, he or she would have wanted to persuade the philosopher that Rilke's poetry was art, and not a continuation of metaphysics by other means. It was about how we have our being in the world: how we use its artefacts to weave temporary meanings. The words alone are not enough. We have to keep rejoining them to the objects to which it is possible for them to point, by way of our enjoyment and enlightenment and contact with each other. There is an obvious relation to what Wittgenstein was doing, but Wittgenstein stayed within the network of words, whereas Rilke sought a *bodied* result. I mean by that poetry that speaks of and to our physical existence, and is thus, to my mind, much more satisfying than a philosophy of language that rather strips away the pleasure. For exactitude is not the only value attached to human communication. Rilke evokes our relation to iron and stone and says for instance that this is how we *are*, embedded in our material world. Perhaps therefore we don't need to know more than what this pillar of stone knows, having endured through millennia. Embedded in materials, located beneath the sky, leading diurnal lives, we shelter ourselves and we build. Of course it's not enough, in an age of science; in the modern age. Even so, from the wall and the pillar, the house and the panther, the king and the work of art, we live among a mass of active co-presences, and that is also our condition, alongside the pursuit of knowledge. Sometimes Rilke finds the fact of that existential condition *schrecklich*, 'terrifying', but often it is also wondrous.

It's hard to argue that Rilke had a social conscience. Though the sight of the poverty and sickness and the possibility that he too could end up that way filled him with fear, he was rather wary of the rise of social democracy; of its protesting presence in the streets, and the circulation of 'red' propaganda.[9] Some critics stress Rilke's 'creaturely' awareness of our common human condition.[10] He felt it and admired it when he travelled among the simple people in Russia. The impoverished streets of Paris held a painful fascination. But in my judgement taking Rilke in this *engagé* direction is an exaggerated attempt to update him. He lived an easier existence when he could.

In fact much of his 'inner'—personal—experience was desperate. No conventional religious consolation came his way for feeling lonely and displaced. The irony is the consolation he has since given to so many readers in so many countries. It's an invitation at once to expand inwardly by way of imagination, and therefore forever to enlarge on a world outside us. Rilke asks us to concentrate on inner resources to be able to find, at all, what is out there. Life is fleeting, we are fleeting. While we have time—for there is no consideration of an eternity we might inherit, only the vast immediacy of our being here—we need to respond and transform what we meet. We need to bring the sum of our experience into some kind of order—the kind that poetry can achieve, beautiful but unreconciled—before we die without any belief in a hereafter. The gist of the *Duino Elegies* is that he might as well be writing for us on our deathbed. The angels can't hear us, but why would that stop us making the effort, right to the end, with poetry to show us the way?

Although he was born in Prague and died in Switzerland, having led much of his short life in Paris, Rilke was a German lyric poet whose work appeared with a German publishing house. His success in his lifetime depended on a Germanophone audience.[11] Though he was greatly influenced by linguistically innovative later nineteenth-century French poetry, and although Ruskin and Walter Pater and the English Pre-Raphaelite painters, and later Rodin and Cézanne and Valéry, introduced aesthetic strains into his work that didn't derive from German classicism and could rightly be hailed as more generally European than specifically German, or Austrian, still the pressure on Rilke's language came from the tradition of the mighty German lyric.[12] In the patriotic years after 1914, the wife of his publisher urged him to acknowledge this bond with German literature; to make it more conscious. Rilke, though a-patriotic at best, took up reading Goethe, whom he had previously claimed to dislike. For the history of German literature this was a good moment. The publisher's wife, Katharina Kippenberg, had her way. Goethe, who moved with similar, paradigmatic ease between nature, human presence and the creation and company of works of art, reinforced Rilke's sense of a bond with the earth and the elements, and it's no bad thing to see what links these two great poets. From his middle years and on Goethe evoked a human existence rich in shared material reality and shared feeling. A similar sense of the real was elaborated by Rilke. Still it was not a case of a literary debt. It was more an unexpected affinity across the span of two centuries, and one of which Rilke would have remained unaware, had it not been pressed upon him.

A much greater affinity was the late eighteenth-century poet Friedrich Hölderlin, whose elegiac poetry Rilke discovered at one of the most difficult times of his life. *'Hier ist Fallen / das Tüchtigste,'* he wrote in tribute to that unique poet who sang the glories of ancient Greece in a German of unparalleled beauty, before his mind forsook him. 'The best we can do is fall in battle.' Rilke always liked this ancient idea, also celebrated by Hölderlin, that an early death was preferable.

> We're not here to stay; even among
> the things we love our minds suddenly fall away;
> our ripe pictures need filling again;
> lakes only occur in eternity. The best we can do
> is fall in battle. Lose touch with our schooled feelings
> and fall into some vague other world, and move on.[13]

Rilke was depressed by the First World War, which is why I've expanded the verb 'to fall' here to mean, in one of several variations, 'fall in battle'. On the other hand, in 1914, he was also reading Proust, and gathering strength to complete that unique cycle of *Duino Elegies* that both beg and defy translation into all the many languages of the world. He could still 'fill out' the most satisfying and unexpected imagery, which is why he juxtaposed bringing images to fruition while life fell away beneath his feet. Filling and falling. The verbs are as close in German as in English.

Rilke was a cosmopolitan, indifferent to nationalisms, as I just suggested, and to national traditions. He was drawn to a certain worldliness, a sort of spiritual party-going at which his genius might be fêted. But he also hid away. Like most artists he was riven with contradictions. Let those contradictions speak for themselves.

He adored the idea of childhood, the first and most wonderful party we remember. In this it is especially agreeable to read him alongside Proust.[14] The magnificent creator of *In Search of Lost Time* seems to have shared Rilke's sense of the magical and glittering, although that should probably be put the other way round, for Proust's party just went on and on. Rilke though would happily go with it. He liked fashion and ritual, and the kind of artefacts that would tempt a magpie and a child. He visited the zoo and walked in the park, attended exhibitions of painting and sculpture, and enjoyed the increasing attentions of high society as he became better known. He claimed that this range of experience, though small, was enough for any of us to know God, although not in any traditional or established sense. Transmuted into poetry the magic of childhood was a just-sufficient gesture in the direction of the truly real, or the eternal.

Can we immerse ourselves in such a thought-world today? It ought to be more difficult to read Rilke now than it actually is. The good reason for that is he had nothing in common with institutionalized religious dogma and ritual. He loved the stone and the stained glass it took to build a cathedral but he didn't stop to listen to the service. Rilke, without apology, created his own verses and images. It was as if he painted his own icons and fashioned his own statues in their niches, created nave and aisle and prayer and prayer cushion, only rarely calling them by those conventional names or expressing himself in the old spiritual grammar. He liked the word for the Lord in Russian, *gosudar*, and the word 'psalter', the same in German. He mentioned the

Bible, and within it the Old Testament and the Apocrypha, but essentially his was a new inner world of unique inventiveness.

In his middle period he is allegedly easiest to read because of his focus on objects and animals. These are the *Dinggedichte* in German: the 'thing-poems'. Those were the poems Wittgenstein wanted to reward with the famous bursary he provided, not the later, more arcane endeavours. Since Wittgenstein dedicated his life to the avoidance of obfuscation, one imagines he became impatient, feeling that the later Rilke became wilfully obscure. But let me make a case for what is sometimes too easy to call obscurity and doesn't anyway relate to any particular period in the work. I'm thinking of Rilke's use of the verb *schwingen*, for instance. Whatever dictionary equivalent the translator might settle on, or the German-speaking reader interpret to herself—and that choice is usually the far too accessible sensation of 'vibration'—this verb suggests for Rilke the stir of creation. When Rilke uses the term *schwingen* he wants to live in that moment none of us can grasp with our senses, when something inanimate moves of its own accord: a moment when life happens to things, when things ripen, and swell, and fill out, and lift—movements all, but movements we can't see, and might only guess to have as much life in them as a puff of wind. Rilke believes that the universe can come towards us as something living. This can happen, or seem to happen, when the experience is of beauty and loss, because these feelings are so strong in us. What, he asks, in a post-Darwinian age is then the *origin* of such a hope? Whatever might be the answer to that, it seems that when we intuit such universal or cosmic moments we break out of the confines of our singular time and space and have some sense of how the world *is* for us human beings.

Rilke is not fumbling with abstractions out of a vagueness in himself. He writes in 1912 at the end of the first Duino Elegy of the startling moment when

das Leere in jene
Schwingung geriet, die uns jetzt hinreißt und tröstet und hilft.

But because of all that I've just said it is indeed difficult to translate. The moment when 'the Void felt for the first time that harmony which now enraptures and comforts and helps us' lacks any hint of that delicate, logic-defying spring into life that Rilke is after: like an inanimate thing starting to breathe, like life auto-igniting in shock, in sympathy with our misery, and becoming emotionally coherent. The place where 'vacancy first felt / the vibration which now carries us, comforts and helps', also misses the target. Neither 'the Void' nor 'vacancy' sounds comforting because abstractions can't keep us company. Voids are for maths and science lessons, and architectural drawings. Vacancy is even stranger. The moment when 'space, aghast... first trembled / to that vibration of the emptiness / which draws us still, and comforts us, and helps us' is much better, because space for most of us is already a place we are in, and can perhaps imagine talking to.[15] One effect of these concluding lines of the first Elegy is that the linguistic problem actually asks us whether we believe in the visionary moment Rilke wants to convey. Even for those disinclined, he's left behind an invaluable record of how it seemed to him, a century ago.

The lines have to be beautiful and elegiac to bring about the mood, but how does Rilke do it? For one thing he recognizes what poets have celebrated for centuries: that human beauty, a beauty of physical perfection, and of love, doesn't just die. The very fear that it might has generated so many poems and legends. Rilke's first Elegy echoes a lament in Greek mythology for the death of the beautiful young Linos. German readers meanwhile must recall Schiller's 'And Beauty Too Must Die', written in 1799. Though beauty is transient in human form, it endures in poetry. Across the centuries Schiller referenced Thetis mourning the death of her son Achilles, while Rilke was always aware of how Orpheus lost Eurydice to the underworld. This loss indeed he would re-enact in his own magnificent poem 'Orpheus. Eurydike. Hermes'.

Yet when the translator introduces a sense of 'harmony' into the Rilkean moment of the universal throb of empathy, we know why.[16] Music is the nearest we can come to feeling a force which has 'the daring' to 'break through what is inert'. In Rilke's day Schoenberg invited listeners to associate this daring with his Second String Quartet. Written in 1907/8, just a couple of years after the D Minor First String Quartet, it carried a radically different message. The fourth movement, 'Entrückung', for instance, was atonal.[17] It suddenly figured music in a new realm. The dictionary definition of *Entrückung* is 'rapture'. The sense is of something that has happened to transform the way a person exists and feels. When we are rapt we are spellbound and, to draw out the etymology of the English word, stolen away. The idea is of apparent physical movement spiritually caused. This is what Rilke and Schoenberg seemed to experience. No doubt it was the fashion in their day: the way of that sensibility transitioning between the romantic and the modern. Rilke left us the evidence for how he had this experience, in, say, the *Duino Elegies*. And so too did Schoenberg when, in the Second String Quartet, his art broke with an entire instrumental tradition. Listeners to the fourth movement who expected the traditional four string instruments to continue their tortured conversations suddenly heard a single ethereal soprano voice.

For all translators there are terrible pitfalls in Rilke. Offering mostly my own translations in this book I am not setting myself above such translations as exist and continue to be made. I only want to suggest where I can that a more relaxed diction, while respecting Rilke's hugely important rhyme schemes, can stop difficult passages in German becoming impenetrable in English, for Rilke himself was not so tight.

Come back to that idea of rapture, or *Entrückung*. Just like *Schwingung*, it suggests movement, but it is not movement from A to B. One dictionary translation of *Schwingung* is 'oscillation'. Perhaps there is the idea of an alternating current building energy. In fact, *Schwingung* asks the question: what would it be for the settled matter of the universe to self-generate into motion? In the age of Einstein, and immediately post-Darwin, Rilke was groping towards new, seemingly absurd, answers, but ones that constantly referred back to Darwin's new version of our origins. So how did those origins *begin*? With Freud, who said there was never one fixed point from which a neurosis began? With Darwin, for whom to do evolutionary science was to plunge into the middle of things, never to know their starting point? I don't think we mind about origins any more than Darwin and Rilke did. We know we can't capture the ur-generic moment of who we are and what we are about. We're just here, now, in the middle of things; thrown into the world, as Heidegger said, also in response to Darwin. Rilke was exploring that feeling.

In contrast to the grand reach of his feelings, Rilke's actual world was, as I said, much smaller. The new technology that found occasional reflection in his poems was, apart from a school-boy meditation on the phonograph, concentrated in his Paris experience. It included electric light, electric trams, street lamps, motor cars and the not-so-new photograph. A photograph—and a brief meditation on what kind of a thing it was—would help him write a single poem about his father. The street lamp, *Kandelaber* in German, featured spectacularly in another poem to which I find myself returning over and over, 'Archaic Torso of Apollo'. Later Rilke would say that the poet he was should treat all things—by which he meant everything from features of nature to manufactured objects to works of art—equally. Now that was a masterstroke, because it meant that confronting—standing opposite—the most familiar and most banal object always opened up a world.[18] A world that could be described in an older spiritual language could by the same token also be simply bizarre. For Rilke defamiliarizes objects and procedures in daily use, just as did Joyce, and Wittgenstein, and he was a modernist in that.[19]

He was born into a time fascinated by how the phenomena of the world strike us as we go about our lives. The philosopher Edmund Husserl, with Rilke another great intellectual product of the late Austro-Hungarian Empire, but half a generation older, was one of the first to turn the fact that we are never free from being struck by *something* into a new form of enquiry. According to Husserl's phenomenology, our consciousness, like an open eye that cannot help but see, always has a *something* in mind, tangible and visible, or not. The theory itself is like a short Rilke poem, and Rilke actually wrote about the eye of the panther he saw in the Paris zoo. With his all-consuming eye does this creature see more than we do? The eye forms an image and then swallows that image into its depths. Phenomenology happened to philosophy because in the later nineteenth century the horizon of European poets and thinkers became visually and audibly and tangibly ever more busy. The bustling world of manufacture was suddenly full of things and events. The growth of European cities and their populations, and all the tools millions of people now needed to live, and all the objects they consumed, changed the content of consciousness.[20] Rilke fell in with many poets' disapproval of what industry and urbanization were spoiling. Where was quietness? Where was the capacity to pay attention, without distraction? (Yes, even then.) But visually what fascinated him were the juxtapositions: the panther behind bars, the fading hydrangea, a man inflicted with St Vitus's Dance, the grandeur of an eighteenth-century palace, and the first signs of traffic. He enjoyed them, at the same time as he noticed what jarred. He was caught up in modernity, but, unlike Brecht, say, with his poetic tribute to asphalt, not quite of it.

Because he was enamoured of childhood Rilke loved what he saw and ignored what a child couldn't understand. He looked at paintings and sculptures in a way that continued and preserved his innocence. His inwardness, it struck me a long time ago, when I first became a Rilkean, wasn't so much naive as, to use that word borrowed by Schoenberg again, *entrückt*: belonging to a different sphere. (Schoenberg's music was in turn inspired by a poet whom Rilke greatly admired, Stefan George.) For Rilke it was as if the spiritual absences he felt could be refined into near-presences, through poetry. His was theme and variation on what was not there, probably never was, except in the miracle of art. It was that obsession with the genesis of meaning again. Humanity had the capacity to transcend itself through imagination. Human hands, to adapt one of his fondest images, were made to reach out to an order of things that was absent but not empty. No doubt his poetry was a move towards preserving the inner world he had built for himself as a home; even a neurotic home; but the torment underlying it was radical and unconsoled. The panther's eye seems to see something, but then swallows it up; perversely keeps whatever it is from us.

TWO

The Restless Domain

A year after Rilke died, in January 1927, when Robert Musil celebrated his work in a long and enigmatic memorial speech in Berlin, he said Rilke had 'to do neither with philosophy, nor scepticism, nor with anything other than how we live things [*das Erleben*]'. That still seems absolutely right. Many critics have preferred to interpret Rilke, following his own hints, as a poet 'who praises' life. But, as Musil knew, Rilke was existentially much more unsettled, and so was his work. Musil then proposed two categories of poem, to help us understand where to place Rilke. There are poems that 'in a fixed world can heal or complete something in us; ornament our world, boost our feelings, let something new escape or begin... and there are poems that can't forget the uneasiness, the inconstancy and the fragmentariness hidden in existence as a whole'. Rilke, he felt, and again I agree, belonged to the second category. As Musil put it, for Rilke, 'the world rests like an island... on the entirety [of our feelings]'. That was what was happening in a Rilke poem; something total about our feeling for existence, but also deeply unstable. 'When he says God, this is what he means; and when he talks about a flamingo this is also what he means; that's why all the things and events in his poems are related to each other and can change places like stars which move without our being able to see it.'[1]

What is the uneasiness and fragmentariness at the heart of our experience of being here? Where does it come from and how does Rilke express it? Rilke, continued Musil, wrote 'a poetry which may lead us to a new sense for things, a new sense for God, and... following on from the medieval idea of devotion and the humanist ideal of culture... to a new picture of the world'. That was an enormous claim. But there was a sense for Rilke's readers at all times, and especially for the twentieth-century artists of all kinds who drew inspiration from him, that he did change the picture.

We could put it another way. Whatever was to be the West's new picture of the world in the twentieth century, Rilke's endeavour was central to it. There was a sense that a certain style of living and feeling was over. The political revolutions of the first two decades were only the more immediate and obvious evidence. The shift was from a nineteenth-century, bourgeois, humanist society into something that had as yet no fixed name. Brecht looked forward to the communist transformation of society and invented a new form of drama to hurry it along. In his view art—*die Kunst*, that great domain comprising all our imaginative making—should provide no more sops to middle-class complacency. Rilke could never follow that practice. He was of an entirely different sensibility. But, as Musil detected, he too was addressing an audience whose sense of direction and permanence had been radically undermined.

Darwin and Nietzsche were the prime movers of this other kind of revolution, and that's why, with respect to Darwin, Musil described Rilke's unsettled new humanity as *gellertartig*, 'gelatinous'. That would otherwise be a strange description of human life. But painters over the last fifty years had often interpreted Darwin's origin-of-species message as resembling a primeval sea.

Out of it new shapes arose, as life evolved. Rilke did not toy with the horrors of animate forms that were prehistorically less than human. But he accepted the very blurred and unstable boundaries linking history with prehistory, human with animal, flesh with stone. In the 1908 poem 'Archaic Torso of Apollo', a mysterious shimmer emanates from the stone plinth on which the torso rests. The plinth, though made of stone, has been carved to resemble a lion's skin. The stone might be thought to retain the memory of a once-living animal. I doubt Rilke had an answer to what binds culture and nature, human creativity and deep time. He was neither a scientist nor a philosopher. But he stated the question as it appeared to him: what was that glow? Whatever it was, it was something art, and the artist, could bring to present attention.

What would happen, for instance, if you subtracted the glow in this instance? At the very least, if *this* object didn't glow, then it wasn't the Archaic Torso of Apollo as a work of art, just a bit of stone:

> It would just be a misshapen boulder
> beneath its opal globes of shoulders
> and wouldn't glow like a wild beast's fur;
>
> if it didn't break like a star
> out its own body; for there's nowhere
> it's not looking at you. You must change your life.[2]

Freud imagined a chaotic unconscious functioning at a level beneath our conscious wishes and generating ever-new thoughts and images. His disciple and apostate Carl Jung imagined that there was an ur-source of creativity he called the 'collective unconscious', greater than any single creative individual could possess, and potentially common to all, underlying our creative activity. Rilke also had this feeling of imagery and form reaching back through time, changing its material makeup. As he was now writing a poem, someone once sculpted this Apollo. He asked—and that was part of the miracle that the poem evoked—what about this 'nature' that provided the stone? What about the passing of 'time' that weathered the statue? There was a slight effect of alienation, in order that these ultimate questions could be posed, but very lightly posed, as had to be, for this was not a treatise. The poem concluded with a message to a 'you' that was a message to himself and all of us: in the presence of a work of art that goes as deep as this you must change your life; otherwise you're not grasping it deeply enough.[3]

As he put it in another poem, eight years later:

> Almost everything can make us feel,
> at every turn we hear the cry: look!
> A day when everything seems unreal
> can in future be the gift we took.
>
> Who decides whence our life will stem?
> Who divides our time from years gone past?
> What way of being, having lasted,
> will know things in us, and us in them?
>
> How can cold things get warm with us beside?
> O grass O slope O dusk O village,
> suddenly you almost show your visage
> and stand embraced by us, to our lives tied.
>
> It is all one dimension. Everything is routed
> through an inner space where birds silently fly
> veering through us on their way. While I,
> the sort of man who wants to grow: in me a tree has sprouted.

I take care of myself, and in me is roof and wall.
I protect myself, and in me is hearth and fold.
When I became a lover of the beauty of it all
she, its image, lay beside me, unconsoled.[4]

Rilke's famous poem of August/September 1914, 'Es winkt zu Fühlung', is a manifesto, as if answering to that demand to change his life. It says, this is where I have arrived, as 'one who wants to grow'.

Rilke talks throughout the poem of time and space. They are what our physical situation makes us feel. We have our being in the here and now that time and space make possible. It is an extraordinary realization. It shocks and moves us emotionally that this is how we exist. But how is that? We're stranger than we think. We're creatures puzzled by the gift of existence. Rilke can make that gift more clearly visible: not give it a face (*Gesicht*) but bring it into general sight (*Ge-sicht*). He can do that because he's close enough to reality to call it by a familiar name. Creation, so often in other poems described as shy, is not afraid of him, but, as he wrote in so many other poems, he was often fearful of it.

None of this is easy, because the way Rilke expresses it is so bound up in the way he uses the particles of meaning in German to assemble his own ever-shifting universe: one now visible, and now, as he would suggest, not so much invisible as in hiding. Or this universe is a woman he takes as a lover, and the woman yields to him, but is not reconciled to what she must lose—her essential mystery, her intactness—by that act.

Around 1914 Rilke's task as a poet was to overcome his fear of experience—a strange complex on his part of far too sensitive involvement, and creative dependence, and existential disorientation—and coax whatsoever was timid and reticent about life to make itself better known. And this is what the poem also shows us.

Pay attention!—*Gedenk!*—he writes in the second line. Literally: think about it! But then a single word in a poem will often mean many things at once, in this case through its etymology, and through its relation to other key words in the language. In German (which, reader, when you change your life you must learn), *denken* is to think, *Gedanke* a thought, *Denkmal* a monument, *Gedächtnis* memory and also the capacity to memorialize. Think, therefore, reflect, meditate and, if you have the talent, create lasting works of art that grasp how time and space work for us.

This thinking is our human way. We bring our mentality and our creativity towards whatever does not have our kind of consciousness, doesn't use words, doesn't remember, and forge a bond. Our world is full of things that blow and flutter and run and fly and show themselves as green and white and red and gleam and glow; or just stand there, age-old, and so we approach them in *our* way. In my translation above I have taken the liberty of translating the imperative *Gedenk!* as 'look!' because that way the poem presents better in English. The justification would otherwise be that for so many centuries the mind and the eye were taken to be aspects of the same human power to comprehend the world as it strikes us. Rilke also often interchanges the senses, as ways of knowing. They should all be alert and our mentality should process with the utmost delicacy and precision what they find.

The 1914 poem as well as being a manifesto is a general key to Rilke. It explains why there has to be a vocabulary of instability and faint motion in the poetry as a whole. His starting point so often was the indefinite flow of things and the possibility of magical transformations of substance. As he observed in the first Duino Elegy, 'Human beings differentiate too much.' Between classes of beings, between epochs, between stationary and dynamic: *we* differentiate too much, and that is only the beginning. Often, and paradigmatically in 'Wendung', another 1914 poem, translated as

'Turning Point', he writes rhymed verse that glides through parallel realities. The rhymes are what evoke those parallel realities, and that is why it is so important to retain them in translation.

At all times in his life he is given to considering his achievement to date, and the emotional cost to him. He once wrote of his friend, the painter and illustrator Heinrich Vogeler, that it would be wrong to see him, Vogeler that was, as somehow romantic and escapist. Vogeler

> was a man of our time, struggling, like we are, seldom happy, just as we are, and full of complicated feelings. A person living in an entirely defined, but very narrowly limited reality, to which all his experiences and impressions stood in conflict. A person to whom everything appeared strange and improbable, so he could only relate it as a fairy tale and comprehend it as something that had once been… His own fairy tales… were experiences projected beyond his reality, and which he attempted to express with the limited means of that reality.[5]

In fact I don't think this was a description of Vogeler, who seems to have been a quite different man, but of Rilke himself. It defined the task and how to go about it. The poet must cross from a world of facts and differences into one of limitless possibility and fluidity, and he or she must make that crossing over and over.

In 'Almost Everything Can Make Us Feel' the crowning response is to see the beauty of the world and to love it.

> Geliebter, der ich wurde: an mir ruht
> Der schönen Schöpfung Bild und weint sich aus.

> When I became a lover of the beauty of it all
> she, its image, lay beside me, unconsoled.

I've taken a certain liberty with the syntax here, while retaining the rhyme.[6] True of all translation from German to English is the vast difference in the syntax, to which a creative solution must be found. One has to try.

Let me explain how I tried to find a solution here. An image of the beauty of creation rests beside Rilke—lies on his shoulder, as I imagine his thought—and there she weeps until she can weep no more. Rilke has in mind a post-coital sadness, a kind of cosmic loneliness in the face of that great togetherness. In my translation I've made him a lover, rather than struggle with a phrase like 'the now well-beloved', which makes him, following the literal German, the object of another's love. I've also gendered and personified as a woman that 'image of the beauty of creation' to bring out the meaning behind the two of them lying side by side. Though the passive mood is often significant in Rilke—because of the need to coax that truth out of nature, not assail it—in a consummated moment of love it does not seem to matter much who was the one first to feel the commitment.

'Unconsoled' is a different kind of choice, in place of 'weeping her fill'. I have in mind that line at the end of the first Duino Elegy where we feel sorrow at emptiness in the wake of those who have died young.[7] The idea is that Rilke attributes that feeling of acute loss also to the universe in its relation to us. It is another facet of Rilke that he gives to the universe a range of feelings sometimes akin to our own, sometimes not. Here the cosmos is a woman who feels the sadness of surrendering to love. It's surely not an uncommon feeling.

Rilke is often most satisfied by love when exploring the eroticized bond with the universe into which he has channelled his deepest feelings. Conventional human bonding, your world and mine, seems to him paradoxically to create a sense of being alone in the world. Against that his ur-love for all that is out there, all that is not us, is a gateway, endlessly to reimagine what a human life might be. A poem of August 1907, 'Die Liebende' ('A Girl in Love'), attributes this yearning to a girl, or a woman in love:

> *Das ist mein Fenster. Eben*
> *bin ich so sanft erwacht.*
> *Ich dachte, ich würde schweben.*
> *Bis wohin reicht mein Leben,*
> *und wo beginnt die Nacht?*

A stanza that begins with childlike simplicity, gazing out of a window, lifts itself into a dream of flying and ends with the fascination of boundlessness: a boundlessness that applies to 'me', whoever 'I' am. It applies to my being-here, and it applies to the night, in which 'I' will one day no longer be. *Schweben*, literally to hover, to float, to be airborne in no particular direction, is another of Rilke's favourite words. And so we see again how the dream of limitlessness—'what, amid this unfailing / endlessness am I though?'—opens up the speaker's imagination after the lover has left her bed.

This translation of two lines from the fifth stanza is James Leishman's. J. B. Leishman, a university teacher of English literature, self-taught in German, was the first translator to embed Rilke lastingly in the minds of English readers this side of the Atlantic. I only feel his opening—'That is my window. Ending / softly the dream I was in'—is not quite right. For it sets up one of those hard and fast distinctions between sleeping and waking which was just what Rilke wanted to avoid. The German original nowhere suggests something 'ending'. Rather there is such a gentle waking from sleep that the speaker is already flying in existential bliss, not caring to distinguish between light and dark.

The girl in love has woken so happily that she knows no difference between 'my life' and 'the night'. She simply exists, neither clinging to the one, not fearing the other. Rilke preferred as a way to be just this kind of enchanted lingering; preferred it to moments of decision. Spring and autumn, dawn and dusk, drowsing and wakening, all bring with them the apprehension of things beginning or ending. But change makes us sad. But then again, when actually does the change happen? Here Rilke's imagination offers to rescue us. For change is never the moment of our fullest experience. That's too stark. We're most alive when we don't yet need to distinguish between this and that. Our existence, in which whatever love does to us is one of the greatest feelings we can have, is caught up in a swirl of processes. The glowing animal pelt inscribed in the stone, the ancient statue that still moves us as art in 'Archaic Torso of Apollo', are equally embraced in the swirl.

For Rilke to extend his post-Darwinian fascination with evolution into art history, and from there to reimagine the Archaic Apollo, was a magnificent artistic gesture.[8] It even turned the subject of art history into a poem. For it asked: could there be a prehistory of art, of the materials that existed before they were gathered together, and of the idea that worked them? All 'thingliness' has a prehistory in unnamed materials not yet gathered together. Meaning too is a long time coming into being.

Rilke tried to imagine the process, as we've seen. There once was an artist and there once was the skin of a lion on which he rested, or imagined resting, his work, which was a piece of carved stone. But we can't name the artist, nor even properly know what he depicted, for the statue we see has neither arms, nor lower legs, nor neck, nor head, and no records exist to enlighten us. It is in this sense, I think, that Rilke writes, with regard to this putative Apollo, of 'his unheard-of head'. Again the phrase is difficult to translate because 'unheard-of' has several non-literal meanings, not indicating the limits of what we can know but the limits of what we can accept. Unheard-of behaviour is, in the language of the school report, 'outrageous'. Is it outrageous to art historians that in this instance the ultimate provenance of the statue and its original integrity can never be pinned down? Perhaps this is why Mitchell calls it a 'legendary head'. Yet the very word 'legend' evokes people talking, from generation to generation: talking of some magnificence we'll never see. It suggests heritage, and, via its derivation from Latin, the idea that we know about that statue because we've been reading about it.

But Rilke's implicit question is not about heritage at all. It is rather: how did this thing, *ein Ding*, a piece of stone, become a *Kunst-Ding*, an artwork? How does culture map onto prehistory? He wants, if I'm not wrong, something closer to what the philosopher Heidegger meant by the work of art going to work and thus first properly becoming an artwork. What Heidegger, via some intricate German wordplay of his own, seized upon, was the notion of 'the work of art going to work'—*das Werk am Werk*. It was the idea that from time to time a work of art springs alive.[9] At others it is as inert as the materials from which it is made. It is simply stone: simply wood.

The stone springing alive as art is the crucial topic of the poem, which is a sonnet. This torso, writes Mitchell,

> gleams in all its power. Otherwise
> the curved breast could not dazzle you so, nor could
> a smile run through the placid hips and thighs
> to that dark centre where procreation flared.

Rilke then makes clear what we already know, namely, that if we did not respond to this object as art, if it did not communicate itself as art to us, 'Otherwise this stone would seem defaced'. But 'defaced' is not quite right, for here the sense is that this armless, legless, naked torso without a head risks being hideous, 'grossly out of shape', to us, if we can't feel it as art.

Rilke writes *entstellt*, distorted, twisted, literally forced out of place. Consider then just one more time, how he demands to know whether a Darwinian cosmos can accommodate spiritual moments such as here, a piece of stone going to work as art. Spaces where meaning can happen are *Stellen*. But where a piece of stone is no longer capable of attracting our attention as art, it might be said to be deprived of such a place in the order of things: *ent-stellt*. The usual translation would be 'distorted'. But in Rilke's peculiar language the meaning based on the derivation is of cosmic matter or space which is 'without that proper quality in which meaning can spring to life'.

German interpreters of Darwin in Rilke's lifetime longed to preserve the uniqueness of the human species and thus keep traditional cultural enchantment alive. Evidently the Bible was wrong to put a figure of 4,000 years ago on the creation of the world, but the magnificence remained, crowned by human achievement. Theodor Haeckel, an outstanding biologist who was also a superb graphic artist, published books on Darwinism that were also stunning visual poetry. Wilhelm Bölsche was a hugely successful popularizer of Darwin who became known above all for his three-volume work entitled *Das Liebesleben in der Natur* (*Love-Life in Nature*). The idea—really the late nineteenth-century German idea here, as a way of interpreting Darwin—was that, the fortuitous nature of evolution notwithstanding, culture still had nature under control.[10]

Even though control was an alien idea, and he did not feel nature and culture in conflict, Rilke was part of this moment. He participated in this historical moment by exploring 'an inner space and a depth in reverse'—something over which Darwin could have no say.[11] It's this inwardness of his I'm pursuing in this book. Darwin can have no say over it, but it includes Darwin, does not dismiss, or negate, or hide from him. Rilke addresses through Darwin a huge expansion of our existential consciousness. It's not a religious moment, but if the meaning of the word had not been eroded by casual use, it might be described as awesome.

THREE

Sexuality, Childhood and the Beginning of Things

The woman, also the person, who knew Rilke best, Lou Andreas-Salomé, first encountered him as a sexually driven, artistically obsessed twenty-one-year-old. She was thirty-six and had a degree from the university of Zurich. He had taken a few university courses. They had intellectual and artistic interests in common, despite the disparity in age, and she immediately took him as her lover. It changed his life. Changed his name too, for she thought that socially he might fare better if he became the unambiguously male Rainer, rather than the ambiguous René(e).[1] He conformed, and made it his professional name, though he remained René to his mother.[2]

We don't know all we might about the tumultuous, passionate first four years of this relationship, June 1897–August 1901, when it was sexually active, though in that time Lou called herself Rilke's wife.[3] By agreement the lovers destroyed nearly all of their letters, and those that survived were censored, first by Lou's own hand, and later by their editor for publication.[4] Yet there is an enlightening commentary which is often overlooked. After the affair, and beginning in 1903–4, Lou wrote a short, revelatory book on eroticism, *Die Erotik*.[5] Although when the book appeared in 1911 it was in response to a publisher's commission, and had a larger audience in mind, the five essays, and in particular a long final footnote, were seemingly addressed to Rilke, and I will read them in that way.

As a pioneer in the field, a feminist of sorts and a future psychoanalyst, Lou analysed the many guises of sexuality, gender and what convention called love. Turning to a larger public, she in effect held up her relationship with Rainer Rilke as a model of liberation from a religious past. For with its unexpected interplay on both sides of masculine and feminine elements, uninhibited by traditional teaching, it had been

a relationship [in which] all sexual echoes are then possible, echoes of every spiritual hermaphroditism, including its physiological harmonics, and finally every amorous behaviour towards one's own sex.[6]

That swirling Darwinian vision which was about to change all our romantic inwardness already belonged to Lou and Rilke and startled and liberated them.

He was twenty-one years old, she thirty-six, and they taught each other how to use their sexuality. For one so liberated, her practical sexual life was strangely stalled. Their relationship unexpectedly consumed her in the brief period of their 'marriage'. He for his part simply lacked experience, and confidence. He was a phallocentric man, and a vigorous lover, and yet he had that disconcerting girlishness.

Once their passion was spent—Lou forced the relationship to a close—the memory of it became a testing ground, in her mind, for how sexuality needed to refind its place in a sensitive and intelligent modern world. The Church had long guided sexuality's conventional understanding. But the Darwinian revolution, the idea that the world that had not been created according to God's will, weakened the Church's authority. Lou's insight into a modern sexuality freed from divine supervision was so exceptional that Sigmund Freud treated her as a rare equal. But many people found the new sex bewildering, which is why the emerging philosopher–publisher Martin Buber commissioned Lou's monograph, to offer guidance on a crucial aspect of what was new about twentieth-century society.[7] The question the post-Darwinian era raised was: if biology determines the shape of our affections and our place in society then how, as makers of culture, do we respond? Lou, Rilke and Freud offered their liberating suggestions.

For Freud sexual intercourse was an act of 'aggression tending to the closest union'.[8] His inspiriting definition contained no reference to moral or reproductive context, nor to gender. Bisexuality, and/or gender fluidity, were fundamental to human experience, as was a sex-like passion for all sorts of people and things.[9]

Rilke was immensely interested in sexual pleasure. His work has left a trail of evidence as to how he used his sexuality to expand his poetic consciousness. Sexual feeling almost created his inwardness, his *Weltinnenraum*, because it was so overwhelming, and created such an intensity he could build on. But that meant it could hardly be what is conventionally meant by romantic love. He did desperately love Lou, but when that relationship foundered as a sexual partnership, he taught himself to become more emotionally detached from other women, and, in effect, he married his work, and never left it.

In this respect a great irony underlies the poetic oeuvre. At least two of his poems, 'Tear out my eyes; I still can see you' (1897/1901) and the 'Liebeslied' ('Love Song') of 1907, beginning 'How should I contain my soul / that it doesn't touch on yours?', are among the finest romantic lyrics ever written.[10] But there is art, and beside it life, and the artist in Rilke wanted to keep them apart. That he was madly in love with Lou, and dangerously dependent, when he wrote 'Tear out my eyes', you can see in the paragraphs in his letters to her where his repeated devotions begin to emerge as poetry.[11] But then again he only published 'Tear out my eyes' in 'The Book of Pilgrimage' (1901), in a context where it seemed to refer to a monk's love of God.[12]

As for the 1907 'Love Song', in which he yearned to keep his soul from touching that of his lover, the message seemed to offer the greatest concern for the loved one. Yet in practice, over ten intense years, he had learnt how important it was to him to keep his life free from the emotional demands of others. As he would later put it to his estranged wife Clara:

> Please let me be and trust me. Don't ask anything... of me, not even in your mind. I'll feel it otherwise, and it will occupy a place in my heart that needs to be kept simple... Don't be shocked. I am so exaggeratedly sensitive, so that it only needs an eye to rest on me and that spot goes numb. I just need to know the stars are looking down on me, that see everything all at once from their distance, and see it whole, and so don't fix anything rigidly, and leave everything free, in all things...[13]

It was a marvellous explanation, but probably not much consolation.

Rilke lacked a capacity for happy intimacy after Lou but found great purpose in his sexuality. For he realized that genital excitement stimulated imaginative renewal and adventure along the poetic road. As opposed to marriage, which interfered with his work, the uninhibited use of his body was a tool to provoke his poetry. He felt the pining, the lusting, the solitude, the jealousy, the yearning. But that wasn't the point. Exploring the sexual–emotional response fuelled his art. In the same way as a generation of English poets slightly younger than his own would reach for substances to expand consciousness, so Rilke used sex to open Aldous Huxley's doors of perception.[14] So he anticipated D. H. Lawrence in finding something cosmological and cosmogonic in his own sexuality.[15]

Rilke and Lou talked endlessly about the sexuality they revealed to each other. It was related to childhood, the way they saw their parents, and their creativity as writers. While they destroyed their letters, they poured what they learnt into their separate work. Eleven years after their overwhelming four-year intimacy ended, Rilke wrote the third Duino Elegy, which was astonishingly explicit about his sexual adolescence and its autoerotic raptures. 'It is one thing to sing of the beloved. Another, alas, / to invoke that hidden, guilty river-god of the blood.'

> The lord of desire who, often, up from the depths of his solitude,
> Even before she could soothe him, and as though she didn't exist,
> Held up his head, ah, dripping with the unknown,
> Erect, and summoned the night to an endless uproar.[16]

It took translators into English three-quarters of a century before they dared name this event.

Among the truths the very young Rilke wanted to vouchsafe to his lover was that socially he had struggled to find an object for his 'love' before he met Lou, and that creatively, still, he revelled in a perfervid activity that moved 'the dark book of the beginning' before his eyes. Was that humanly and socially acceptable? Lou, a woman almost as gifted and astonishing and sexually unconventional as he was, surely told him he needn't be ashamed. In one way, as she wrote to him at the time: 'You are so simple.'[17]

The phrase about the dark night of beginning, '[das] dunkle Buch des Anbeginns', crystallizes a poem called 'The Angels'. It was published in *The Book of Images* (1906) but actually written back in July 1899, when their raging liaison was two years old. He was in love and in lust and distraught when she abandoned him a year later.

Lou had her own memories of that time, not least a new awareness of how different individuals were, with some prematurely awake and others erotically slow to mature. An ideal of tenderness so ruled some people that it suppressed their desires. In society they might be 'discredited through devotion to an ideal of delicacy', especially when the same society at its other extreme had a 'robust idea of physical culture'.[18] She meant, of course, that while some men (and surely women) could be brutish, unfeeling lovers, others were just too timid, too deferential, too sentimental, too evasive. There were things here, physical and psychological tendencies, and the relationship between them, that a modern culture interested in happiness had to understand.

In their intimate time together she would encourage Rilke 'to behave as a creator' and thus master his sexuality.[19] He was an artist, and artists had to find their unique way. Perhaps the advice came early on, for it formed part of what he had to say in 'The Angels' of 1899:

> Their mouths are tired.
> Their bright souls have no seams.
> All the while desire (as if for sin)
> passes through their dreams.
>
> Each one quietly roams
> the gardens of the Lord.
> Each walks between the many tones
> where his power and song are stored.

Only when they spread their wings
do they cause a wind to rage.
Now God with hands of a sculptor-king
seems to move page by page
through the dark book of the beginning.

Rilke as a poet was one of those angels.

He had great affection for the Bible, including the Apocrypha. He told the young poet who sought his advice in 1903–4, and again in 1908, in the book that became *Letters to a Young Poet*, that the book of the Christian faith was indispensable to him. He asked Lou to recommend an edition of the Old and New Testament. Many Biblical allusions found their way into the poems throughout his career. Still 'God' or 'the Lord' remained a vague reference and the angels were his own invention. They were there to help him in his earliest creative task, through and beyond his desire for Lou: how to marry the sometimes sweetly, sometimes cruelly redemptive Christian stories of a Christian sexual upbringing with the visceral tug of the Dionysian.

His realm of 'the spiritual' was a place where the Dionysian (the phallic) and the Holy (the angelic) could walk side by side. The eponymous angels of the 1899 poem have 'tired mouths' (a staggeringly erotic phrase in the alliterative '*müde Münde*' in the original). Longing possesses them: '*eine Sehnsucht (wie nach Sünde)*'. 'As if for sin'. 'Sinful somehow'. They go about silently in God's garden, but we feel their presence when God the sculptor turns the pages of the dark tome of creation. Rilke brings such refinement, and fresh imagination, to the biological making of human beings, and to the old Christian story of sin in the Garden of Eden.

Lou answered him in *The Erotic* with a view of sexuality as 'the primitive, the awakening of that which is most archaic in man'.

Primitive, and yet the source for 'a primordial and spontaneous human creation, the creation of the divine'. Put another way, for this is how the poet experiences his sexuality, the erotic opens up an experience of creativity, such that 'it is as if the coming into being of the world, and the birth of the self, were being re-lived, re-experienced'.[20]

In the cultural dimension Lou had two answers to the role autoeroticism played in Rilke's artistic vision of the world. One was that an 'objectless love' was a phenomenon worthy of a name.[21] 'As if the object of love were not only itself, but also the leaf quivering on the tree,' as she put it, in a way that might have come directly from discussing it with Rilke.[22] Secondly, the narcissism she detected in both herself and Rilke did not exclude, in each case, reaching out to a lovable world beyond themselves. Rilke's sexual self-directedness was his way to empathize with others. So convinced of this was Lou that she later challenged Freud to drop his condemnation of narcissism as such.[23] Rilke's exaggerated concern with himself, his narcissistic journey within, *could* become the basis of his art.

I wonder whether, as a psychoanalyst focused on the divergence between sexual satisfaction and loving relations, she had in mind what actually happened, namely that Rilke instrumentalized the many brief relations he had with women over the years; that he felt the pain and physical frustration of breaking off, but also inflicted that condition on himself deliberately, as if to keep in touch with that 'coming into being of the world, and the birth of the self'. Lou certainly distinguished between love and sex and stated plainly that in terms of love the effects of sexual ecstasy could be illusory; even while such bliss made us individually aware of the glory of existence.[24]

Rilke had another intimate question for Lou which fascinated her, since it was one she also asked herself. What actually makes a man a man and a woman a woman, genital identity aside?[25] Are we not all a mixture? Notoriously in childhood Rilke's mother had treated him as a girl. His father in response insisted on the boy's military training. The young poet struggled and felt those stereotypes had mummified him. Lou replied: 'artists are often bisexual.' They are capable in their art of 'the affective expression of the other's sex'. They possess a 'spiritual hermaphroditism'.[26] But others feel this way too. Not just artists.

In his creative imagination Rilke often addressed himself to youthful, presexual female creatures, delighting in their delicacy. His muse in the late *Sonnets to Orpheus* was 'almost a girl... who bedded herself in my ear'. In a poem to night he addressed 'the sister inside me'.[27] This was the kind of feeling that convinced Lou, if she were to take Rilke as an example, that narcissism in general was not a limitation on empathy. It was a description she recognized also applied to herself. It was possible, moreover, even with two people as self-involved as they were, to find some common harmony and confidently speak of 'us'.[28] Lou believed it more than Rilke himself did, I think: that the 'we' has an identity all of its own, beyond the separateness, gendered or otherwise, of the two lovers.[29] For Lou all sexuality was androgynous, in its nature and in its origins. Darwin had written as much, and the 'we' created through the sexual bond restated it. Freud's act of aggression leading to unusual closeness was very much proof that a strong sense of 'we' was possible. However, Rilke resisted quite strongly, as a man, the proposition that in the beginning there was no sexual division. Hence his emphatic statement of his maleness in the third Duino Elegy. He believed his sexuality connected him to the male function in the history of our species. Yet within the poems did he associate very strongly with women in love. Mostly these women, versions of Rilke himself, were gently disorientated and melancholy in love, but sometimes they were violent.

Another message from Darwin was that not only the boundaries between man and woman, but also between the human and the animal, and the human and the landscape were not definite, and tended back to a common ancestry.[30] As Rilke the apprentice biologist heard it, and as Lou instructed him when she was reviewing Bölsche's *Love-Life in Nature*, sexuality belonged to a luxuriant ur-realm.[31] Genital love was a phenomenon of life on the planet, under the stars and sky. Rilke found some reflection of this vision in the naturalistic poetry of Arno Holz, but far more important to him was *Jugendstil*, the Austrian-German equivalent of art nouveau. Naturalism was uncompromisingly harsh, as if measuring life by means of scientific apparatus. But *Jugendstil* was elegantly androgynous, and its love of art for art's sake quickly led it away from raw human acts of the flesh towards a fresh romanticism. Stylized couples intertwined like plants.

The new erotic possibilities for art in the age of Rilke can be seen in three famous renderings of the human embrace between 1880 and 1910. In 1882 Rodin brought the humanist idea of the heterosexual couple to a new height of idealization and tenderness in his white marble sculpture *The Kiss*. By 1895, with a charcoal sketch similarly of the whole body, Edvard Munch had substituted homely intimacy, and a certain shyness, even furtiveness, for classical grace. It was as if the artist was turning away from idealization but was now unsure what to celebrate. Peter Behrens, meanwhile, in 1899, showed only the heads and faces of two almost identical beautiful human beings, lips touching, hair interlocking. These were a new kind of lover, who each lost their sexual individuality in passion. They were also quasi-mirror images of each other, as if narcissistically attracted in the first instance. The young Rilke was living all these possibilities in his love affair with Lou, and she with him.[32]

While gender stereotypes were unravelling in Germany, as in Britain, Rilke could see in his study of art history that androgyny had never been far away. From the gender-fluid angels in Renaissance art to the sexual ambivalence of the Pre-Raphaelites, male and female were intermixed.[33] Dante Gabriel Rossetti blurred the gender boundaries with his tall, beautiful sirens. Like ships' prows—an image Rilke would later use[34]—his strong-necked women were manly and yet gloriously and gracefully feminine. Edward Burne-Jones dared to paint effeminate men.

The undoing of gender stereotypes, encouraged by women entering the world of work, and their wider social presence that followed, also made way for the portrayal of women as capable of unexpected erotic violence. One of Darwin's messages was a reminder that, sentimentality aside, *all* nature was 'red in tooth and claw'. Neither the domesticated animals we admire and love, nor the 'pure' women whom good men were expected to take as their wives, were as tame and innocent as tradition had taught. Physical aggression to the point of gory murder was not restricted to the male gender. In Austria Gustav Klimt and Alphonse Mucha empowered women as lustrous sexual predators in the wake of Darwin's revelations. Richard Strauss set Oscar Wilde's play *Salome* to delirious music. Salome reached orgasm with the bloody head of John the Baptist on a plate. Rilke as late as 1911 would take an interest in the equally violent, sexually intoxicated Judith, murderer of Holofernes.[35]

O, that I am Judith, I come from him, from the tent from the
bed, his head trickling, thrice-drunk blood. Wine-drunk, drunk
on incense, drunk on me—and now sober as dew.
Low-held head above the morning grass; but I, above in my
going, I erect.

Brain suddenly empty, images flowing out into the earth; but I
am still pricked in the heart by the whole breadth of the night's
deed.[36]

A striking feature of Judith's violence is how Rilke presents it as
a regression to a going-on-all-fours; how human self-awareness
counteracts that brute fury; how nature itself is sober compared
with human self-intoxication; how the brain's images flow out
into the earth, like blood, where they will be absorbed. But then
the humanity in us has a conscience, and will not forgive. Judith's
remorse insists that the human is distinguished from the animal
morally. Sexuality though risks blurring that distinction. Lou con-
tradicted Rilke just as he was writing the Judith poem: 'We have
a sacred right to stoop,' she said.[37] In sexual excitement, whatever
the cause, inevitably we risk regression.

The encounter with Darwin is something we can see constantly recurring in Rilke's treatment of gender and sexuality.
The vegetalizing of human sexuality present in Behrens, and in
Rilke's earliest illustrator, Heinrich Vogeler, proved early on a rich
source of imagery, and a way of accommodating the human in
the cosmic. The preference for a fine-spun and lyrical vegetable
and mineral beauty over the muscularity of the Renaissance and
the rotund fleshliness of the baroque was everywhere apparent
in the *Jugendstil* art journals Rilke read and contributed to around
1900. His own future publishers, Insel Verlag, produced highly
ornamented books with specially commissioned drawings, cal-
ligraphy and endpapers.

Ancient and modern myth and legend pictured the new fascination with gender ambivalence at one remove. There was a
tendency to make humanity itself more feminine, which did not
mean soft. Glorious women appeared on the page like soldiers
for beauty, armed with jewels, and they held up the pillars of

great structures, displacing Hercules. In their midst flourished a cult more interested in Eve's fantastic birth from Adam's rib, as a model for human procreation, than in the brutishness of carnality. When painters in an earlier Christian age had equally wanted to remove animal violence from the sexual act, Renaissance painting in northern Europe had minimized the elements of sexual difference and the element of physical force entailed in the male prevailing over the female. In Lucas Cranach's *Adam and Eve* (1526) the two players possessed bodies almost identical and Adam was not an aggressor. The figures had a flatness on the canvas that together with a hint of humour drew the sting of sin from sexual congress and showed it to be a charmed human moment. Centuries ahead of their time, it seems to me, though not all critics of the painting agree, the animals on its margins are gentle fellow animals, among whom ur-man and ur-woman, defined by their genitals, take their place. Marc Chagall, meanwhile, painted non-carnal creation for the age of Rilke, with, in 1911, an almost cartoon, surreal version of Eve emerging from behind Adam's shoulder.

Rilke, never quite arriving at surrealism, despite the girl muse nestling in his ear, himself vegetalized the act of creation beautifully. The very last poem of the third and final instalment of *The Book of Hours*, 'The Book of Poverty and Death' (19–20 April 1903), celebrated St Francis as the great progenitor.

> And when he sang, yesterday itself turned back
> as did all that was forgotten;
> the nests fell silent,
> and hearts only wailed in the sisters
> whom he touched like their husband-to-be.

> But then the pollen of his song dispersed
> softly from his red mouth
> and made its way dreamily to those full of love
> and fell into the open corollas
> and sank slowly down into the fertile soil.
>
> And they received him, the immaculate one,
> in their bodies, which were their souls.
> And their eyes closed up like roses,
> and loving nights filled their hair.

A few lines on, configuring death as the second act of life, Rilke went on:

> And when he died, as noiselessly as without a name,
> it came to pass that he was scattered; his seed
> ran in streams, his seed sang in trees
> and peacefully looked upon him from the flowers.
> He lay and sang. And when the sisters came,
> it happened that they wept for their dear husband.

This poem, so painterly and so tender, and which has almost never appeared in English collections,[38] is Rilke's great early hymn to non-carnal love and reproduction.

A most unusual poem, 'Woman in Love', meanwhile, begun perhaps just a few months earlier, but not finished until 1906, told the story of a girl's birth into womanhood. Overwhelmed by desire,

> losing myself, out of my own hand,
> without hope of conquering
> what comes to me, as if out of your side

this woman, lately a girl, faces up to her sexuality for the first time, 'seriously and directly, as to something alien'. Whereupon she declares:

> in these spring weeks
> something has slowly broken me off
> from the dark unconscious year.[39]

With human beings embedded in the landscape and the seasons, sex was not sinful, not created lapsarian by a punitive god, not conventionally gendered and not burdened by innate guilt. And yet the ways of love, and the flesh, remained puzzling. Rilke's poetry is steeped in sexual and religious feelings that, having freed themselves from an older, more reassuring context, are difficult to classify. When a woman addresses her absent lover, when a nun addresses Christ, the erotic power of the relationship opens out or changes its focus into a puzzled questioning of what it is like to be here, to be a person existing on earth at a particular time and place. Rilke's point of orientation is what Heidegger meant by *Dasein*. If it's a matter of our post-Darwinian being here, from the moment we are thrown into existence, until death brings our end, how is our sexuality part of it?

Rilke drew deep inspiration from the ways of girls: not because he was sexually attracted but because he loved how they were, and could empathize, as if their bodies and feelings were his own. His 'Von den Mädchen' of September 1900, 'On the Subject of Girls', was an attempt to sort this out. He began by addressing them:

> Girls, there are poets who learn from you
> To say, what you, in your aloneness, are;
> And they learn from you to live the widest lives,
> The way the evenings through the great stars
> Become familiar with eternity.

None may give herself to a poet,
Even if his eyes are looking for a woman;
For he can only think of you as girls:
The feeling in your wrists
Would break under the weight of brocade.

Leave him alone in his garden.
He welcomed you there as eternal beings
On the walks he took daily,
Beside the benches that waited in the shade
And in the room where the lute hung.[40]

He often associated the feminine with what was soft, quiet, happy to wait and receive—virtues that seem to us gender-stereotyped today. But, as I've already suggested by highlighting the poem 'Judith's Return', these portraits need to be set against legendary instances of the sexual aggression of both sexes. Nor was Rilke timid in such matters. In 'Leda' (1907 or 1908), he repurposed the antiquated verb *halsen*, based on the word for 'neck' and meaning 'to embrace', for the swan ramming its neck into the flailing hands of the girl. This visceral assault delivered to Zeus the double pleasure of genital intercourse with Leda and becoming fully the swan whose beautiful body surprised him before he took it. 'Pietà' (1912) meanwhile moved ever closer to a profound attack on the values enshrined in the traditional religious story.[41] Rilke both cherished the Virgin Mary's sweetness and chastity and felt impelled to reject it. A German critic speaks of 'the demands of a woman's nature' asserting themselves through Mary. Rilke borrows this iconic figure and turns the Bible into legend, in order to assert 'the right of women to insist on the ferocity of their feelings'.[42] In this devastatingly abbreviated poem, full of swelling and hardness, Mary suffers Christ's physical birth and his death as her two great passions. A third suffering is insemination. The insinuation of Rilke's repetitions, linking pregnancy with moral grandeur, but also with male engorgement, are such as to foist threefold pain on the woman by the man. Once again in Rilke the physical male overwhelms and causes pain to the female, no matter that the woman is the Virgin Mary and the man her son Jesus Christ. At the end of this piercingly brief poem, moreover, Christ is lying inert across Mary's lap, as spent in death as Zeus in the lap of the ravished Leda. Rilke is not working towards a particular typology of the sexes. Rather, he delivers a sense of the strangeness and often violence of human desire and devotion, one sufficiently disquieting that critics have mostly stepped around it. In yet another poem, 'A Nun's Lament' (1909), to which we will return, a woman who has given herself as the bride of Christ, a nun, scratches him in lust and still he refuses to love her.

To the time of his intense sexual conversations and experiences with Lou, however, also belonged Rilke's recent and persistent memories of innocence. He wrote the positively Proustian 'From a Childhood' in March 1900, about his mother coming into the sleeping child's bedroom. Several poems then followed, finally collected in *The Book of Images*, about childhood and two about being a boy. The last of them was 'Kindheit' ('Childhood') (1905–6):

> And to look far off into it all;
> Men and women; men more men, women
> And then children, who are different and bright;
> And here a house and now and then a dog
> And soundless terror changing back and forth with trust—.
> O sadness without reason, O dream, O dread,
> O depth without ground.[43]

Connoisseurs will recognize in the fourth line, '*und da ein Haus und dann und wann ein Hund*', a glimpse of a much more famous line from the contemporaneous poem 'Das Karussell'. In 'The Merry-Go-Round' poem of 1906, the rhythm of the returning circus animals is finessed by the almost mystical recurrence of 'here and there a white elephant'. Here in 'Childhood' it is similarly, if less picturesquely, the same children who glimpse a wider world through gaps left by the adults clustered around them. Rilke believes, prior to puberty, in the universal capacity of the child to see 'differently and brightly' and to alternate trust with dread. Just like androgyny this capacity fed directly into his poetry. There dread, or terror, was the most famous Rilkean emotion of all.

Only what actually did it mean to see the truth of our spiritual existence as *schrecklich*? The last two lines quoted above from the 1905–6 poem run '*O Trauer ohne Sinn, o Traum, o Grauen, / o Tiefe ohne Grund*', sound out a terror that just goes on and on without a name. As Rilke piles up the names for states of mind alongside each other, 'sadness without reason', 'dream', 'dread', all take on new associations through their alliterative proximity. *Traum* and *Grauen* sound unbearably close. The sadness for no reason leads to the dreaming, but also to a kind of metaphysical anxiety, namely, that we feel 'depth', but at the same time we fear our profundity isn't attached to anything. The ground must give way beneath us, whoever, whatever we think we are. Just as Musil said.

All the while the boy whose memory has provoked this meditation continues to sail his boat on a pond. He stares at his pale face in the water. The adult remembering the boy is trying to remember '*entgleitende Vergleiche*'—similes that glide away like circles on the water.

In a companion poem from 1899 which begins: 'Boy, what is that tune you're playing?' it's the child's soul which is on show, wandering through the gardens, while his adult self prescribes what must happen to this 'song stronger than your life' if it is 'to live in what flows and is many', there 'to grow wide and wise' and avoid an excess of tenderness and artifice.[44]

Finally, in a 1902–3 poem where Rilke is fully a boy, 'Der Knabe', he is a cavalry hero as if out of a children's book of legends. The scene, set at night, is reminiscent of the passionate and fatal adventure of Cornet Christoph Rilke, the tale of his ancestor that the young Rilke told so enthrallingly it first made him a famous writer in Germany.[45] The boy in the poem drives through the night with wild horses and dreams that

> the houses fall to their knees behind us,
> the streets slant against us,
> the squares try to evade us; we seize them[46]

Our existences are random, our sexuality, often imperfectly and misleadingly socialized, is a sign of our primitive origins, and yet we often live happily, delighted by the sensations of everyday life, delighted, indeed, by all the other pictures the poet can dream up for us. In another 1901 poem Rilke felt inclined to list 'many small happinesses' as an emotional counterweight to the difficulty, including the sexual difficulty, we have in actually expressing who we are:

> People are just voices, fragments, and chance.
> A chain of good times, whose days and fears advance.
> Disguise soon spoils children, locked in what they wear,
> masks speak already, the face is not there.[47]

It's the accidental nature of cultural life Rilke ponders, as he wonders about childhood, about the ways of men and women, and the continuing possibility of addressing 'God'. When evolutionary science took hold—and it did so more powerfully in German high culture than anywhere[48]—the fragility of all our previous ways of organizing the meaning of life—natural, psychological, religious and philosophical—became apparent.

Traditional culture, focused more or less on the Christian story, was routed. Yet it left intact our many small happinesses (the 'chain of good times' in my translation above). All we need, Rilke feels at the end of the second Duino Elegy, is 'Some pure, narrow, cherishable human way of things, a strip of fruitful land that we can call our own between the river and the stony ground.'[49] Humanity, ungendered, is a narrow strip of possibility. We make poetry out of it. We re-enter nature on our own cultivated terms.

FOUR

Shall We Still Try to Believe in God?

In Rilke's life all the big things happened early and at once: love, God, who I am. The questions seize him with such intensity between the ages of twenty-two and twenty-five they are hard to separate, as he matures and grasps his talent.

Why in this context should 'God' be important? As I hope I've made plain, Rilke was not a conventionally religious man. God for him was 'one who possibly exists' or 'one who only seems to exist' or 'who left a long time ago'.[1] But he was a worshipper, as a psychological type, not a wit.[2] Diderot, that driving force of the French Enlightenment, sorted his characters into these categories. In the brazenly secular mid-eighteenth century, wits disbelieved in the sincerity or credibility of any belief. Rilke was different because he wanted to believe, and praise, what he found. When he despaired he became morbid, so he was never frivolous or cynical. Even without God the rich human response to God mattered: mattered for art and for human character.

Musil wrote: 'In a certain sense [Rilke] was the most religious poet since Novalis, but I don't know if he had religion at all. He saw things differently.'[3] The novelist Saul Bellow has an interesting passage in which typical mid-twentieth-century American Rilke readers, assuming their poet to be mystical, reject 'a crude world of finery and excrement'. In Rilke's name they spurn 'a proud, lazy civilization that worships its own boorishness', and disdain 'the fat gods'.[4] For some people the temptation is to read Rilke like that, and Bellow suggests it happens in places and times when 'most people are unpoetical'. Bellow himself knew Rilke better. With God in mind, possibly, Rilke existed on some distant, totally ahistorical periphery, standing for something, although it's difficult immediately to say what; and he himself was unique; but how?

Rilke's poetry, from Ahasuerus to Moses, John the Baptist to Jesus, tours the Christian horizon. It embraces the mute suffering of the Virgin Mary, the magic of the raising of Lazarus and the harrowing prospect of the Last Judgement. In the poetry and the letters, and in his novel *The Notebooks of Malte Laurids Brigge*, he returns over and over to the parable of the Prodigal Son. His range and style of reference derived from his Catholic childhood. The faith of his mother and her Roman Bible underpinned his fascination with Judaeo-Christian imagery and Christian stories. Later both Testaments of the Lutheran Bible, and the Apocrypha, were his teachers. Yet what God was for him was distinct from saintly pictures and heroic tales, and, indeed, he was at pains to discard those too-familiar pictures: not because they were graven images, but because they were distracting kitsch, their spiritual power long since mortified. Nor does he centre his interest on Jesus Christ. In the early poetry especially it is God who is his direct addressee. Rilke talks to God as 'you', as one would talk to a friend or a lover or a family member. This God is not a person, but a kind of living focus. As a bare minimum God exists grammatically as 'you' in order for Rilke to say something about 'what is real for me'.

Rilke's mother Sophia bequeathed him many problems, physical, psychological, psychosomatic, perhaps even sexual. 'I'm still a beginner at life and find it hard,' the troubled son told Lou—Lou who became his lover, his better mother, his analyst and his greatest friend over a lifetime.[5] Yet, as Lou knew, it was his biological mother's troubled existence, as he inherited it, that set Rilke his creative tasks. Phia Rilke, as she preferred to be known, born Sophia Entz, after separating from Rilke's father, took piety as a life crutch. She has had a bad press for much of the lifetime of Rilke scholarship, but actually much about her seems admirable today.[6] For she was a passionately independent woman against the tenor of the later nineteenth-century high-bourgeois age. (In this Lou was just like her.) Phia travelled widely and alone, and tried to make her journeys meaningful with occasional cultural journalism. She was slim, attractive and lively. Presumably what stopped her finding another partner was the indissoluble nature of a Catholic marriage. She became instead intensely neurotic, with a constant stream of physical troubles that would not have surprised Freud. Her symptoms real and imagined left her in need of constant medical counsel. Hypochondria was part of the burden laid at her son's door, who became a fussy valetudinarian in his turn. One of her great-granddaughters, the archivist and curator Hella Sieber-Rilke, who has read her writings, has observed:

> Phia Rilke's refuge after her world collapsed was her solid Catholic faith, which, if it gave her no inner peace, was nevertheless helpful to her as an external structure and resting place. The Church, less so the depth of her religiosity, created around her a new world of illusion, surrounded her with rites, ceremonies and the adoration of saints. Her empty days were divided up according to the exact following of all the Church's precepts.[7]

The same editor has since published all the son's letters to his mother, so we can see the sense he made of this distressed heritage.

His mother's piety enraged him. He found that her whole existence lacked reality, as he complained to Lou.[8] But he forbore to tell her directly. Rather, in the early days, when she too was a writer, he offered her his professional advice. After she sent him her article about a religious experience she had in Arco, Italy, at Easter 1899, this was his comment:

> I wanted to feel that this happened in Arco and could not happen anywhere else. The church of St Anna, the light and glow of Arco would have needed to find their way into words some-where—not in broad gushes of enthusiasm and not in depictions forced into being part of a spiritual event, part of the process of this inner liberation—the writing and the intention would then have been clearer. But it belongs to a very long-practised art to weave the landscape in this way into religious experience, and the immediate danger for you would have been to become too broad and circumstantial and perhaps sentimental too. *It's my opinion, by the way, that what is of the highest value is for pious minds to take their feelings and work outwards: to express outwardly the longings and sensations of their most profound experience. In this sense what is said by way of a confession is too short, it would have to flow out of the whole atmosphere, so that the reader could feel how such an exalted and simultaneously humbled person could do no other than to sink to their knees and let their sins flow away like a secret stream into the sea of divine forces.*[9]

The emphasis here is mine. It seems to me remarkable as a description of what Rilke himself would try to achieve.

In his *Letters to a Young Poet*, Rilke would become famous for talking about himself while giving advice to another. Here he was unwittingly already doing the same, to the extent of setting out a programme as to how, as a poet, he, Rainer Maria Rilke, would deal with religious emotion. To push the sensations outwards, into the landscape, would allow him to ground the inner life. He would make that life real through the quality of his art, and through pinning down as closely as possible the occasions that made those works of art happen. Rilke was not pious like Phia, but he knew the richness of the Christian world view she fed on. His unique quality was how he rerooted familiar religious feelings in a shared external world; how he transplanted them into a broad natural landscape. This was his way out of inwardness as piety. He would take religious feeling out of its confinement in a church, dissociate it from rehearsed gestures and from neurotic self-evasion, and create a context where the expression 'divine powers'—*göttliche Mächte*—could still mean something.

It was in this way that his project for the twentieth century took shape. If talk of God seemed like the most puzzling gift Phia Rilke bequeathed to her son, so too, for us, the shift in sensibility he bestrode seems difficult to name, though we can talk around it. When William James published his *Varieties of Religious Experience* in 1897 that was part of the same abrupt cultural redirection. Suddenly so many people in the Christian West had experiences that didn't seem to belong to an intelligent modern world any more. They accepted intellectually the science-oriented and materialist devaluation which the Enlightenment and Darwin brought but they remained attached to their religious responses aesthetically and emotionally. Indeed, they depended on those values to call themselves 'inward' or 'religious' at all.

And so, under pressure of his age, Rilke began transposing ecclesiastical piety into poetic legend. That was his gift. People who might have wanted to be believers could assume his work as a new foundation. His was not an answer *why* such quasi-religious feelings exist, against the scientific evidence and despite it, but a new way of showing *how* they do: the forms they can take. In the

1960s the mystically inclined English novelist Iris Murdoch laid great store by Rilke for this reason..

He spoke early and sweetly of *'der liebe Gott'*. This expression meant something like 'dear father God' or 'the old man in the sky': disbelieving, but affectionate, not scornful. The phrase was a way of reminding himself that his and Lou's psychological and intellectual interest in religion, not uncommon in the wake of James, was more sophisticated than that of the average man or woman in the street. Lou, by the time he met her, had published so much on the topic, both fiction and non-fiction, that she had amassed a substantial collection of essays to propose to a publisher.[10] Her teenaged years, in which she fell in love with the clergyman who was her tutor, and he with her, were traumatic, and culminated in her first novel, *The Struggle for God*. That relationship, never enacted, had occupied terrifyingly ambiguous ground between shared religiosity and sexual passion. Rilke followed her as a writer on such topics, half a generation later, with his thirteen stories *Vom lieben Gott*. Except that the tone was quite different.

The translator who rendered this 1899 work *Stories about the Dear Lord* got the title just right, I think, and it is still worth reading, for this is what Rilke thought of as 'spiritual'. (I take it the word has become difficult to use without careful definition today, so I will try to attach it to specific works and named feelings in all that follows.)

One stimulus to the 1899 stories had been, on a visit to Florence and Rome, the encounter with Michelangelo Buonarroti. Rilke had gazed up at the richest of Biblical motifs painted on the ceiling of the Sistine Chapel. He had examined those marvellous hands, seemingly of the sculptor, reaching out to take, or accept, the hand of God. Michelangelo showed in his own letters and poems how God reached out to the artist, as his complement and almost as an equal.[11] By 1899 though, when Rilke was travelling wide-eyed in mostly rural Russia, Russian folk tales began to jostle with Michelangelo in his head, as alternative ways of depicting God. The stories subsequently revelled in fantastical, non-Biblical accounts of God's antics and God's voice, mixing the Renaissance with Russian Orthodoxy and folk art. The involvement of the hands in the search for God would become one of Rilke's own great motifs. He also took over, already in *Vom lieben Gott*, and in poems throughout his career, Michelangelo's idea of God's indwelling in stone. A sense of 'from inside the stone'—the very stone on which the artist was working—was the beginning of Rilke's feeling for the world's inner space, that phenomenon or sensation he called *Weltinnenraum*, the place where as a poet he functioned. Soon after he also attached it to peasant Russia, where the piety of daily life entranced him.

The Book of Hours, set in Russia, was begun at the same time as the *Dear Lord* stories, and Rilke never surpassed the sweetness and intensity of feeling he poured into its first two books. *Das Stundenbuch*, especially those first two sections, 'The Book of Monastic Life' and 'The Book of Pilgrimage', was tightly structured, fluent verse close to prayer, and it seemed to ask with mesmerizing directness: shall we still try to believe in God? These good people in Russia do.[12]

The poetry of *Das Stundenbuch* flows majestically and with the greatest of ease.[13] Seizing on Rilke's own later critique, critics have seen those qualities as a fault and called the poetry facile. But I have to disagree.[14] It is astonishingly intense and daringly simple, and it happened because the first Rilkean 'landscape' God lived in was Russia. Attributed to a Russian monk praying in his cell, Rilke's extemporizations on the theme of belief created one of the most powerful religious poetry cycles of the twentieth century. Here was a gripping voice, an 'I', talking reverently, colloquially and passionately to a God, a 'you'. The poet needed a role, but, just as important, God needed someone to believe in him.

> What will you do, God, when I die?
> I am your vessel (when I am turned to dust?)
> I am your drink (when I am turned to must?)
> I am your cloth and, wear what you must,
> with[out] me you lose your sense.
>
> After me you will have no house where
> words will warmly tuck you in.
> Still for a while, when your feet are tired and your sandals fall,
> I will be inside them, your all.[15]

Nothing of Rilke's verse is easy to translate because of its two foremost features, imagery and rhyme. These make demands that seem impossible to fulfil without sacrificing a third feature, namely the syntactical logic of the original, and a fourth, to do with intelligible ellipsis. But by setting many translations side by side the reader without German will get the closest impression of Rilke's original. Here, I believe, I am offering the reader a faithful rendition of the spirit of a beautiful, too-little-known short poem.

After Rilke returned from his travels (with Lou, who was Russian-born), he called Russia his homeland. He meant his spiritual homeland. He had found a land which still had room for God. To a German-speaking public about to undergo a philosophical and religious revival, in the face of pressures from industrial modernity, he seemed to ask: can you afford to abandon God? He seemed also to embrace the Nietzschean idea that it was human beings who had recently killed God.

Thus the monk asks what humanity risks losing if the will to believe in God dwindles:

And your pictures stand before you like names.
And if the light within me ever dies,
so I no longer recognize
you, then a pale glow will fall idly on the frames.

And my senses, soon grown tame,
will be homeless. They won't be with you.[16]

Was it that the Western way of Christianity, the Renaissance legacy, of conjuring God as perfection, had become so difficult to accept? Certainly the Russian way with God now seemed more inviting, for it accommodated darkness—a concern with the night—and difficulty—what normally went unsaid—and inarticulate things.

Darkness holds the whole world tight:
figures and flames, animals and me,
and, as it takes them in its favour,
lots of people and many a powerful essence,
it may happen that a great presence
makes itself felt as my neighbour.

I believe in the night.
I believe in all that has not been said before.[17]

Just a few years after Rilke, the titanic German novelist Thomas Mann would also ask: is not Russian spirituality the way out of our German pessimism? Schopenhauer and Nietzsche have taught us to flee from the spiritual insufficiencies of the world into a religion of high art. But surely that removes us too far from all that we love materially and directly, visibly and tangibly, about that same world, with its figures and flames, animals and

me. Poet and novelist were both asking: what can be the legacy
of our nineteenth-century inwardness as we face a new age of
unbelief? Twice in the opening pages of *Vom mönchischen Leben*,
written on the cusp of the new century, Rilke has the monk note
the date on his calendar:

> I live strictly, as the century ends.
> A wind has come up as a great leaf has blown.
> What God, and you and I, have inscribed on it as known
> now high up turns in someone else's hands.
>
> A fresh page glows strange,
> everything may yet change.[18]

Further, the monk has the sense, acquired 'from foreign books',
that Michelangelo too lived in changing times, and will always
come back to us 'when an age, coming to an end, / wants to take
the measure of what it is worth'.[19]

In prose, expressed casually, Rilke wrote of Russia: 'This is
the land of the unfinished God, and out of all the gestures of
the people streams the warmth of His becoming like an infinite
blessing.'[20] The key idea here is of 'the unfinished God' who needs
the human contribution. Rilke's *unvollendet* means both imperfect
and unfinished. The monk offers himself to God variously as a
vessel on a high sea, a mirror, a useful 'apparatus' and a dream
that can be dreamt. God, be my guest! We'll build cathedrals. I
offer you wings. Yet human beings are very small creatures, barely
of significance, so their role, mine as monk, should not be exaggerated. 'I am in the world so slight and still not small enough, /
to stand before you as a thing.' 'You are so great that I no longer
exist, / the moment I draw close to you.' 'I am one of your least
significant creatures.'[21]

The tension here lies in potential human arrogance. To be hopeful is perhaps already to presume too much.[22] It has been suggested, rightly, I think, that Rilke presented a spiritual Russia of waiting and abiding as a counterweight to all he had learnt of Renaissance magnificence. Michelangelo and God competed to achieve perfection, their activity humbling an imperfect humanity. In his 'Florence Diary' Rilke had noted that Florentines of the day could hardly doubt that their pursuit of worldly power and glory had heavenly sanction. But the God he came to know in Russia couldn't clothe and feed himself; couldn't build a house; except in our imagination. And so the poetry was set to capture a longing rather than an achievement—a longing that God might accept human help. The sentiment had nothing to do with a 'perfection of the mind' that some admirers and critics have attributed to Rilke.[23]

Likewise Rilke is often said not really to belong to the history of German poetry, until he began to make that history himself. But it is characteristic of a great deal of German poetry from the mid-eighteenth century forwards that it works in a mode closely related to Christianity.[24] It was above all to the Protestant theology student Hölderlin whom Rilke would pay tribute, and to some of Pastor Eduard Mörike's loving poems about the materiality of the world that his own would be compared. Mörike, like Rilke, wrote in praise of the things of our world that God might need. But that was an affinity critics noticed, whereas the poet who stood on the threshold of the nineteenth century was Rilke's own choice. Hölderlin filtered modern religious sensibility through the Greek, not to profess a belief in gods as opposed to the Christian God, but rather to keep open the imagination to alternative heroic, pantheistic and mythical possibilities.[25] Rilke in his 1914 poem of tribute to Hölderlin almost addresses him as God, as well as the greatest poet: 'You, you glorious creature, your whole life, the way you avowed it, your task was urgently to capture it in images, and the lines took shape like fate, there was death in the mildest of them, and you entered it; only a god went ahead of you and led you out the other side.' As Rilke sees it, Hölderlin's landscape, just like his own, is the night. Moreover, his making of his poem is like the moon drawing across the sky. 'And down below in that nightscape of yours / a landscape lightens and darkens in shock at its own holiness, / and you feel it each time you move on, and are gone.' '*Die heilig erschrockene Landschaft*'—'a landscape in shock at its own holiness'—is the key phrase, and homage.[26]

And still Rilke is different, by way of being, despite himself, more philosophical about religious feeling.[27] As we reach out to touch the objects we love he has an almost childlike curiosity that something might be hiding in the spaces between them (an image he used in 'The Angels', where the Book of Creation was also a musical score). The further implication of this serious playfulness, perhaps, is that where we habitually look at objects, and name them, we forget about the spaces in between. Or we look at the foreground and ignore the background. Or we listen to sound rather than silence.

> My life is not this demanding task,
> when you see me rushing past.
> Against my background I am a tree.
> Of my many mouths, how many, three?
> The one that closes soonest is me.

> I am the silence between two tones
> which repel each other from their bones:
> because death the sound so pressingly groans—
> only in the dark interval of their moans
> are they reconciled.
>   But then the song is still beautiful.[28]

'*Gesang ist Dasein,*' he would declare many years later, in the third Sonnet to Orpheus. Song, or poetry, attentive to silence and absence, is our existence. Of course, it's not unusual for artists to claim their art as their existence. Yet again Rilke is different, with his sense of poetry as a gathering-in, and a weaving. It is a specific art: *Ge-sang*, a collective noun for the singing we do, but also *Ge-webe*, a tissue of woven threads brought together, stresses the way of fashioning the artwork. (I write them with a normally incorrect hyphen to bring out the collective aspect, which Rilke emphasized for his purpose.)

The underlying idea of *The Book of Hours* is to establish the right attitude to God. It rehearses a willingness to step in but also spiritually to make do, not to expect too much. Rilke wrote a beautiful short poem on this theme a year earlier. The poem offered a sacrifice, not to God, but to Life. Dated 16 April 1898, and set in Florence, it hymned the ripening and then gathering-in of the day and its slow merger with the benevolent darkness. Rilke had already found this idea of a good darkness before he went to Russia. It was there in Florence, too, in a complex, opulent, touristic world yet seemingly redeemed by the art of stone, and distant hints of past worship.

> Here so silent life acts out its sacrificial wont.
> Here the day deepens still. Here the night inches
> round a dream like a tower round a font.
> Here life cinches in
> its heart and light and finds its power ensconced
> in intimations: of lovely women and princely pomp,
> and of Madonnas whom thoughtful thanks have prompted,
> and of a monk in a cell who flinches...[29]

My abiding impression of *Das Stundenbuch*, years ago, was of a thin line dividing the world we know from whatever we yearn for.

Only a thin wall lies between us,
and that is chance; for it could happen:
a call from my lips or yours—
and it would silently fall in, without ado.
Because it is built of pictures of you.[30]

Those conventional pictures of God, those preset visions of the old man in the sky, or the perfect man, or the bejewelled saint, block our own imagination. They may lure us in a weak moment, but really for truth's sake we should complain, and reject them, for they get in our way.

Come back then to the human hands, which, after Michelangelo painted a finger almost touching God's, on the ceiling of the Sistine Chapel, have something celestial about them whenever Rilke mentions them.[31] Pressed together in prayer, human hands are not far off God. In Rilke perhaps they are hands drawn by Dürer: two extraordinary parallel images in German iconography. Rilke's hands concentrate as they press together. They are trying to abolish the empty space which opens up between them. However hard they press against each other, however, the gap never disappears. And so, even as we remember what Michelangelo said about God being inside the stone, we keep returning to the gaps, the wounds, the torn places, the emptinesses in between, to the open mouths, of *The Book of Hours*.[32] With stark and startling imagery Rilke set about refining the absences which human beings commonly feel when they contemplate the meaning of their lives.

What the heart misses, when it has no answers, in Rilke's experience, has a philosophical equivalent. There are those traditional humanistic arguments we would love to work, to convince us of the quasi-metaphysical meaning of our lives. But they never do, they cannot. Derrida called them 'aporias'. Both Rilke, angelic in a most ambivalent sense, and Derrida, a Jewish latecomer so often seen as diabolic in the late order of the West, were possessed by that classic Judaeo-Christian anxiety that names and images and logic preclude the God we yearn for. The names and images and logic murder God, in Nietzsche's Zarathustran formulation. So say Rilke and Derrida. That's why we must confine ourselves to the spaces. This is why Derrida, a strange late mystic, overfills his pages with multilayered expressions that mean little; why he leaps over the barriers of grammar like one of those sprites from the margins of a medieval Bible, presenting us with an impish diversion from the main text we feel we must concentrate on. So Rilke fills the intervals and spaces of sense experience with imagery that, such is his claim, will let no picture settle into meaning. The technique is to adhere very closely to the simplest facts about our human existence, and then ask those questions of God tentatively and very much later, with all answers infinitely deferred.

Where, for instance, does God live? In *The Book of Hours*, almost in passing, his address is stated as the very last house in the village.

> You are no more centred in your aura,
> where in the terpsichorean furore
> of angels music misleads distant ears—
> you live in your last house of all.
> Your whole heavens search in me and beyond my walls,
> because I and my senses have gone silent on you.[33]

Or God lives in the house after the last, which seems much more definite. But that is how grammar misleads. We can no more find him at home than before.

Or it may be that God doesn't see or hear the poet come knocking. Still the Russian monk thinks it is God who is in need. He offers to be the dream God is dreaming. God, like Rilke, has difficulty breaking through to a shared reality.

Around this time, another Rilkean monk bemoans God's failures. The people await the Last Judgement, but 'All-seeing one, I'm afraid you left a long time ago'.[34]

Since it is a Christian orthodoxy that Rilke has lapsed from, we must wonder what role Christ plays in whatever attenuated religious sentiment is still possible on the cusp of the twentieth century. Critics who say Rilke had no time for Jesus have surely missed the pathos of his calling God 'you', *Du*, as if in Christ's place. Christians have long since befriended the human Jesus and talked to him in their hearts. But instead Rilke takes God as his companion. He all but ignores the Godman, his birth and his crucifixion, as if what might be historically verified doesn't interest him. Instead he demands of his friend God this piercing, life-changing intimacy.

> Because once one man wanted you,
> I know that we can want you too.
> Even if we reject all that is deep:
> if a mountain has a seam of gold,
> yet no one now knows how to mine the fold,
> one day the river will make so bold,
> and seep into the quiet laden wold.
>
> Even when we don't wish it:
> God ripens.[35]

The prayer is offered early in 'The Book of Monastic Life'. 'The Book of Pilgrimage', meanwhile, rejects the traditional idea of 'God the Father'. Better to think of God as the monk's son. Indeed, the monk's own momentary adolescent rebellion turns a full circle in imagining God as *his* child, *his* son as an adult and *his* son as an old man.

This is our father, they say. And I—
I should call you father?
But that would to be cut myself off from you. Rather
you are my son. I will know you,
as one knows one's unique child, know you
as a man, and as an old man.[36]

It seems to me a dramatist has worked this image, taking from the traditional Christian story the intimacy of the faith's deepest and most fundamental bond, freeing it from the traditional players and turning the intense feeling into a new mystery. This has much to do with Rilke's interest, shared with Lou, in the psychology powering the conventions of faith, and what might be made and remade of that extraordinary human energy.

How could one otherwise place that tumultuous love poem, the one brimming with sentiments inspired by Lou, that immediately follows the seizing of God as one's own son? Here the same sentiments are addressed to God as if from a monk who confesses, 'And my soul is a woman in your presence.'

Tear out my eyes; it's you I can see.
Stop up my ears: it's you I can hear.
And I can walk to you without feet.
And I can talk to you without lips.
Break off my arms: I'll hold you
using my heart just like using my fingers,
seize my heart and my brain still lingers,
and if you set my brain on fire,
I will carry you on my bloody pyre.[37]

The great religious emotions of emotional steadfastness, devotion and service are anthropomorphized in the bond of romantic love. We human beings can feel nothing greater.

The development of Rilke's ideas on God, from *Stories about the Dear Lord*, where God is a neglected old man locked up in a tower and never visited, to *The Book of Hours*, where God is absent, to the *Duino Elegies*, where the angels don't even hear the human cry, throws up too many common themes to mention here. The first half-line of the second Elegy, *'jeder Engel ist schrecklich'*—'every angel is terrible'—may be the most famous Rilke ever wrote. But the terror is somewhat empty without its surrounding imagery, nor is 'terror', in English, enough on its own. Terror, shock, horror and awe all mark the moment. We're halted in our tracks by the grandeur of things; as in that *'heilig erschrockene Landschaft'* in Rilke's tribute to Hölderlin. The world at first light is shocked by its own beauty. So are we, overwhelmed, but not unhappily. The moment may be sublime, but it is not a terror that is frightening. William James had analysed such moments in believers' lives.

Between the landmarks of Rilke's religious experience there is not a great distance between the absent, needy God and the unhearing angels, only a shift into a less conventional, mostly non-Biblical way of speaking. The monk has gone. The poet is more a man of the world, just. He knows what a fairground looks like, and how life in a small town might go.

In the last published work, the *Sonnets to Orpheus*, Rilke told us that the poet's role, at least *his* role, was to praise what he found. But the legacy of religious inwardness in the Christian West was losing its grip on people's credulousness, and their patience. His brilliance was to make poetry out of that too:

> The kings of the world are old
> and no one will inherit.
> The sons don't mature before they die
> and their pale daughters forced to conspire
> with putrid power lie with men without merit.

The rabble smash the crowns for money,
and the man now master of us all
forges that metal into new machines
that clumsily serve his will;
how unhappy those machines are.
Iron ore is homesick; if it could leave
the coins and wheels it would,
because the life they teach is corrupt.
And out of factories and tills
it would return to fill up the veins
of the open mountains,
which would then close up.[38]

Rilke turns the intensity of loss back out into the world, and there he finds correlatives for occult yearning in the tinsel of the fairground, as well as in the mysterious company of animals and stone. All this is in his compass, not simply 'praising'. He has to keep his imagination alive; so he keeps looking around for where to let it linger. There is that extraordinary image we saw just now of the Russian monk offering to live in God's sandals; to be the vessel and the drink, and the house and the comfort of dwelling there. The whole vision is really a wonderful extended image of human hospitality towards a possibly non-existent guest. There is the hope for a very tentatively existent God to be safe at night when the poet renews his offer—really a lonely search—to find new spaces to move into the next day.

FIVE

Paris (1)

Surviving the City

In the summer of 1901 Rilke met, not for the first time, the art publisher and critic Richard Muther, and they talked with enthusiasm of the bold artistic scene in contemporary Paris. The city was the capital of European aesthetic experiment, and Muther was about to publish a book of his own about the preceding, foundational century.[1] Comparing themselves with Paris, German artists were passionately aware of their late start in painting.

Muther stepped into a time of artistic excitement as a popularizer, businessman and genuine art-lover. Several of Rilke's recently acquired German friends, as his life moved on from intimacy with Lou Salomé, had studied art in Paris. Muther visited them in the artists' colony in Worpswede, near Bremen, where they lived and worked. The talk under a vast, low, north-German sky was of nothing but the avant-garde. Rilke's ambitious and unusual new sculptor friend Clara Westhoff, soon to become his wife, had even studied with Auguste Rodin. And so began Rilke's Paris, in a season of 'People at Night', talking, drinking wine and planning the future.[2]

The two young artists married on 29 April 1901. But then the birth of their daughter Ruth on 12 December 1901 plunged their life into difficulty. There was no money. With marriage Rilke's entitlement to an allowance from his uncle had abruptly ended, a development he hadn't foreseen. The couple based themselves now in Worpswede with friends, and now with Clara's parents in nearby Westerwede. Rilke found it hard to work. So when Muther suggested he go to Paris and write a monograph on Rodin, building on his wife's connection, he seized the opportunity. 'What any artist wants: [is] to benefit from chance, to take advantage of coincidence and make it work for him.'

He arrived in Paris late in August 1902, hoping, above all, to bring more substance to his poems. His resolution recalls the same advice he had given to his mother, to write more evocatively. It was as if he feared drifting, and living out a fantasy, only imagining he was a poet, while daily life closed in on him. He had been cast off by Lou and married Clara in very short order. Clara can hardly have known the man she had married, and nor did he properly know himself. He needed to 'open himself to the world more', Lou said.[3] He needed to manage the difficult features of his personality: 'what you and I called "the other" in you, the man who is so quickly depressed, quickly excited, one moment afraid of everything and the next completely caught up in something'.[4] Describing herself as someone naturally inclined to be happy, Lou saw that Rilke was the opposite. He had an alarming combination of qualities likely to make his life—and those of people around him—difficult. She pledged him her lifelong friendship and support when their romance ended, and when she later trained as a psychoanalyst, her experience of Rilke's temperament was one of her motives.

Rilke surely did 'open himself to the world more' in the two volumes of *Neue Gedichte*. The *New Poems*, which he wrote during and between subsequent visits to Paris, and published in 1907–8, no longer spoke with the incantatory 'I' of *The Book of Hours*. They were something other than 'love-poems to God'.[5] Objectivization was their distinctive feature. That capacity for impersonal contemplation has commended itself to a certain kind of Rilke reader ever since. But that is to look beyond the intensely difficult preceding years, and to screen out crucial elements of the man. It was a troubled, subjective, God-seeking poet who lingered, and who now took himself off to live in a foreign metropolis.

In 1902, having mostly lived in quiet places, either provincial or rural, Rilke was simply not prepared. With a population of 2.66 million, making it Europe's biggest city after London, Paris shocked him with its poverty and ill health. So distressed were his first months that he chose the Boulevard de Port-Royal, a street of four hospitals, to open the other great work that would emerge from his Paris years, *The Notebooks of Malte Laurids Brigge* (1910). Paris brought home the trauma of whole swathes of humanity lacking nourishment and shelter. The plight of the poor was all around him, and it was potentially his own plight. Penniless and with no social ground beneath his feet, he began to notice, alongside his familiar god of the gaps, the plight of courtesans and beggars, the maimed and the sick. He also became intensely observant of animals, whose mysterious beauty and dignity evidently belonged to a different order of existence from the human. Famously he spent hours in the zoo contemplating the caged panther and the stalking flamingos and the 'perfectly rhyming' gazelles who became highlights of the *New Poems*. Art galleries and museums drew him in, but it was the teeming, impoverished streets themselves that were revelatory.

The Rilkes left their child behind and Clara followed her husband to Paris in the first week of October 1902. But their painful lack of an income soon overwhelmed both of them, and whatever they hoped Paris might do for their art. They could hardly afford to rent a studio and a room each, which was Rilke's condition for being married at all, and Paris pushed them to the limits. Back in Worpswede the painter Otto Modersohn had confided to his diary in Rilke's wake: 'He's in Paris, with Rodin, she'll be going in two weeks, if she has the money. They've taken the child to her parents. The future totally uncertain... How appalling: first marry and have a child, and then think about how to earn a living.'[6] Rilke's move to Paris also began a lifetime of insufficient, much criticized relations with others.

With a spring break of three months in Italy, he lasted in Paris on his first visit until June 1903. Even then his return to Germany felt like a personal defeat:

> The city was against me, opposed to my life, and was a test that I didn't pass. Its noise, which was endless, stole into my serenity, I could still feel its awfulness when I was back in my sad room and my eyes drooped under the weight of the pictures they had seen that day. On top of that I was ill.[7]

The same long and winding letter to Lou, 'confused and hasty', continued:

> Must I be afraid for myself?... Perhaps [my neediness] is just a consequence of this awful city that weighs on me, and for which I am too feeble and prone to depression; perhaps they are just reflections of the fears that arose out of our poverty; there were so many of them in our year in Westerwede, and here, where poverty and collapse are so close... I'm writing in the middle of packing.

Yet, secure again in rural north Germany, amidst his beloved greenery and birdsong, on the edge of 'a great northern plain, whose remoteness and silence and sky are to make me well again', he began to put the Paris experience into a complicated but bearable context: it might eventually benefit his art.[8] In eleven dense pages of retrospective description sent to Lou between 13 and 18 July, he compared his Paris trauma to how he had suffered in his teens at military boarding school. He was feeble and depressive but he survived.

One consolation was to read Baudelaire. Charles Baudelaire had left marvellous poems, *The Flowers of Evil*, of how each night after the Paris lamplighter went about his business the city would say an eternal farewell to another hundred of its poorest and most wretched citizens. Baudelaire had found a way not to succumb to the misery.

> Dissatisfied with everybody, myself included, I would gladly redeem myself and retrieve my self-respect in the silence and loneliness of the night. O souls of those whom I have loved, O souls of those whom my poems have celebrated, strengthen me and sustain me… O my Lord and God, grant me the grace to produce a few lines of poetry which will convince me I'm not the dregs of mankind, and not inferior to those I despise![9]

Rilke particularly loved this prose poem, with the title 'One O'Clock in the Morning':

> It's got a great ending; it stands there, stands up straight and finishes like a prayer. A prayer by Baudelaire; a real, straightforward prayer, made with the hands, unskilled and beautiful, like the prayer of a Russian.

Baudelaire's French was difficult to understand, but Rilke read him aloud sometimes in the middle of the night, and repeated his words 'like a child',

> such that he became close to me and lived alongside me and stood palely behind the thin wall and listened to my voice growing quieter. What a rare togetherness there was between us, a sharing of everything, the same poverty and perhaps the same fear. O, a thousand hands set to work on my fear, making more and more out of it until out of a remote village it became a great city, where unutterable things happened. It grew all the time and took away from me, removed from my feelings, all that was green and serene. I couldn't bear it. It began growing in Westerwede and houses and lanes arose out of the state of fright I was in, and the hours that passed there. And when Paris came, it grew very quickly into something huge.[10]

The truth was the problem was not Paris, or not only Paris. It was in Rilke's own soul, which he had to cope with. So he began to picture it as a replica reality, with its own houses and lanes, where he could outlast his crippling bouts of fear.

He would construct his world view out of the building blocks he had to hand. From his experience to date, he had discovered religious simplicity as an antidote to fear. The humility he had recently encountered in Russia left him awed by the ability of the peasants to pray. A longing to devote himself to simple things merged with a desire magically to reimagine rooms, villages and perhaps even whole towns where he *could* exist. Some of this imagery was already at work in *The Book of Hours* (where not Baudelaire but God was behind that thin wall, offering to guide his soul). There had to be some kind of intimate friend he could call *Du*, even if he only seemed to exist.

He probably always felt the significance of rooms for his poetry. Many of us rest our souls in rooms and watch the metaphors grow out of them. Once Lou had put to him her own imaginings:

The feeling for me of my past, become dark where I thought it light, dominated by an unconscious will to live among certain lives: has it happened to you, that the past becomes a room with the light suddenly switched off, and what you feel is that other lives, now all eclipsed, have written your own?

Rilke captured the mood in a poem of 1899, 'Am Rande der Nacht' ('On the Edge of Night'):

My room and life are this vast thing,
may they invigilate the nightfall outside.
For they are one, and I'm a string,
resonating, bridging
rustling distances far and wide.[11]

This was a distinct Rilkean feeling, religious only in a most attenuated sense, but describing in tremulous detail his earthly presence, in benign darkness and amid human silence.

As for his need to transform, *verwandeln*, what he lived, it entailed rebuilding every immediate environment: room, house, village, wherever he found himself. Perhaps that sounds banal. The task of all artists is to transform their material. But Rilke had this special gift, as the Scots poet Hugh MacDiarmid would put it,

Where what begin as metaphors all turn
To autonomous imaginative realities all pursuing
Their infinitely complicated ways...[12]

The transformations were often generated by fear. Fear, I do believe, was the deepest source of his work. *The Book of Hours* was memorable in lovingly transferring the fear to God, reversing the relationship, so that Rilke, otherwise immured in his own anxiety, could become the source of comfort. But in the ensuing *Book of Images* (1906), combining earlier work with Paris impressions, and in the *New Poems*, and even in the *Letters on Cézanne*, naked fear was everywhere. Metaphor transformed the fear and rhyme contained it. You can see it throughout the work, that rhyme holds Rilke's fears at bay, almost as if he were casting a spell on himself.[13] And that's also why rhyme is essential to understanding him, and why translation has such a task.

Rilke used a range of conventional words for fear (*Furcht*), anxiety (*Angst*) and terror (*Schrecken*) more or less synonymously, together with the verb 'to be afraid of' (*bangen*). Sometimes the context was immediate and down to earth, like the fear of a child, or of a woman alone *in extremis*. But often it was quasi-metaphysical and/or Biblical. 'The angels are so afraid,' begins 'The Annunciation'. In that poem the feelings of shyness and foreboding are attributed to the angels. So, in their wake, we might translate the famous opening line in the *Duino Elegies*, '*Ein jeder Engel ist schrecklich*' as 'Every angel is fearful'. But equally the fright might be ours in seeing them. From his earliest work Rilke turned emotional responses both ways, and made fear sometimes passive and sometimes creative. In 'God in the Middle Ages' the people are respectfully and deferentially afraid of God. On the other hand Rilke tells us that cathedrals, like poems and like paintings, are all responses to the shock of existence. He thinks that Cézanne felt something similar.[14]

For himself he becomes all too often afraid, pathologically so, we might suspect. In that 1899 poem 'People at Night', with its observation of the faces of others all 'fearfully distorted', he takes fright at human sociability drawing him into something he should resist.[15] Darkness is the poet's hour. Others should not invade it, with their gesturing and their chatter. In the company of others Rilke feared losing track of himself. Here was one of those perverse moods that so disturbed the otherwise happy Lou. Suddenly and ferociously he wanted to be alone. More terrifying, but part of the same semantic continuum, was what Rilke felt confronting metaphysical emptiness and death. In the 1914 poem 'Christ's Descent into Hell', the *Furcht* and *Schrecken* abound. This is a work of abject terror, about unlimited and remorseless pain. But all forms of Rilkean human/divine existence are riven by anxiety, unmediated by the legend of Christ's sacrifice. Only trees and animals and stones are free from metaphysical angst.

'The Book of Poverty and of Death' (1903) was published, somewhat anomalously, as the third part of *The Book of Hours*. It shows us Rilke taking his terror with him to Paris, and giving it a new, or redoubled, basis in social distress. The same kind of anxiety, urban, social and psychological, will make *Malte Laurids Brigge* a great work of modernism. The 1903 collection meanwhile contains poems once regarded as 'apostrophes to God' that 'did not readily lend themselves to translation' but are now much more popular.[16] They are to my ear strange works, with the root fear translating itself into a facetiousness one doesn't readily associate with Rilke the poet of the God of the Gaps. But they are part of the picture and part of what places him as an early modernist.

The challenge of the city, of which Paris is at once the paradigm and the only one Rilke ever really knew, turned out to be a far greater threat than Darwin to the value of humanity, because, said Rilke, it was a horrible place to die. In 'Lord, Give Each of Us Our Own Death', written in a few weeks' respite in Viareggio in April 1903, he thought of the end of life as a ripening. But living in such a place of madness and perversity as the modern city, how could one hope to experience a rightful natural end?

> For we are only leaf and husk outside.
> The great death by which we all abide
> is the fruit we envelop.[17]

Another poem about urban rottenness, seemingly indebted to Baudelaire, features the deprived lives of poor young women, 'with their disappointing experience of childbirth lived in obscure backrooms, their long nights of whimpering without hope, and cold years without the strength to struggle'.[18] Still the most important lines for understanding Rilke's development is a stanza telling us how in the city 'my voice grew in two directions':

> The first to reach for some distant place,
> the second to be the angel, benediction and face
> of all my lonelinesses.

A few lines on he breaks out in fury:

> The great cities are untrue; they make illicit
> the day, the night, the animals and the child;
> their silence tells lies, they lie with their wild
> noise, and with things that are complicit.

Long passages invoke the grandeur of what we would now call 'old money', as compared with the brashness of metal and glass and business. Just as there was a true wealth, so there was once a true poverty in earlier forms—feudal, mercantile—of society. God should take the poor out of the industrial city and give them back their dignity and their Biblical meaning.

Then blessed are they who have never gone from home
and quietly stand exposed in the rain;
for them the harvest will bring much grain,
and their fruits be like the honeycomb.

They will endure until the last in the land,
long after the rich man whose sense is faded,
and their hands will raise themselves up, unworked, pure,
when all the peoples and the social classes
are jaded.[19]

Many readers over the years would like Rilke to have been a political poet, which he was not. But these unfamiliar lines, full of Biblical and German musical echoes, mark the very great conservativism in which Rilke and other writers of his day sheltered from the urbanization and industrialization that, belatedly in Germany, overwhelmed them.[20]

Meanwhile, it's possible he himself became aware that spiritual angst was not the only, nor certainly the most effective way for art to approach social misery. One hope in 1906 accompanying the publication of *The Book of Images* was that readers would realize not all his work was 'purely aesthetic'. He deliberately added to that collection of characteristically inward poems a cycle, 'nine leaves with a title leaf', that had social content.[21] It was a vain hope of Hugh MacDiarmid to compare Rilke to Lenin.[22] But 'The Voices' were definitely a new venture. They gave a chance to 'the destitute' to speak in the first person: the beggar and the blind man, the drunkard and the suicide, the widow, the idiot and the orphan, the dwarf and the leper. The tone of the originals is, as I touched on before, a kind of facetious impatience with a world that has neither kindness nor mercy. The humour is bitter. The dwarf has an ugly face. He goes forth as a human being wanting to appeal to others, but no one likes him because of his appearance. Besides, at his height all he comes up against are dogs for whom he's not even worth sniffing. The implication is that art can hardly leave these facts aside. And yet surely it is not these poems, admired by translators especially today, that we need Rilke for.[23]

From *The Book of Images*, 'Autumn Day' (1902) was by contrast a study in intense 'inward' emotion, tightly compressed. One of the great poems of German literature, 'Herbsttag' juxtaposes the blissful ripeness of summer's wake with a cold winter wind blowing down deserted streets. It recalls Hölderlin's 'Half of Life' from a century before. But perhaps the affinity, so early in his career, was not conscious, and Rilke's poem alone is a soaring achievement:

> Lord, the time has come. Swollen summer has come around.
> Cast the sundials into shadow,
> let the winds blow across the ground.
>
> Order the fruit to ripen now, in this time's last sunshine;
> grant it two more southerly days,
> press upon it your perfect ways
> and force a final sweetness into the darkened wine!
>
> Who has no house now will never build one.
> Who is alone will stay that way,
> stay awake, reading, writing letters, aye
> he will, and will walk the streets till he is done;
> anxious, as the leaves fly up in disarray.

One of the greatest critics of German literature, Erich Heller, has asserted that those streets, '*Alleen*' in the original, do not, in fact, belong to the city, and that therefore Stephen Mitchell's translation of them as 'boulevards' will not do.[24] But Heller's assumption that Rilke is thinking only of himself here, pacing the grounds of a country house where one of his rich patrons had given him refuge, seems quite wrong.[25] He did find a way of dealing with his unease and his penury in the city by residing, often alone, not necessarily happily, in icy borrowed castles. He had been saved from trying to make his way in Paris by a long stay in a Danish castle most recently. But Mitchell was not wrong at all with his sense that this poem had, ultimately, an urban setting. All one might object to about the Mitchell translation is that boulevards sound far too alluring to an English ear, as having everything to do with an image of Paris as enchanting. That would be misleading. In the beginning was Rilke's own disenchantment; also his fear of how quickly a feeling of well-being, home even, could reverse itself. Much more important in any translation of *Herbsttag* is therefore to retain the idea of *building* a house and finding a home, two of Rilke's lifelong themes. Whoever we are we *must* build a life and make a home or be destroyed. Active verbs in the imperative mood give this poem its charge. God commands nature to make its work perfect. The same verbs record Rilke stating the human task. Push back against the despair the city can inspire. Find inspiration there. Using rhyme as his essential technique, he shows the reader how *he* builds a refuge in art, as *we* seek a roof over our heads. The poem replicates the harvest. It is itself a store against winterly anxiety. Fear of winter never left him. A poem written on a return to Paris in autumn 1913 exclaimed: 'Now we must bear the days that deny us / and endure on the edge of our resistance.'[26] Two years later again he cried out in the fourth Duino Elegy: 'O trees of life, are you made for winter?'

And so glancingly we come back to his fears, which had many sources: physiological, like these fears of the cold, and of an underworld barrenness; social, because he couldn't get on with people and had no home; socio-economic, because he feared becoming an impoverished outcast, and, yes, in a way political, because the fruits of capitalism dismayed him. He had called Russia a spiritual homeland because, as he experienced it in his soul, it was a rare and still extant mirror of eternity, compared with an industrialized and urbanized Europe. But the truth was Russia did not create the burdens Paris did.

The project continued to find that little bit more reality that Lou insisted on. One day she would quote in an essay of her own one of his poems suggesting he had succeeded; that he had found his gift.[27] But in fact 'Narcissus II' is a harrowing poem, for it is about desperately trying to get out of himself and his constant collisions with the world—that very high degree of sensitivity-cum-irritability Lou had detected—and find some way of making his talent fruitful.

> This thing, then, sometimes leaves me be,
> dissolves in the air, wanders in the grove,
> slips away—painless—and is no longer me
> and glows, then, free from feeling loathed.[28]

At one point he asks: did she really see me like that, as deadly and incapable of love? The truth was she did. Riven by a kind of enmity towards others, arising out of an excess of self-direction, he was lucky to survive.

SIX

Paris (2)

Sculpture and Eternity

After his first visit in 1901–2, despite the shocks to his soul, Rilke would have returned to Paris much sooner, had he only had a post, and an income. A letter to Rodin already in September 1902, reprised in September 1905, when he finally did return, made that clear. We forget, talking of that lovely, yet to be written novel, by me or any of his other admirers, *Rilke in Paris*, that he was away for three years, right at the beginning. But then he came back. For the city that outraged him also excited him and broadened his horizons, and that was so much to his good. Paris in fact demanded he forge himself a personality 'in the world' and not just exist in the repose of his own soul.[1]

Always lodging on the Left Bank, in the fifth or sixth arrondissement, over an intermittent twenty-three years and ending only in 1925 on the eve of his death, he had seven Paris addresses. He loved the parks and the galleries and the zoo at the Jardin des Plantes. Even his daily visits to his favourite cheap restaurant, Jouven, he found worthy of recommending to the young poet Kappus, who had written asking his advice. Eat well. 'Do not dull the clarity of this need, and all those deep, simple necessities by which life renews itself.'[2]

There was something enfeeblingly Platonic about his younger self, which needed an ideal realm to retreat from reality and feel safe. He grew stronger, and success helped, but he was always wary of the least compromise. 'Fame is ultimately but the summary of all the misunderstandings that crystallize around a new name.'[3] He was the kind of artist who had to preserve himself from the crowd—from journalism, from tourism, from any kind of mediating triviality in the pursuit of experience—and who may be hard to understand today.

The *New Poems* of 1907 and 1908, about 'things', reflected a Rodin-like plasticity and there was a deep new influence there. They might, moreover, be read by a psychologist as demonstrating just the 'objectivity' and 'thingliness' he needed to reduce his personal anxiety. Yet there are only about twenty that really achieve that vision, out of more than 170. It has been convenient also to make the *New Poems* Rilke's most accessible and down-to-earth work. Still they *are* superb, no doubt about that. They arise out of moments when he contemplates 'The Panther' (1902–3), or 'The Blue Hydrangea' (1906), or, to return to that great favourite of mine, 'Archaic Torso of Apollo' (1908).[4] His ability to see goes so deep that the objects stand forward in all their organic delicacy, sleek animality and startling solidity, as works of nature and works of art. With 'Archaic Torso' the process is redoubled: the object viewed becomes a poem, but the object itself is already a work of art. The transaction goes back and forth between art and life and back again. Doubling is also at work in 'The Merry-Go-Round, Jardin du Luxembourg' (1906). For here was a poem composed more like a painting. These poems were extraordinary excursions into what Rilke's art meant to him. But they also considered what art was as such, and what bound verbal, painterly and haptic art together. The 'things' chosen as points of departure were often given a Symbolist reading in the first decades of Rilkean criticism. But that seems a misplaced approach now.

> Though [the work of art] springs out of infinite distances, even from the depths of the sky, it must return to itself, the great circle must complete itself, the circle of solitude that encloses a work of art… it must not demand or expect anything from outside, it should refer to nothing that lies beyond it, see nothing that is not within itself; its environment must lie within its own boundaries.[5]

This, as it happens, was Rilke in 1902–3—the same dates as 'The Panther'—describing the work of Auguste Rodin. But clearly he was talking—and perhaps even exclusively—of his own creations.

Famously Rodin urged Rilke to work and work: '*Il faut travailler et travailler.*' He was also, excepting Tolstoy, the first artist of supreme stature whom Rilke met in person and the only artist he ever watched working. On 2 September 1902, Rilke 'took the ferry across the Seine' to interview the sculptor, or, surely, to be interviewed, in his atelier at 182 rue de l'Université. 'We talked a lot—so far as my peculiar speech and his time allowed,' Rilke wrote to Clara (whose role as his correspondent far outstripped her role as his wife). The Master continued to work while they talked. 'He had a little plaster thing in his hand and scratched away at it.' Meanwhile all around them, heaped up in the studio, was work upon work, mostly of the human body, in various stages of completion. Rilke noticed a sculpture of a hand. There were also Rodin's own living hands, so rich in sculptural gesture, so capable of 'forming' and 'holding' things. When Rodin spoke and pointed to his work, moreover, it seemed 'as if things were growing out of his hand'. Rilke examined a bas-relief called *Morning Star*. It showed the head of a very young girl, 'with a wonderful young brow, clear, lovable, light and simple', and beneath it a man just waking up, shading his eyes with his hand before such brightness. The studio was altogether full of work, and 'everything small had so much greatness that the space in workshop H seemed to expand into the immeasurable, in order to contain it'.[6]

A day later Rilke, aged twenty-six, by invitation, took the train from Gare Montparnasse to visit this imposing artistic grandee, in his prime at the age of sixty-one, at his country villa. The tall thin Louis XIII house at Meudon, pale stone framing pink brick, didn't please him but the setting was a delight, with yet more workshops and a huge glass pavilion transferred from the Paris Universal Exhibition of 1900, where Rodin received his first solo show. The lawned grounds sloped gently down the Val Fleury back towards Paris, with the trains in the valley toing and froing from the city visible and in regular earshot. Inside the pavilion, dazzled by the whiteness of so much plaster, Rilke seemed to confront 'the work of a century', 'an army of work', even while he had the sense that the life every piece breathed was 'an articulation of one man's will and one man's strength'. '*Schwingungen einer Kraft und eines Willens.*' *Schwingungen* were moments when inspiration took wing, when art really went to work. *Schwingen*, as we've seen, was the word Rilke used when he wanted to convey life coming into being, whether under its own impetus in the universe or at the hands of the artist scraping away at his Pygmalion. Or it could refer to a deep feeling awakening in his own heart.

The Meudon house, though a museum, has retained an intimacy today that can make you feel that at any moment the master might walk in through the door and join you at the table, or that you might encounter the unhappy Rose Beuret, romantically compromised and not to be granted the dignity of becoming Madame Rodin almost until Rodin was on his deathbed.[7] She was by Rilke's account pleasant enough to the visitor and invited him to lunch 'whenever he was in the vicinity'. She may have liked him because he was attuned to women. The location is an outer suburb of Paris now, but of the pleasantest garden-dominated kind, with winding streets, an occasional bus and almost no traffic. Perhaps its situation a century ago helped to generate another common theme in Rilke, when he cleaved to the edge of things, here on the edge of the village, and imagined another realm springing to life just beyond, like the place where 'the plaints' would live ('We were a great race... our fathers worked the mines... we used to be rich') in the tenth Duino Elegy. Where in the poems there were not edges of villages there were hems of gowns and 'the rind of our resistance', and other wonderful frontier possibilities. But perhaps I see Meudon that way because I too love the edges of cities.

His first Rodin essay Rilke wrote almost immediately, through October 1902, and there was something faintly Dionysian, in Nietzsche's sense, in one of Rilke's chief observations: that Rodin represented the rediscovery of the body, where the Renaissance had focused on the face.[8] Nietzsche had famously speculated on Western philosophy as a misunderstanding and an underappreciation of the body. The tension in his work between the Apollonian and the Dionysian was another way of talking about new conditions for art and the human soul in modern—post-Renaissance—times. For that change 'bore the stamp of old mysteries that, rising from the unconscious, reared their dripping heads like strange river gods out of the singing blood'.[9] In his lecture on Rodin five years later, Rodin himself was the river god. (And finally, completing what linked three great artists of early modernity, that phallic river god would become Rilke himself.)

It wasn't that sculpture didn't know the body before, but that Rodin, with his attention to surfaces, and his positioning of the body in space, subject to weather and light, captured it anew.

L'Homme qui marche (*The Walking Man*) struck him as if the master had invented a new verb for walking.[10]

Rodin was immensely flattered by the essay, as soon as he could read it in French. And so the second time Rilke begged him for material support, he offered him paid residence at Meudon. Rilke arrived in September 1905 and stayed until mid-May the following year. The post, usually described as secretary, was never well defined, and it is surprising those two bears in a lair lasted so long. But it brought Rilke back to themes that worked so well for him, and while assimilating Rodin's practice to his own—the hands, the panther, the cathedrals, the Dionysian creativity, the figures of Orpheus were all common ground, as Rilke saw it—he could pursue his own art.

In the 1907 lecture, which became his *Auguste Rodin: Zweiter Teil: Ein Vortrag* (Auguste Rodin: part two: a lecture), he recalled that one of his tasks in 1905–6 had been to frame the 'more than a hundred and fifty' impressive Rodin drawings 'in the masses of cheap white-gold frames that had been ordered'. When he saw them again, exhibited, at a Paris show in autumn 1907, what captivated him were fifteen or so new drawings, 'all from the time [1906] when Rodin had followed King Sisowath's dancers on their travels, in order to admire them longer and better'. These were the pencil sketches of the terracotta and plaster Cambodian dancers that would become among Rodin's most admired work. Rilke, in a letter to Clara (15 October 1907), called them 'gazelles transformed', 'the two long slender arms as if of a piece pulled through the shoulders'. From the panther that was a model on Rodin's shelf, to the Buddha image in the Meudon garden, to Rilke's own 'The Gazelle', Rodin's vision heightened Rilke's own, as he translated sculpture into poetry. Of course, he saw the panther and the gazelles at the zoo, but the heart of the matter was learning to take such objects as his own 'things'.

Another great event, perhaps the high point of their material and poetic coexistence, was the joint outing, on 25 January 1906, to Chartres. They stole away from Paris by train on a raw and icy day, and 'Madame Rodin' came too. Rilke had a project at the time, contrasting 'the spire-less towers of so many medieval French cathedrals and the spired towers of most German and Austrian ones'.[11] A happy visit to Notre-Dame in Paris, with the sculptor who was everywhere received with reverence, had probably set it in train. Rodin 'is the only person (it seems), to whom all this comes and says something'. Rilke was right. Architectural sculpture was about to be recognized as art, after long languishing as something less.[12] As for what they saw in Chartres, in the presence of an historic building terribly neglected, there was 'a slim weathered angel holding a sundial and broadly smiling down, unbelievably beautiful in its decay, with a face full of joy at being able to serve, on the entire passing hours of the day'.[13] These rich encounters produced four great poems: 'L'Ange du Méridien (Chartres)', 'The Cathedral', 'The Porch' and 'The Rose Window'.

Why would anyone suppose it less than a miracle that Rilke and Rodin lasted as long as they did in harmony? They never quite quarrelled but Rilke desperately needed his time for himself. The very few private letters Rilke managed to write that winter and spring included one hungrily answering an offer of help from another quarter that would relieve him of his present duties. Rilke explained a plight that any writer, any artist must know:

After certain profound and in a way frightening experiences that strangely encapsulate and bring meaning to everything that was there before, there would have to come, there must come a time for me when I can be alone with my experience; to make it mine and to transform it; for I feel this terrible pressure from all that I have not yet transformed; I don't know whether

99

I'm coming or going. This spring... has become a task... I'm thirty-one this year, and all other circumstances suggest that if I could take myself in hand with a view to my progress, I could make a couple of works happen that would be good and would help me inwardly, and perhaps even outwardly might lead to some security in my life, something I haven't had from previous books, but which is so to speak not ruled out for the future.[14]

The same letter continues that Rilke would like to leave but doesn't dare do so abruptly, all the more as Rodin, 'having been ill, is tired and still not recovered, and needs my help, as slight as it is, more than ever'. Still we know he does then bring about his departure, with Rodin sacking him on 11 May.

Later, apart, Rodin and Rilke would find new respect for each other. Meanwhile, why would anyone suppose it strange when an artist puts his own work first? Her own. Though she always suffered from the consequent material circumstances, and the social hindrance of being technically married when her husband was constantly absent, Clara Rilke understood independence for her poet-husband, as for herself. Moreover, it was one gift of clarity and sympathy that Rilke brought to his marriage; that he deeply sympathized with his wife's position as an artist. He wrote that the problem of the woman artist left him speechless.[15]

So he left Meudon to take stock, to write up, and to move on. He would try to profit where he could from giving a lecture on Rodin, including in Prague. All the while he probably didn't realize how much his essential Rodin essay of 1903, and this 1907 addition, contained so much as if about his own work that he had set out a programme for *his* once and future work; had established *his* attitude to bodied things—*Dinge*—in the world.

There is a dark patience in Rodin that makes him almost nameless, a quiet superiority and a capacity to wait out his time,
something of the great patience and generosity of nature, which
begins with nothing, in order in silence and all seriousness to
embark on the long road to what is plentiful.[16]

There is patience in the dark eye of the panther too, and in Rilke
himself.

Though he hardly needed persuading, Rodin convinced Rilke
of the 'infinitely great experience' of a life spent working stone
and the need to accept 'the burden of looking'. In recognition
of the fact, Rilke placed two 'Apollo' statue poems like mythical
doorkeepers, or house gods, to preside over the two volumes of
New Poems. 'Early Apollo', from July 1906, was, in this respect,
his first counter-gift to Rodin: a sculpture, in words, about the
power of stone:

> Often it happens: through trees seeming dead
> a spring morning shines, the weather glows fair;
> just like that now: nothing in his head
> can stop the blinding glare
> of lines that almost cause our death;
> for his gaze is not yet shaded,
> and his temples are cooler, not wrapped in a wreath;
> though his brows are a garden glade
> where tall-stemmed roses will later grow
> whose leaves when they fall, will, one by one,
> as the mouth moves, over its moving loosely blow;
> though the mouth is still now, blinking, not using
> its power, only its smile fusing
> its lips, as if in song to be undone.

Was there ever a more erotic poet writing about the life in *stone*? It's not that we're voyeurs here, but at best unsubtle apprentices in what it might really be to dream of consummate love. Rilke's observation about the Dionysian revolution Rodin's work embodied is pertinent here, for it seems to suggest how Rodin taught him to widen his sense of how the body could speak:

> There was not one part of the human body [for Rodin] that was insignificant or unimportant...

Moreover, a body

> consisted of infinitely many movements. The play of light upon these surfaces made manifest that each of these movements was different and significant...

And

> Rodin had now discovered the fundamental element of his art... the surface.[17]

This then becomes the way Rilke gazes on the stone body of the statue, how he calls the mouth 'the mouth of the body', and brings the whole presence of this early Apollo erotically alive (actually far more than Rodin's own work, to my mind).[18] I suppose that's the Dionysian implication, that the mouth is the organ that makes entry into stone possible; it's the mouth that opens and closes and whose motivation is flirtatious and secret. Likewise the poem is full of erotic promise, through its teasing speaking. In both the statue—a tribute to a work Rilke had seen in the Louvre—and the poem of the statue, all the inanimate surfaces, of the word and the stone and the plant, flirt with human flesh. As the roses grow tall and erect, falling petals graze the silent stone mouth, teasing its sexuality, wanting its mouth to pucker into a kiss. Rodin had little erotic power by comparison. Indeed, he could be crude, whereas Rilke scattered his sexuality, Franciscan-fashion, about the cosmos.

'Archaic Torso of Apollo' from two years later, that magnificent poem to which I keep returning, impacts on our consciousness with the same glow as the 'Early Apollo'. Only here—and we must compare the illumination of the two poems—light falls onto the surrounding stone as if from a low-burning street lamp. Rilke finds in the statue's incomplete body the same reserved but powerful sensuality as in the 'Early Apollo', and claims to have learnt a secret Rodin taught him about incompleteness. Rodin's girl without arms, *La Meditation*, had impressed Rilke as a way of redoubling the sense of emotion held within.[19] Similarly, although the Archaic Apollo has no head, we learn from the poem that it smiles a virile secret from its loins.

Rilke tried to work out through Rodin what he felt about the value of the human. He decided that the sculptor made a cathedral of the human body (at the same time as that body was the outcome of Darwinian adaptation):

Here in the body Rodin found the world of his time as he had recognized the world of the Middle Ages in the cathedrals. A universe gathered about this veiled mystery—a world held together by an organism was adapted to this organism and made subject to it. Man had become church and there were thousands and thousands of churches, none similar to the other and each one alive. But the problem was to show how they were all of One God.[20]

He admired Rodin for putting his statues in the open air. But by 1907 he felt Rodin's 'things', of the kind that once belonged *in* cathedrals, were problematic, for the contemporary age no longer expressed itself that way. Taking himself back to the first time he stood in Rodin's crowded studio Rilke wondered why the things were 'not trying to work out their value'.

> And so I asked myself for the first time: how is it possible that they're not trying to work out their value? How is it that this immense oeuvre is still in the ascendant, and where is it headed? Does it no longer think of its maker? Does it really believe that its place is in nature, like the rocks, in whose presence thousands of years pass like a single day?
>
> And it seemed to me, in my shocked state, that one would have to get everything already done out of the workshops, in order to be able to see what needs doing in the coming years...
>
> Ever since that moment I see the tragedy of [Rodin's] work as lying in its greatness. I feel more clearly than ever that in these things sculpture has found in itself a power unrivalled since antiquity. But this plasticity has been born in an age that has no things, no houses, no externality. For the inwardness of the present day is without form, is ungraspable; it flows like a current.

Hold off on that rather counter-intuitive use of 'inwardness' for a moment. What is Rilke saying? That Rodin can give form to what is otherwise vague and constantly shifting and self-transforming? Yes, no doubt. But at what cost? Underlying his achievement is a monumental exercise in power, to stop the tide of the modern and the result is something strange for contemporary civilization:

One might almost concede: these things have nowhere to go… Do they not avow their own tragedy, these brilliant creations that have pulled down the heavens upon themselves? Abandoned, don't they just stand there now? No building will ever contain them. They stand in space. What concern are they to us.

In antiquity temples were the place for sculpture. In the Middle Ages sculpture filled cathedrals and climbed up gates and towers.

But where should Rodin's things go? Eugène Carrière once wrote of him: 'He [Rodin] couldn't work on an absent cathedral'… [Rodin] saw that his things were homeless a long time in advance. His choice was either to smother them in himself or seize the sky for them that surrounds the mountains. And that was his task. He raised his world in a great arc above us and placed it in nature.

Rilke's message was wonderfully clear. Rodin's humanism, magnificent as it was, didn't fit in a world in which humanity had become more like an electric current. The body no longer stood still. Inside humanity was a surging dynamism yet to create the art objects equal to a less permanent way of living. Its 'inwardness'—the word used somewhat differently from the theme of this book—was at present pure potential, or the expectation of quite different forms of art in the future.

The Rodin essays were of a piece with many of the *New Poems* in returning again and again to Rilke's own question about the future of 'man' and the 'inwardness'—in our sense—which for so many centuries had seemed to distinguish the human from the beastly and the cosmic. These days it seemed that inwardness had no content at all (though he, Rilke, was doing his best to generate a content). The 1907 essay, though far less well known than its predecessor, actually broke with Rodin's form-giving humanism and asked for a more appropriate modern art. Rilke said that because the 'thingliness' of the world had changed, art too had to change. It's things that take our life and our art into their compass, not the other way round. There are things and we are their surfaces; there are things whose surfaces attract us. Rilke wanted to transform the picture of the thoughtful species. He wanted us to see that looking at things in terms of *their* inwardness could give us a new lease of life and a way out of our confusion.

'The Swan' was actually written at Meudon, when Rilke was living in a charmingly furnished cottage in the grounds. He was living well, and learning a great deal. But he needed to revert to his own themes: that is, not only thingliness, but death. Hence 'The Swan'.

Something is stopping the swan from gliding on the pond as he should. He nervously lowers himself into the water, thinking of death. Death troubles people. With Darwin they no longer know what the end means. But then the swan reassures himself that death will receive him gently. 'Endlessly sure of himself, ever more regal and ready to speak', he now concedes to swim.[21]

Here was Rilke still just managing to speak for himself, in the overwhelming presence of Rodin.

I've already suggested one way of imagining the inner life of things, as opposed to our own, was to search for rhyme, as if that was a clue to meaning out there. It helped Rilke to remember rhyme, as a phenomenon, when he looked at Rodin's work. Out of that conjunction seems to have come 'The Gazelle' of 1907. Here, at the zoo, or in the sculptor's workshop, was a magical creature, herself like a perfect rhyme: the more perfect for coming and going again ethereally.

Another temptation was to find meaning—as only Rilke needed it, Rilke who wasn't a sculptor but a poet—in the virtues of stone. 'The one thing / that will infinitely increase your life / [is]... the awakening of stones, / depths turned round towards you.'[22] Twenty years later a draft for the eighth Sonnet to Orpheus gave the sentiment a dramatic twist: 'You should know nothing more than that pillar of stone.'[23] For Rilke, to praise stone was to praise something close to eternity: that sense we do have, or did, until perhaps half a century ago, of nature and culture, of the ancient and of the Renaissance worlds, existing in some great continuum.[24] It incorporated Lou and Rilke's shared belief that others before them had built the life they stood upon. Progress lay at the heart of modern humanist exceptionalism. Against that there was no progress in stone. But there were always aesthetic possibilities.

New insights into the prehistory of the world gave Rilke the sense of firmness beneath his feet which he could associate with stone. A line in 'The Last Judgement', a dense five-page poem from 1899 he presented to Rodin back in 1902, ran: 'then all times rise out of the stones.'[25] Rilke had discovered the poetry of archaeology, and of geology.[26] The power of stone, the chorus of voices stored up in it, seemed to yield a mystical perspective from which to view the very claim of what the past was. A new sense of the deep past had much to do with the pervasive Darwinism of the era. The sense, brought home by excavations across the globe, from digging into the earth, was of lost peoples and their achievements. And yet did that not mean that one day 'we' too might be lost? If in fact the sense of continuity was already doubtful in Rilke's time, perhaps the thought was that at least stone would endure.

Rilke's compatriot and rival lyric genius Hugo von Hofmannsthal celebrated the deep past in a memorable couplet:

From the lids of my eyes I cannot banish
the vanished woes of peoples past.

One of Rilke's own responses came in an 1898 poem, 'When the clocks are so near':

I can never be alone. It will never be.
Many, many who lived before
steered themselves to a far-off shore
and wove
and wove
to make the man I am: this he.

In *The Book of Hours* he had needed to be a stone to gain God's attention, and to be stone was another way of surviving; of not being fearful and alone.

Stone had another aspect in Rilke's work, though, and that was that it stood in for an extreme tendency to passivity. As the answer to his life, the temptation of passivity never left him.

Still Paris and Rodin had taught him this 'pure seeing', '*das reine Schauen*', as an alternative way, a braver way for sure, a more interesting way for us, to venture forth.[27] You could see in the way Rilke was in two minds about Rodin that he was intensely attuned to the new without knowing what it could be. He could not know that soon after his death stone would become dynamic and modern. Brâncuși was already at work, and Moore and above all Barbara Hepworth lay just around the corner. None of them needed to imagine cathedrals in which to place their work. Their work, which now rested in nature, restored something almost prehistoric to the human form; or made it ahistorical; or showed it be the product of a wonderfully reimagined biology. Rilke, I think, would have been a great admirer, had he lived another twenty years.

Stronger, buoyed up by success and continuing inspiration, Rilke meanwhile rediscovered Paris in 1907. He could see now that he had not paid his native Prague enough attention. Prague too was a city of stone. Still the monumentality of Paris had him in its grasp. The *hôtels* that presented towering closed facades to the street seemed to tease him with their impenetrability. Surely they hid now monumental, now delicate materiality, the wealth of ages, from his gaze. He grazed their surfaces on his daily walks.

> One has a premonition of the coolness of a vestibule, with cold, uncommunicative walls that take part in nothing, like servants at the table, and are only there to hand round the lamps in the evening. One has a premonition, one believes that these palaces have majestic inner rooms, there is something in one's blood that belongs there and for a second the scala of all feelings lies between the heaviness of ancient Chinese porcelain and the lightness of being in the voice of the grandfather clock...[28]

Three days earlier he had laid his hands on the granite of the Obélisque in the place de la Concorde, 'where, in the indentations of the hieroglyphs, in the recurring depiction of the owl, an ancient Egyptian dark blue is preserved, dried up like on the inside of mussels'.[29]

Another side of his experience in Paris was, against his terrible earlier experience, trying to live well. He owed this to himself as a person as much as an artist, and it reflected ideals he had tried to live by through 1903 and 1904. These he wrote down in those letters to a chance correspondent, Franz Xaver Kappus, which Kappus collected and published shortly after Rilke's death as *Letters to a Young Poet*.[30]

Sometimes it's tempting to imagine Rilke absurdly setting out each day in Paris in Search of Lost Faith, and finding Nietzschean treasures, 'superabundant substitutes', out of which he could make his art and his life. But sometimes he was simply happy. I mentioned the idea of the novel *Rilke in Paris* which I would interminably write and/or love to read to the end of my days. His own novel *Malte Laurids Brigge* is partly a Paris diary, a record of highs and lows, but mostly reflecting the terrible struggle of his first visit. When there were lows it helped to project himself into this ultimate lost soul, whose path he would explore but ultimately not follow.

Meanwhile he gave life-sustaining advice to himself in the form of giving it to Kappus:

> Sex is difficult; yes indeed. But difficult things are sent to challenge us, almost everything serious is difficult, and everything is serious. If you can just accept that and arrive at your own attitude to sex then you will no longer need to fear losing yourself and squandering your greatest possession. You have to work it out through your disposition and the way you are, out of your experience and your childhood and make it wholly yours, not influenced by convention and morality.
>
> Bodily pleasure is a sensual event, no different from the pure contemplation or the pure sensation of what the tongue feels when you take a beautiful fruit into your mouth; it is an infinitely great experience which is given to us, a knowledge of the world [in the way] all knowledge has a fullness about it, and a glow. It's not wrong that we are in receipt of it, but that we misuse and squander nearly all of this experience and people use it to spice up the tired aspects of their lives and as a diversion instead of as a moment of self-concentration leading to the highest experience.[31]

As for love in the city, one has to accept sometimes to be lonely:

Love is... a sublime occasion for the individual person to mature and to become something, to become a world, to become a world for themselves for the sake of another. It's a great, immodest demand made upon a person, something that makes them special and summons them to distant challenges.[32]

Another city theme was how to live alone in a room, and Rilke treated it both literally and metaphorically. Don't lead a monotonous existence. Don't give in to spiritual laziness.

For if we think of individual existence as a room, bigger or smaller, so it becomes apparent that most people only get to know a corner of their room, a seat beside the window, a narrow strip where they walk up and down. That way they have a kind of security... We though are not prisoners.[33]

In his room no doubt he paced like the caged panther in the zoo, at times. His Paris rooms were inadequate. But he learnt to manage his self-imposed unfreedom and he and his four walls and dreary furniture became bearable companions. The lodging he moved to immediately after Meudon was 'not too small but not very airy, full of worn-out things, but which don't press their memories on me'.[34] The best was on the first floor of the Hôtel Biron (now the Musée Rodin), from where he could gaze out of the full-length light-filled first-floor window down into the garden. The location in the sixth arrondissement was so good that Rodin copied him and moved in below. Or perhaps it was his last, in the town house known as the Hôtel Foyot, 33 rue Tournon, just opposite the grandest entrance to the Jardin du Luxembourg, beside the Senate, and round the corner from the majestic seventeenth-century rue de Vaugirard. In this stone building, at last worthy of him, he stayed in Paris for the last time in 1925. It was undoubtedly a lonely and rather grim existence for much of the time, and those who criticize him for now and again repairing to the castles of rich friends might remember what for most of his life the alternative was.

SEVEN

Castle-Dwelling and Human Ties

B y 1911, in the wake of the *New Poems* and *Malte Laurids Brigge*, Rilke had become a celebrity. One definition of success is that money, support and company flood in when you least need them. Long desired rewards, love even, have to be juggled with leading a creative life at all.

Rilke was grateful for the offer to spend the winter of 1911–12 in the castle at Duino on the cliffs of the Adriatic, after painting a grim picture of his winter ahead in Paris to the Princess Marie von Thurn und Taxis. She lent him a car and a driver for the long journey south and east, to her family seat just outside the port of Trieste. He arrived in October, yet if it was solitude he needed, he had to wait until after Christmas for all the princess's other guests and family members to go. The castle, 'like a great body without much soul', alternately battered by the bora and scirocco winds, did not endear itself as a location and the sea did not really increase its appeal.[1] Nor, as he opined in a letter, without further explanation, did he like a region dominated by 'Austrian multi-lingualism', a mixture of German, Italian and Slovene. He may have felt that the languages undermined each other. Diversity has not always been a cultural ideal. Yet, if fortress Duino had its shortcomings, he was about to turn its address into a legend; almost a stand-in for himself. When years ago I saw a motorway signpost to Duino my heart skipped a beat. I knew Rilke was worth the detour but how could he be just a couple of kilometres away?

In his followers he has created such ties to places because the places stand in for the poetry. It's good to be able to walk around them. To take Rilke's Duino walk along the cliffs (although it has always been closed when I've tried) is frankly easier than reading the poems. But if you have read them, then suddenly Rilke is with you. The experience is vast. It might be the beginning of that novel you always wanted to write. Or a way of framing your life to date that you've never grasped before. It's as if the time spent walking in a place about which so much has been written needs your answer too. Write a postcard to friend, or an essay for yourself. Remember what you made of 'Rilke'; the hours you spent in his company; before you go home. Home may also look different, when you arrive back. In fact, I've always been sceptical about visiting writers' houses. The work to me means so much more than the person. But I love places and want to invest in them. I love the places and, adjacent to them, the work that has brought me there. The case of Rilke is also a special one insofar as *he* didn't have a house, or home, just these places he passed through. The thought behind so many of the poems was to live richly in the moment—hardly an unusual ambition for a poet, but one which Rilke fulfilled superbly. 'To make the world slowly ours, with words and fingerposts' would be the task.[2]

> O despite the fate that awaits us: the grand overflowing
> of our lives, spilling over, in parks—
> or figured as stone-sculpted men. See there, where
> the high gates close, beneath the balconies, they stand like trees!

O the brass bell, that opens its gorge
daily to stir the deadened day.
Or the column in Karnak, one column, forged
to outlive temples on endless display.[3]

But this, to quote from one of Rilke's last poems, is to get ahead of our story.

As of New Year 1912, for all his belated outward success Rilke hadn't actually written anything for two years. Then, suddenly, come mid-January, he was able to set down the first and second of the *Duino Elegies*. The ten-part cycle begun in those weeks brought together his favourite themes in arresting new combination. Each theme and its variations was a sustained and magical weave of words, issuing in a narrative of scores of lines. While he waited for the creative moment to ripen he had confined himself to reading and writing letters to people presently in his life. It had been the faintly desperate routine he had described in 'Autumn Day', not because he was miserable, but because he was waiting. Waiting.

There were six letters to Lou between the beginning of January and 16 March, all several pages long, uniquely using the familiar *Du*, and fourteen to various acquaintances, including to his publisher and to his wife Clara's psychoanalyst. Several were keen responses to other writers. Talking about art, he flirted with the thirty-year-old Countess Manon zu Solms-Laubach, whom he had met in Capri six years before. There was also a reply to the Hölderlin scholar Norbert von Hellingrath, commiserating with his having to stay in Paris, the city that made unbearable demands. Von Hellingrath, the first to collect Hölderlin's own elegies and publish them in 1913, broadened Rilke's knowledge, a process that would culminate in the September 1914 tribute 'To Hölderlin'. But it was a professional bond, not a personal one. Generally, Rilke's letters gave him an outlet to set down his thoughts and he did not especially require a reply, because his mind was already on other things. Only when Lou's letters arrived did he walk up and down the garden reading them as if he were learning a passage by heart.

It was not an empty life, but it was a writer's life. He got up each day oppressed by having something more to achieve, and wondering how to manage it. From a high window he saw the gardeners busy in the garden. They could get on with their task. Why couldn't he? Reading diverted him, and gave him material to entertain his correspondents. Of that reading Goethe interested him more and more. Previously Rilke had thought the psychology of Germany's greatest writer, and greatest cultural institution, lacked sufficient despair. But encountering Goethe's *Italian Journey*, Rilke found a real vein of tension to tap. The *Journey*, reworked from a more vivid diary, told the story of how that poet and polymath escaped the narrow human ties stifling him in the principality of Weimar and travelled south incognito. Freed from public office, and a difficult relationship, Goethe rediscovered himself in Italian art, antiquity and landscape, and with Italian women, and began his life anew. It's hard to see how this aspect of Goethe—encouraging any creative soul to leave the familiar and the familial behind—could *not* have appealed to Rilke.

He was also reading about the fourteenth century, when he decided people had led a rich religious existence inside themselves. Nothing in the external world of the day could match it. (The great medieval cathedrals were an obvious exception.) Compared with the 1300s, when gold was a beautiful thing to hold in the hand, how different was the present day, when gold was just money. The imbalance between the inner and outer life led to 'all that is forced, ignoble and self-conscious' about 'our present drama'.[4] You could see where his own poetry fitted there: to correct the balance also in the twentieth century; to restore spirit to Western materialism. He taught not cultic introversion, but heightened awareness of how to live with nature and things. It was an immense task.

The people Rilke wrote to, and some he did not, helped him pursue his work in ways they themselves could probably not imagine, just by being there. In company he could 'be for [people] roughly what they expect me to be', although 'I am not really present', he told Lou. When he had been writing *Malte* on Capri, in the winter of 1906–7, he sat together in the evenings 'with two middle-aged women and a young girl and they showed me their needlework and sometimes one of them peeled me an apple'. There was nothing 'of destiny' in this acquaintance, 'but I felt something like the mystical power of nourishment of the Last Supper'. The hope was that people existed who 'would be satisfied to radiate their presence and [yet] not expect anything'.

James Leishman made connections between Rilke's life and work that still today no commentator would want to overlook. The second Duino Elegy led him to the letter to Lou on 10 January 1912, from which I've been quoting, and in particular to this passage in which Rilke stated his emotional needs so clearly.

I think it was once in Naples, standing in front of some ancient gravestones, I was suddenly seized by the idea that I ought never to have contact with people in more forceful ways than were shown there. And I really believe that sometimes I can express everything that is bursting in my heart, without loss and without consequences, simply by resting my hand softly on someone's shoulder. Would that not be, Lou, the only conceivable progress [I have made] in terms of that 'holding back' you recently reminded me of?[5]

The eighty lines of the second Elegy are, like all the *Elegies*, a tumult of feeling and imagery. Unlike the shorter poems of the

previous decade nothing is rhymed, but pictures of life and meas-
ures of feeling fall wondrously over each other to declare: 'Look,
these trees really *are*; and the houses we live in still endure.' The
lines proceed with such a determined rhythm that appeals alike
to angels and to lovers unfold judiciously. Their quantities are just
right. It is only that Rilke feels he must hold this intensity back
from his relations with actual people.[6] He mustn't get too close.

This is Vita Sackville-West's translation of lines 95–114:

> Have you not been amazed at the discretion
> With which all human gestures were portrayed
> In Attic statues? Were not love and parting
> Laid on their shoulders with so light a touch
> As though they knew them in a different guise?
> Recall their hands: they touch without insistence,
> Despite the strength that in the torso sleeps.
> They, in their mastery of self, were wise;
> We've travelled far from thence and are condemned
> So to caress each other; for the gods
> Press heavier on us. Yet this concerns
> The gods. If but we also might discover
> Some narrow, pure, restrained humanity!
> Some strip of fertile land to make our own
> Between the current and the stones!
> For our own heart outstrips us, even as theirs did;
> But we are now no longer capable
> Of rendering it in mitigating image,
> Nor yet in godlike bodies,
> Wherein it finds a nobler moderation.[7]

'They, in their mastery of self, were wise' is a fine, simple line,
not contrived at all, as some English commentators think Rilke

is.[8] We need knowledge and self-control to handle ourselves well. That 'we've travelled so far from thence' and become emotionally messier creatures suggests that we have fallen from heaven, but here in peculiar Rilkean terms. Vita introduces the extraneous, though still Christian, idea of humanity being 'condemned'. Yet Rilke, who has worked to transform and transcend his religious background, without ever forgetting it, is lighter. Things are simply thus. There are these two realms, often divided, yet by the thinnest of membranes. We may always hope to encounter grace, just over the other side, seemingly in the next room, just a step away. It's possible.

The peroration after the section break—'If but we also might discover…'—though a little awkwardly translated by the Sackville-Wests, is a superb mixture of regret and sober longing.[9] The romantic, modern way we live—the fierce pulsing of the heart[10]— causes us too much disturbance:

> If but we also might discover
> some narrow, pure, restrained humanity!

Stephen Mitchell strikes a more modern tone with his:

> If only we too could discover a pure, contained,
> human place, our own strip of fruit-bearing soil
> between river and rock.

Yet the effect of abandoning Vita's blank verse is emotionally flat, as if what Rilke advocates isn't urgent at all.

Sackville-West captures the pure sadness of our lack of restraint, and the blindness. We forget how classical art softened human excess. The 'mitigating image' and the 'nobler modera-tion' can teach us everything. Yet in our present age these ideals of the self are just memories in a graveyard. (Well, yes, and that was a century ago.)

The 'eight-page' (in the original handwritten) letter to Lou on 10 January points up the contrast between the public Rilke, without urgency, and the private man, often so anxious. 'I'm a warmer, happier person e.g. with my companions in Capri than the person I actually am alone and when I talk to you.'[11] Yet he wanted no one to take his solitude for a sickness. Indeed, his desire not to be thought of as *krankhaft*, sickly or morbid, shaped the two letters he meanwhile wrote to the psychoanalyst Dr Emil Gebsattel. Rilke struck a tone both polite and searching as he wondered should he follow Clara into analysis.[12] Clara had complained he had this stubbornness and intransigence that allowed him to cut himself off. True, he replied, but 'drive out my devils and I'll lose my angels too'.[13] He had practised *self*-analysis for the last twelve years. That was what writers did, and that way was better for him. An analyst would take the red pen of a schoolmaster to his precariously constructed self and work.

> I know there are things wrong with me... but, believe me, I am totally caught up in the inconceivable, outrageous magnificence of my existence which from the outset was temperamentally impossible and yet progressed from one rescue to the next, as if over very hard stones, such that, had I considered not writing any more, almost what shocks me most is that I wouldn't have written down the entirely wonderful course of my life, however unusually I have experienced it. Oh, all around me I see miserable fates and hear about chance happenings and it sets me thinking. Can you understand, my dear friend, that with any kind of soothing survey and classification [of my feelings] I would be afraid to disturb a much higher order of

things, which, after all that has happened, I must accept is for me, even when it destroys me?[14]

Perhaps a feature of the impossible temperament—in the original the character he was born with—was the effeminacy to which Lou first drew his attention. Against that he had recently made friends with the deep and searching writer Rudolf Kassner, 'who can make something of what is feminine in me'.[15] Ten years hence the eighth Elegy would carry a dedication to Kassner, surely dating back to their 1912 meeting.[16]

The Duino cycle reaches a certain point with its eighth instalment, and the way Leishman summarizes it suggests that Elegy too had its origins in Rilke's winter 1912 reflections. 'Already certain fundamental defects or weaknesses in human nature have been lamented [by Rilke]: our transitoriness, our inability to accept it as a condition... our fear of death.' Kassner thought Rilke was wrong to demand that we live in a spiritual world where, again in Leishman's summary, 'there is no time, no past or future, no end, no limit, no separation or parting'. Kassner urged a belief in Christ the Redeemer on Rilke. The Christian idea was that mankind could progress in time because of Christ's sacrifice. But Rilke did not accept that Christian faith, through contrite conscientiousness, was the only way to achieve a moderate, tempered existence.[17] The eighth Elegy, with its famous line about 'the happiness of the gnat', was his rejoinder.[18] Rilke found moderation and forbearance in animals. The stars made him think of a continuous openness to eternity. And he decided to live within those horizons, on the one hand paying attention to the tiniest feature of creation; and on the other recalling his own insignificance in the ongoing cosmic expanse.

The conversation at Duino pitched Kassner's progressive vision of society, inspired by the New Testament, against, according to

Kassner, Rilke's fondness for the Old Testament. Yet to my mind Rilke's real fidelity was to an often savage, ahistorical nature more than to a God who enjoyed revenge. In their debate Kassner represented the Apollonian and Rilke the Dionysian point of view, to employ Nietzsche's fundamental modern choice. Rilke's variation on the Dionysian, in place of the high culture of the Renaissance, and of the moral institutions of Christianity, was to love 'the openness / deep in the face of the animal' and 'the pure space ahead of us / in which the flowers live and die.'

The philosophical implications of these conflicted thoughts about humanity ran far deeper than anything Rilke had to say about actual human beings. Yet the poems had the courage to weave together the great themes with all the smaller irritations. The mixture makes them still so readable now.

A constant irritation for him was his mother. From Duino he mentioned her to Lou again. Her egregious Catholic piety embarrassed him. Some people might understand, be able to describe and even admire such a nature, he wrote, but for him Phia had no self-awareness and no proper connection to reality. Her feelings of devotion and compassion were vague and unreal.[19] As we see it now, the psychological problem was surely that the son was too much like his mother. He too was prey to unreality, but saved by his talent. He would write a furious poem about her in October 1915, complete with her daily cleansing visits from Jesus. The theme was 'Everything I build my mother tears down'. Or 'My mother always insists on bursting in'. The balladic-like repetitions of 'ach wehe'—oh misery—cast Phia as a demon.[20]

Rilke was not close to his father either, but after Josef Rilke died on 14 March 1906, Rilke, in his 'Portrait of My Father as a Young Man', tried to sympathize with him as a person. The portrait, a faded photograph, was of a man almost not there except for the dreams he must have had, and the splendid military uniform he wore. The life concentrated in him in the photograph became ever harder to grasp. The poem, about the father's death, and the poet's own mortality, reflects on the transience of them both. How is it that either of us have ever been here? It is decorative but stark—Rilke's world view in a few words.

While he processed intense feelings in Duino, including thinking once again about both parents, Rilke's best correspondents served up situations Rilke could deal with easily and even enjoy. They didn't make demands or provoke crises. Two of his young readers in the winter of 1912 wrote to say they had been deeply affected by Rilke's novel, published in 1910. *Malte* was the story of a sensitive young poet's impossible life in the Paris where both he and Rilke struggled. The novel though was not really about its story. Not to give them a lesson in literary criticism, but Rilke cautioned against taking too much to heart this intense, meditative tale of decline and destruction. His readers might do themselves some harm.[21] Still, it was a 'very clever young girl', solicitous of his well-being, who wrote then offering to buy Rilke a dog, since he was alone. 'Dear child!' He wrote back to say he had befriended a local dog in her honour. She enclosed some photographs of herself. He asked what she looked like in the one she hasn't sent, of her in her seventeenth year.

He tells a fellow writer that he doesn't have a large window on people. Those who die young, and women in love, are his index of humanity. From there he can open up dimensions of intense feeling to power his visions.

> Have you taken to heart Gaspara Stampa's story,
> enough to understand how any girl might feel
> whose lover has left her; the idea that
> she might copy that intensity?

Gaspara was a young sixteenth-century noblewoman who, after loving and losing, could barely recover her will to live. Rilke fed on the rarefied sense of loss he found in Gaspara's two hundred sonnets.[22] Women were the great lovers throughout history, he concluded in the first Elegy. Their passions conquered the transient and redefined the spiritual. The male sex, even Dante, fell short.[23] Rilke was wrong in his low estimation of what men can bring to love. But that was another way of insisting on the limits of his own romantic devotion. Whatever he felt, love, or something less, he took for his writing.

There are things to get straight here. I mentioned earlier how the much anthologized 'Love Song' of March 1907 was actually a renewed plea for the loved one not to come too close, and not to expect his total involvement.

> How can I position my soul not
> to touch on yours? How can I
> keep it open to things beyond your doors?
> I would so much want to find a spot
> lost in the dark, a quiet place,
> not yours, and which would remain my space
> wherever your deep feelings go.
> Yet everything that touches you and me has wings,
> seizes us both in one stroke of the bow
> and makes one voice out of two strings.
> Who has tuned us to what instrument?
> And which fiddler has been sent
> to play us? How sweetly we sing.

This 'Love Song' says it's folly to get too involved, and yet, ignoring the model of Attic moderation, it's what we do. It really is a fine poem, that doesn't deserve to have its less attractive psychological origins, of Rilke's flight from commitment, thrown in its face.

Its partner was that poem where Rilke experienced romantic love *without constraint*: 'Tear out my eyes; I still can see you'. That very early poem to Lou expressed the feminine intensity in love that then nearly destroyed him. In that way *he* was Gaspara Stampa, who also wrote poems to survive.

> Like Stampa he had learnt to keep his balance:
> should our oldest pains at last not
> profit us? Surely yes. Now's the time, dear lover,
> to tremulously cast free of the beloved and
> endure: like the arrow that flies from the bow
> and transcends itself in all its concentrated power.
> We must move on. There's no place we can simply stop.

I've expanded the famous last line of the first Elegy, '*Denn bleiben ist nirgends*', to make clear how, in the original context at least, it fitted Rilke's recurrent need to escape intimacy and start again. Of course, there is a philosophical dimension. But the temptation to inflate those four words with a precious nomadism of the soul is to state more than is written.[24]

It was Rilke's achievement, as poet and man, to move on from Lou. But if ever we wanted a new definition of love we might look at the very shape of their correspondence, starting in 1897 and lasting till his deathbed in 1926. They are so tightly bonded. In a volume of 505 pages, their physical passion is over by page forty-four.[25] But the loving friendship, the deep attachment and, on his part, the dependency, never end. Dying, it is from Lou that he takes his last leave: *proshchai, dorogaya*. Goodbye, dear one. He learnt Russian to be nearer to her. Imagine Tristan and Isolde, rather than dying together, had agreed to separate but never to part. It's true it goes a little against the romantic grain. On the other hand it reminds us that Lou and Rilke were deeply real.

Before Christmas 1911 he wrote her a poem, perhaps marking ten years since they had parted as lovers. The unofficial anniversary was round about that time, give or take a few months. The result, which possibly embarrassed her, really was a love poem.[26]

II

> Who else will put into words
> what happened to us? We caught up.
> Before we had had no time. I matured
> in a great burst of youth left behind,
> while you, my love, went through
> the wildest childhood, courtesy of my heart.

III

> It's not enough just to remember. Living like that,
> in those sheer moments: that thought must become the
>   ground I stand on.
> It was when the most bountiful, measureless answers
> struck me. I don't have thoughts. I simply am and my being
> stirs in me for the sake of you. I don't conjure you up
> out of those sadly vacated places where you once were;
> even the places you aren't are still warm from you
> and more real and more than any loss. Longing
> is too unspecific. Why should I
> cast myself aside, while your influence rests lightly
> upon me, like moonlight on a window seat.[27]

Rilke's marriage to Clara pales by comparison, and in that one feels sorry for all of them. There is a sad poem from early summer 1906, when Rilke is still with Rodin at Meudon. Entitled 'Marriage', it suggests that rather than the 'feminine' 'suffering' soul in helpless love, in this relationship he has been 'the man', with the effect of 'expending' his wife and 'confounding' her and meeting the easily aroused fears of her fragile soul 'like a descending stone'.[28]

As for his attachment to their daughter Ruth, the poem he wrote 'on her tenth birthday' from Duino on 12 December 1911 was, with its oblique and distant talk of stars, pitiful, like the estranged parent turning up at the party with the wrong present.[29] He knew it was an inadequate relationship but that he could do nothing about it.

People all around him criticized Rilke for neglecting his family. When wife and young child were effectively abandoned, Lou thought Clara should call the police.[30] In a letter at Christmas 1919, only published in 2009, never before translated into English, Rilke faced up to these accusations, which had begun soon after Ruth was born. It was, quite unexpectedly, a letter to his mother. She had complained that he never wrote. He acknowledged the failing, urged her not to take it to heart, and then confessed so much more:

> Oh, my life long I've had little talent for being a son, a grandson and such things, and by the same token I must accept the reproach that as a father I have been careless and inattentive. Other things made such urgent demands upon me that by way of them I thought I could forget things that would otherwise have been imperative. If only I had *more strength*, how willingly would I have taken the one and the other upon me and here and there lovingly played my part. But there is enough *only* for my work, and for the tasks and achievements that one way or

another are connected *with it*, the requirements of art become ever more relentless, the further one progresses with it, and since it is fortunately the case that you value my activity and hold it in esteem, so please grant it, grant it sometimes this priority over me, without jealousy and without concern. I ask you once again: *thus*! [in English in the original][31]

The emphasis was also Rilke's own.

Our moralistic age finds Rilke's behaviour towards his wife and child hard to accept. 'Rilke was a jerk,' is a favourite indictment from the American poet John Berryman. The critic Michael Dirda has called him 'one of the most repugnant human beings in literary history'.[32] Back in little England, Philip Larkin—himself a thoroughly nasty type when it came to women and much else—accused Rilke of living off women. More recently the poets and editors John Pilling and Peter Robinson noted that 'Rilke never managed his domestic situation (a marriage and a daughter, Ruth) with anything resembling responsibility or imaginative grasp. [He squandered], as it seemed to some, all the emotional reserves thereby left untouched largely on *Bildung* and self-development.'[33] How pompous can academic literary criticism get! (And is it literary criticism at all?) The novelist Nicole Krauss does best when she concludes: 'Freed of the weight of wife and daughter, Rilke forced himself to work every day.'[34]

That work, paradoxically, painfully, helped redefine love in Western society. Take that how you will. Foremost in an early twentieth-century scramble to show love had its own splendid history, independently of the Church, Rilke was one of the first to identify the sexual with the 'innermost'. By that he meant cherishable but pagan feelings quite distinct from Christian *caritas* and family piety. Love so understood was inseparable from religious and cosmic impulses. But there was nothing moral or social about it. Nothing that could found an institution. That disturbs those of us—most of us?—who want to live passionately, but also kindly. Then again Rilke was unique, and just as he appealed to his mother, so he appeals to us: grant me this. Let me be the way I am. I'm made to sacrifice everything for my poetry.

A debate raged in the first half of the twentieth century about the place of passion in Western society, and he was caught up in it. Many humanists were suspicious of unbridled feelings that the Darwinian revolution, and the dwindling of bourgeois standards, seemed to have licensed. The best-known scholar to publish in the twenty years after Rilke's death found that the intense sexual love such as joined Abelard and Héloïse hurt the sanctity of marriage, and must be renounced.[35] Denis de Rougemont, who held this view, was challenged by a woman scholar who suggested that men and women enjoying loving fulfilment, unfettered by social convention, marked a moment in which humanity reached new heights.[36] Both writers knew Rilke's work.

A touchstone for understanding modern, post-Christian love was the rediscovery of Plato's *Symposium*, which Rilke urged upon one of his Duino correspondents in the winter of 1912. Reading the Plato Rilke must have agreed with Diotima, that love carried the mind into another realm, and it was the mind that mattered. After Rilke's death it would become almost commonplace to define romantic love as humanly mysterious, and to see the erotic as a distinct kind of love, alongside charity, compassion and love of one's parents.[37] Love was a human resource but it wasn't necessarily orderly or pious. Modern thought, twentieth-century thought, had to consider all those forms of love together, in a way of which Plato surely would have approved.

Rilke chose to make physical passion serve his poetry. The last two lines of the 1914 poem 'Es winkt zu Fühlung aus allen Dingen' (Everything out there inspires our feeling) are like a private manifesto.[38] We noticed it before, the post-coital image in the last two lines, with the poet ('The lover I have become') and the 'fair world' lying alongside him. The world is gendered female and figured as a sexual partner. Her head now rests on her lover's breast and she weeps. She has submitted to him. It's an image that helps to stabilize his position in life: a cosmic marriage entered into by one who feels himself very much a phallic man. It reminds me of Nietzsche's last girlfriend, the sun. Of course it's desperate. But it reminds us of the intensity of feeling locked up inside, looking for an object, and an outlet.

Those feelings, and what we do with them, are our inwardness, he suggested. Some philosophers might dispute the possibility of any value or experience being validly described as 'inward'. But most non-philosophers feel they're wrong. This was the marker Rilke laid down. The inward was the realm, the sensation, and the imaginative comfort that the erotic could create—above all when the love was of the world as such, and not of a specific person.

At a time when a mixture of social licence and psychoanalytical scepticism—Rilke's 'our present drama'—were playing havoc with the sweetest of human ties, to cultivate love was an attempt, which Rilke felt entirely for himself, to recognize the intensity of human feelings that often did not fit in the prescribed, often religious, way of things through the centuries but which created a quite autonomous sense of the power of humanity. Another of the books he praised at this time was the fictional, then seen as historical, *Letters of a Portuguese Nun*, featuring the passion of Mariana Alcoforado for a French soldier. (The work had already commended itself to the English poet Elizabeth Barrett Browning, and, in the same generation, to the German poet Annette von Droste-Hülshoff.) Rilke, who translated the letters, also embedded Alcoforado's example of unrequited love in *Malte*.[39] Love like that was the richest creative fuel; a magnificent source for humanity, but also unruly and destructive, and not necessarily kind to those who wanted to be happy.

If love for Rilke was, in the poems at least, primarily sexual longing, then, as we've seen, he often put himself in situations where he was deliberately far from the loved one, so as to have that energy at his disposal. He so thrived creatively on the pain of separation that he devoted a section of his first Duino Elegy to this self-lacerating practice. The idea was to experience the intensity of 'intransitive love' or 'objectless love' and use it to gain a sense of meaningfulness and connection in the world through the body. Love of this kind might be akin to the sexual ecstasy of the saints imagining congress with Christ. Rilke practises a tradition of martyrdom which painters and sculptors have shown to us as an extreme form of autoeroticism. The religious description of ecstasy is often of a human state somewhere between exultation and despair, intense pleasure and intense pain, of possession by some greater force, imagined as divine love. It is often accompanied by the visitation of angels, as if to restore an image of sexual innocence. But in any case the moment, and the pleasure, are rooted in the complete eclipse of individual will and power of expression. Caravaggio's *Mary Magdalen in Ecstasy* (1606) and Bernini's *The Ecstasy of Saint Teresa* (1647–52) are commonly given as examples.[40] Extremely erotic, they are conceived in a religious framework that allows orgasm to suggest the depths and mystery of an 'inner' life.

But then taking Christ, or the world, as one's lover could also simply and prosaically be called masturbation. Every time I read the third Duino Elegy, drenched as it is in male genital excitation, I say to myself that I don't know whether I can keep up with this, and I'm not sure it would be different if I inhabited a male body either. What I can see, as a reader, and a historian of ideas, is that Rilke had this post-Darwinian idea of a fluid world ever in creation and was moved to put (male) ejaculation at the centre of it. Here was the beginning of things, in a way that each of us could experience. It is extraordinary that the biology new in Rilke's day stimulated, if that is the word, this staggering new imagery. We might think again here of Plato's idea of sensual love, that it was only ever a means to some greater truth. We might ask whether the magical mystery tour is worth the detour, or whether Rilke on love exemplifies a kind of perversion. A number of his poems dwell in a magical carnal solitude.

It depends how you read the late poem 'Eros' (1924) whether you end up relishing the blinding force that hurls two strangers together, urgently to discover what they can mean to each other, and what energy and dependence that might unleash (and hope that neither is already thinking what they will do with all this energy *afterwards*), or whether you support the call for masks and sympathize with the poet's deep inner lament that, alas, he has involved his heart again and is no longer free. 'Masks! Masks! Someone stop Eros from dazzling us!'[41] The bristling and desperate opening plaints sound like a warning, from a compulsive seducer to his latest potential victim; or maybe they are a plea for personal delivery—please don't make that happen to me again—suffused with a confession of weakness.

Lou, whose book *The Erotic* was, as we have seen, deeply influenced by her experience with, and of, Rilke, might more helpfully for posterity have called it 'Five Essays in Modern Love'. She was interested in women's experience, in the limits of marriage, and the fact that love was often primarily about sex. She wrote about the creative energy that love unleashes, about the strangeness of the other person, which is never entirely overcome; and 'what human beings with their feverish intellects have made out of sex' and how they wrap it up and obscure it with talk of moral virtues like friendship and constancy and self-sacrifice.

She further declared that artists have a special licence when it comes to love. They can treat it in a distanced way that in normal life would be considered abnormal or perverse or cruel. They can use the intense emotion to feed their work.[42] Lou and Rilke (though he is a love poet and she a writer on eroticism and psychoanalysis) together still present a cool challenge to our sentimentality.

*

If he was inconstant as a lover, he was not penitent. We remember his advice to the young poet: you have to sort these things out for yourself. Women became his lovers, briefly, and he discarded them. He could live with that.

Yet there was an occasion, momentous and even furious for him, when he confronted not a love affair, but his lapsed friendship with the artist Paula Modersohn Becker, that somehow tugged at his conscience. Paula Becker, as she was when they first met, was one of the two young women in white dresses when he first arrived in Worpswede. She might have been his love choice, except that she was already engaged, albeit to the much older painter Otto Modersohn. Clara was the sculptor, Paula the painter. Rilke wrote his 'Requiem für Paula Modersohn Becker' (Requiem for Paula Modersohn Becker) and subtitled it 'For a Friend'.[43] A long poem, it elaborately explored parallel realities amid difficult human intimacy and belated wonder. Rilke made a point of noting beneath the title that he wrote it over three nights from 31 October to 2 November 1908, in Paris.

It's like a precursor to the *Duino Elegies*. It's the symphony that was written before the symphonies proper were numbered, the prequel that was never included in the official cycle. Rilke's biographer Ralph Freedman writes that this long and passionate poem represents the final act in the drama that had involved Rainer Maria Rilke and Paula Becker during the eight years since they had met. And it clarifies, on the first anniversary of her death, why Rilke's confrontation with it had been largely hidden from view. The dangerous proximity to his own endangered self explains a good part of his ambivalence.[44]

Yes, perhaps. But it's the proximity that is so moving.

Paula died in childbirth, aged only thirty-one. The cause was an embolism that formed in the bloodstream. All had seemed well. She was sitting up in bed, gratified to have delivered her baby, and contemplating what lay ahead in her life as a painter. Having studied in Paris, and absorbed many of the same influences as Rilke came upon after her—Van Gogh, Cézanne, Gauguin—she had developed a unique style of simplified outlines and a rich use of colour to model those stylized figures she portrayed: women, children, herself naked in the mirror. In a work that Rilke loved she depicted herself pregnant, her belly ripe like the fruit that gave all her women and children the natural dignity he admired, a meaningfulness shading into a kind of sacredness for which there was no name, outside of the painting itself. All that he now put into his poem in her memory.

The requiem—it came to be known as 'Requiem for a Friend'— is an epic narrative. It travels to an exotic land and the traveller demands to see the king. He tastes the fruits of those other climes, bribes the priests and admires the statues. One might say, echoing the most famous critical observation ever made about Rilke, that, typically for his poetry, it travels inwardly.[45] But it does not read like that. This fantasy is a real place, or this real place is fantastic. The directions and conditions of travel, inner and outer, real and fantastic, are threads woven together. They create, aided by alliteration and verbal echo, Rilke's peculiar poetic fabric made of day and night, individual and cosmic, living and beyond. He's saying stay with me here a while. This is my tale. Not rhyme does the work in this requiem but lots of tiny shifts of meaning that build up the emotional texture, and the intensity. (And this in turn sounds just like how he described Rodin's technique in modelling a human figure.) Maybe a prefix is added to a kernel of meaning, or changed, or a vowel is modified, or a familiar word is used in such a way that its etymology signifies its meaning, not its current status in the language. All this makes the perfectionist translator's work impossible. Then there is the forward momentum, here a passionate searching in the dark, in the dark of Rilke's Paris room at night, as he attempts to call back his neglected friend from the dead and salute her and mourn her well.

There is a marvellous passage, sometime after the poet's own exotic journey on her behalf, when now it is Paula's indomitable spirit that is travelling. She is like the figurehead at the prow of a ship. She surges on and no ship's captain can hold her back, as she sprints over the waves in the bright sunshine. There is also an elaborate, intensely difficult extended metaphor relating to that blockage in the bloodstream that killed her. In fact blood, sometimes used in his correspondence as shorthand for how he is feeling generally, is here in the poem figured as a presence within; another way of imagining a life-shaping inwardness within each person. It is one of Rilke's themes and here he finds himself talking to this blood of Paula's, sympathizing with its growing tired at all the effort that has gone into making the child; and with the fact that it can't make the final circuit that would have saved Paula's life.

It's clear from all that we know about the life—almost too much—that Rilke by now was defensive about his neglect of those who should have been dear to him. He also abhorred being blamed. If we remember that for him love is a matter of holding back, of not encroaching too far on the soul of the other, then that is the moment he begs: please, no blame. Indeed, that theme of the March 1907 'Love Song' is quietly repeated here, eighteen months later, the poet behaving like a composer echoing in a new work one of his older themes.

The terrible truth at the core of a poem that so much wants the colour and joy of flowers and trees and the lightness of the air we breathe and the lofty magnificence of the stars to be the truth of our existence—is the male sexual act. The man is to blame. All men, in that sense. We find ourselves here in another version of the expulsion of Adam and Eve from Paradise. Elsewhere we fell from grace because our passions were too hectic. Here it is the cost to women of sexual intercourse. Rilke's views on women and their independence were very much influenced by the feminism of Lou and of their campaigning friend Ellen Key. He had this great sympathy for women, especially for women writers and artists. Though it is the social convention and a reproductive necessity, he says in his poem in memory of Paula, no man should take possession of a woman and stop her life. It ought to be possible to say that. The Requiem is thus a lament (*eine Klage*) but also a complaint (*eine Anklage*). There is a thundering emphasis on *der Mann*, the male sex as such, to blame for ending this woman's life and dreams.

Altogether Rilke would prefer reproduction and death to happen the way they happen in the vegetable kingdom and in fairy tales. St Francis broadcasts his seed in *The Book of Hours*. Here Paula eats the seeds of her own death and finds them sweet.

He is very close to Paula in the poem. The tone is extraordinarily intimate. There is a moment near to the beginning when, having welcomed her back from the dead reluctantly—for why would anyone leave that no-longer-bodied bliss, and return to collide with things, and worry, and seek meaning?—he asks her, friend to friend, what she wants of him. What should he do for her? There is an arresting mixture of male confusion before the woman, and genuine humility and desire to do the right thing, when he starts the third section with a dismayed, childlike 'please tell me what you want me to do. Is there somewhere I should go for you?' *'Sag, soll ich reisen?'*

> Tell me, is there somewhere I should go for you?
> Did you leave something behind there, now craving
> to get back to you? I could go to that country,
> a place you never saw yourself though it was just
> at the other side of all you felt.

Partly the intimacy comes from Rilke's belated appreciation of her painting. It was something he neglected in life. He came late to recognizing her talent, perhaps only began to see it now she was dead. Nor in Paris had he wanted to be disturbed in his own engagement with the city, and during his time with Rodin. Still there were times he could look back on, as when she embarked on his own portrait, and in the course of their rapprochement he saw a number of her late canvases. He describes them meticulously in the poem, and with awe:

> That's what you grasped: the fullness of the fruit.
> You laid them in a bowl before you
> and used colour to give them weight.
> And just like fruit you saw your women
> and the children too, the very form of their being
> as if filled out from within.
> And finally you saw yourself as a fruit,
> got yourself out of your clothes, put
> yourself in front of the mirror,

> steeped yourself in it, a way only you could see;
> but your vision didn't say, that's me. It said: this is.

Stephen Mitchell has made a complete translation of this long, little-read poem. It contains magnificent passages, also in English:

> For this suffering has lasted far too long;
> None of us can bear it; it is too heavy—
> This tangled suffering of spurious love
> Which, building on convention like a habit,
> Calls itself just, and fattens on injustice.

What was Rilke saying? That Paula should not have married a widower her father's age, and even if she did, they should not have had a child? That, I think, would be the injustice.

Mitchell continues:

> For this is wrong, if anything is wrong:
> Not to enlarge the freedom of a love
> With all the inner freedom one can summon.
> We need, in love, to practise only this:
> Letting each other go. For holding on
> Comes easily; we do not need to learn it.[46]

Hugh MacDiarmid already in 1931 made the earliest English translation of most of the 'Requiem for a Friend'. His partly rhymed version makes us wonder which English poets first tasted Rilke's art of loving through him:

> I feel your plight and have no name for it.
> Let us lament together—the broken mirror
> And you found naked in your hiding place.

· · · · · ·

No one could think of anything to please.
You knew it, and sat up in childbed there
And from the mirror that was you received
Your own self back, eager as a woman is
Dressing for visitors and doing her hair.

· · · · · ·

                              Customs hither.
We need more customs. Let us show our grief.

· · · · · ·

You grew so homely, taking in your looks,
Like flags the morning after a fête—[47]

Rilke celebrated brilliant, unusual women. He deserves our great
admiration for that.

EIGHT

Three Adventures in Art

As a child and artist Rilke was always attracted to colours and textures, shapes and glitter. His poems luxuriate in sumptuous fabrics and in jewellery he might have worn in another age. His clothes were dandyish when he could afford them—a habit he shared with Baudelaire. There's a famous scene in *Malte* when the young man revels in the possibilities of a dressing-up box in the attic. He's fascinated and then horrified by his reflection in the mirror.[1] And perhaps the clothes themselves had a similar reaction, for Rilke gave to the inanimate object the same narcissistic longing to see its reflection as he felt in himself. He lived a little in the fabrics, burnished surfaces and precious stones, surfaces of water and depths of the rose that came his way. At the end of one of his many poems on Biblical themes the three kings offer the newborn child emeralds and rubies and turquoise—luxuriant words to dress up in. In other poems flashes of light, sun and moon, and an inherent glow in things, like in the Apollo torso, make precious things glint and seem alive, and mirrors duplicate the splendour. Sometimes the mirrors seem like paintings themselves. 'Sometimes you're full of art. Some paintings seem even to have entered you—with others you shyly part.'[2] Or the inside of the rose reflects the whole world. The idea that Rilke was an aesthete is evidently an understatement. Aesthetic and rhythmic transformations embellish his cultural and natural experience relentlessly. His is, as he tells Jakob von Uexküll in 1909, an 'art that shouldn't be seen as a selection of things from the world but as the never-ending transformation of those things into something splendid'.[3] Too much splendour is almost a fault. But the best of Rilke's art, as a painter, is a way of making colours and objects speak for themselves; while, as a poet he finds space in rhyme—in the interplay of the German lexicon—for endless transformations to happen.[4] The two great skills combine.

He might have become an art historian. In 1898, when he was twenty-two, Lou had packed him off to Florence to ground his knowledge of art in a first-hand study of the Renaissance. He'd been dabbling in art history in Prague and Munich for the last couple of years and not to have visited Italy was a failing. Yet in what he took from Florence he showed himself less an historian and more of a spiritual archaeologist. He explored the byways of the gorgeous Renaissance city on the Arno, its churches, its palaces, its galleries and its squares, as if digging to find his own themes there.

> Here so silent life acts out its sacrificial wont.
> Here the day deepens still. Here the night inches
> round a dream like a tower round a font.
> Here life cinches in
> its heart and light and finds its power ensconced
> in intimations: of lovely women and princely pomp,
> Madonnas too whom deeper thanks now prompt,
> and a monk flinching in a cell...
>
> FLORENCE, 16 APRIL 1898

God is dead, he reported, in the 'Florence Diary' he kept for Lou. Or: 'God is the oldest work of art... very badly maintained.'[5] But there is an air of grandeur in the streets, and there are wonderful small interiors, tiny chapels and enclosed gardens, like poems. He wants to enjoy the city, not pass judgement. Often it makes him think of his artistic future in the grandest terms. The task of the present is to complete the Renaissance: to be its after-song. The white blossom was perfect. Now must come the fruit.[6]

> I feel I'm on the way to becoming an intimate of everything that proclaims beauty; that I'm no longer there just to listen in and receive its revelations like silent blessings, that I'm becoming more and more a disciple of things, one who intensifies his answers and confessions through sympathetic questioning, someone who can draw out of them wisdom and allusion, and learn to praise their generous love with a pupil's humility. And through this obedient devotion the path leads to that brotherhood and equality with things that I long for. We protect each other thereby and the ultimate fear becomes a legend to be told.[7]

The wording of this statement, at once intricate and vast in scope, is a programme Rilke fulfils over the years. (It's also noteworthy how it attempts to answer the progressive political pressures of the day by borrowing the political goals for poetry.)

'The Florence Diary' is not much about Renaissance art, nor a great deal about Florence. It is rather a source book for how Rilke, while looking at art and buildings, decides what his poetry will be—and why. Because the Renaissance can still bear fruit, after its flowering, there can be Rilke. God is dead, but as is so evident from Rilke's German, Christianity can still yield riches. It is a matter of our finding the right way to be in the world, after the summation of humanism, and now we can no longer believe God created it; or even that there is a God at all.

Botticelli and Fra Angelico, Benozzo Gozzoli and Andrea Orcagna, draw him in, on his quest. A work 'probably' by this last-named artist, is a 'painting of the triumph of death'. It seems to emerge out of a medieval love song. 'All [the figures] are quiet and grateful for this solitude that they share. A sweet lethargy weighs upon them, betraying itself in the noble folds of their glowing garments.' Just looking at paintings in the Uffizi was a marvellous diversion that surely helped produce such later lines in *The Book of Images* as

> All the garments of the riddle of the world,
> which has for so long kept itself veiled,
> fall within this clasp.[8]

Here is Rilke winding religious mystery around a brooch; celebrating rich garments as if they were a clue to the nature of the cosmos. What 'The Florence Diary' establishes is that we have to see all things equally.[9] Thus the clasp and the cloak and the woman. That endlessly diverse simultaneity is the source of the mystery Rilke feels.

The Renaissance painters backgrounded their great Biblical studies with vignettes of ordinary life. They showed how grandeur and ordinariness might be combined. Rilke learnt a lesson there for when he 'painted' a cathedral during that project he shared with Rodin. His first stanza evoked the towering palace of stone, the second described the village tucked in beneath it. While the cathedral reached for eternity, the village was the children dressed in red or green, 'or whatever material the mercer had to hand', and whose life in the dark narrow streets was a matter of chance.[10] Both mattered equally. But he didn't leave the spiritual geography there. As the poem made landscape out of inner life, and inner life made landscape, the relationship criss-crossed back and forth. In the diary he stated the first part of the equation directly: 'The artist will see into himself as into a landscape. He will be spacious.'[11]

We are told that Rilke 'toyed with becoming a full-time art critic or a museum creator'.[12] But he was more of an art thief, always looking to take what he needed. While reading up on art history he noticed his unwillingness to look away from 'something quintessentially mine... a piece of myself'. He would study, but not to write 'a handbook, some complete conspectus, omitting nothing and arranged in strict chronological sequence'.[13] No, he would do it differently: and, in the beginning, always with Lou in mind.

> And I take the beautiful gift,
> Want to mould it quietly,
> Unfold all its colours
> And hold it, full of shyness,
> Up towards YOU.

And:

> Shall I tell you of my crowded days
> Or of my place of sleep?
> My desires run riot
> And out of all paintings
> The angels follow me.[14]

Three-quarters of a century later, Cy Twombly included some of Rilke's words in a painting of his own made in Rome. It was a tribute and also an admission, of a Rilkean kind, that Rilke's poems have this intense though never quite fathomable relation to paintings, real or imagined, while Twombly the painter cared greatly for words, added to the canvas as if they were supplementary objects, evidence of another resource besides form and colour.[15]

Florence enhanced all Rilke had to invest in colours and shapes and, with that investment secured, called it 'me'. In the diary, 'red evenings... and the Ponte Vecchio... thread like a black ribbon through silk as yellow as the sun. In harmonized tones of brown and grey the city stretches out and the Fiesole hills already wear the colours of night.' His task, vis-à-vis all that impacts upon him, was to choose 'the right bowls into which to place what he has liberated from his consciousness, like flowers and pieces of ripe fruit'.[16]

But come back to Munich, from where the Florence excursion was made. At the time that stately, still monarchical city was the most exciting artistic centre in Germany for poetry, drama, music and design. Rilke had been living there on and off since September 1896. Wassily Kandinsky, the greatest non-French colourist, arrived in 1901 and a few years later the city would become the home of the 'Blue Rider' painters, including the gorgeous early modernist painter of animals, Franz Marc, as well as Kandinsky himself. Rilke looked at many paintings. It was de rigueur to visit the Schackgalerie, a highly conservative collection of stylized nineteenth-century German art. At the same time the city was full of aesthetes like himself, straining against the old-fashioned tendency.

In its place they were living the *fin de siècle* dream. That lovely poem 'Der Knabe' ('The Boy'), though he didn't set it down until the winter of 1902–3, placed Rilke at the heart of the new inventiveness. The poem evoked the glamour of the military life, as a boy dreamt it. It's a theme one can find in grand opera—Bellini—and in the poet Alfred de Vigny's *Grandeur et servitude militaires* (1835). The glorious choreography of battle was so deeply rooted in nineteenth-century European culture that it became part of male childhood. As in Rilke's *The Lay of Cornet Christoph Rilke*, a thrilling narrative he first wrote in 1899, 'The Boy' glorifies swashbuckling soldiery. To gallop through the night by torchlight; to carry a huge flag; to dwell amidst Rembrandtian golden helmets and trumpets gleaming in the darkness: the topic is deeply romantic (although, in practice, during his teenage years as a cadet, Rilke had hated the military experience).

> The houses bow down behind us,
> the streets bend the way we come,
> the squares back away but then we seize them,
> and ride with a swish like the rain.[17]

This magical mood is young Rilke's default, and here the picture is strikingly dynamic, hinting at the sensational simplification of movement that Italian and Russian Futurism would realize, when in just a few years' time late-Romantic excitement would meet a new, modern feeling for speed, rendered by the angular slash.

The boy's dreams of galloping through the night, sword in hand, helmet gleaming, might have come from *Jugendstil* illustrations to fairy tales and legends. The German and Austrian equivalents of art nouveau wove the natural, the supernatural and the devotional into superb new ornamental forms between 1895 and 1910. It seemed every book and magazine was ornamented, as material prosperity brought life and art together, in a new vision of how to live. Rilke collaborated at this time with his friend Vogeler. Heinrich Vogeler was a kind of German William Morris and Aubrey Beardsley combined, with elements of Voysey in the house he built for himself and his friends in Worpswede, and Charles Rennie Mackintosh and Roger Fry in his early modernist furniture.[18] As an artist and illustrator he reproduced beautiful patterns from nature in all kinds of objects in daily use, from cutlery to lamps. He was also a poet, painter and book artist. Together, in what they had in common, Rilke and Vogeler were romantic modern(ist)s.[19] They intimated what was amiss in cities where they did not live—Vogeler became a communist after the First World War and ended his life in Soviet Russia. But as the new century dawned, the two young aesthetes celebrated the beauty of young brides, women's hair, silk, roses and mysteriously gliding boats. Vogeler could have designed a set for Wagner's *Lohengrin*. *Jugendstil* motifs epitomized Rilke's early collection 'Lieder der Mädchen' ('Songs about Girls').

Poetry and visual art were so close at the time that published poems veritably demanded to be illustrated. In 'Songs about Girls' Rilke collaborated with another great illustrator of the period, Ludwig von Hofmann, such that the girls' 'erotic sensations were reinforced by the swirling lines of the grass and the trees'.[20] Hofmann was another prime mover in spreading the message of the English Arts and Crafts Movement in Germany, which, in its turn, coveted the handmade book published on quality paper and with specially commissioned designs, decorative lettering, patterned motifs and crafted endpapers. It was the Insel Verlag that in Germany led this fashion begun in England by the Kelmscott Press, and Insel became Rilke's publisher as early as 1900.[21]

I mentioned Wagner just now, who is so often travestied by monotonous reference to the thunderous, supremely tuneful 'The Ride of the Valkyries'. He was a composer with a vast emotional range, full of quite opposite tenderness, capable of supremely hushed tones and desperate passions, his scores densely woven in the mysterious space between art and nature. It's important to say this because the feeling for that mystery was in Rilke too. His quiet moment was when

Everything has come to rest:
light and dark,
a book. A flower in the park.[22]

But tense and emphatic was just as often the character of his
deeply cultivated involvement with nature:

Quiet friend of distant places,
feel how your breath still fills up a space.
In the bell tower's darkness, under the eaves,
sing out, please. Something tugs at you, doesn't it?
It will make you strong.
Become this, become that, this shape, that line.
Has life done you so much wrong?
The drink may be aloes, but you can be wine.
In this night so much empowered
weave a spell of all you feel, as the road divides,
feel the sense of what has been.
And if the earthly has forgotten you:
tell the earth: I'm still in full flow.
Tell the flowing river: I am.[23]

The creative life of Rilke's early twenties was already a Wagnerian
Gesamtkunstwerk, every aspect of it 'worked through' by imagination. It sometimes seems that only the wealthy can really make
art of their daily lives, then certainly, and sometimes even now.
But there was a sense, in Germany in the late nineteenth century,
as in England fifty years earlier, that it might be possible to create
a thoughtful, bearable materialism for a public forced to become
consumers (as cheap industrial products multiplied all around) and
to complement that material satisfaction with complex, inspirited
poetry and painting and music.

The great resource was nature, for its lovely shapes. Neither a world of manufacturing nor a generation of urban dwellers should forget that gift of beauty, always in store. *Jugendstil* showed art winding itself mythically around nature. The art of love, by the same token, was like a precious plant that grew in the soil. Peter Behrens's 1898 woodcut captured the essence of Munich *Jugendstil*, and twenty years later, as we've just seen, in 'Quiet friend of far places', Rilke's *Sonnets to Orpheus* would retain this sacred–fantastical mood.[24]

The literary journal *Jugend*, where Rilke's earliest work appeared, also published poems by the cultish aesthete Stefan George, much read by the young Rilke, and by Hugo von Hofmannsthal, the Austrian lyric genius who shared Rilke's fascination with the deep human past as revealed by Darwin. All three contributors embodied the same aesthetic by which nature was rediscovered with a new kinship. Myths and legends of the human soul were embedded there, as in Schoenberg's ravishing *Transfigured Night* of 1899, where an abandoned pregnant woman wandered through a wood and was rescued by a stranger. In painting, Kandinsky's stately *Couple Riding* of 1906 was created out of a mass of tiny colour stipples and set against birch trees through which the light filtered enchantingly. The lights of a traditional Russian city—no trace of industry—glowed on the far bank of a river. The whole looked as if it were illuminated, or painted on glass.

One of Kandinsky's aims was to keep hold of beautiful things, and claim spiritual values for art, as the times shifted uncertainly. His style at this stage of his career reached forward to the beginnings of German expressionism, and abstraction, but also back to neo-Romanticism. Rilke's own answer—and he was nearly twenty years younger—was to pick out objects in common use that might be neglected for their spiritual and artistic potential, and list them together like chants. 'The bridge, the gate, the well, the jug; fruit tree, window—' and 'place and dwelling, camp and ground and home'. His vision, spiritual without being religious, countered—and I think he was fully aware of it—the nitty-gritty materialism that socialism presented in every newspaper and on every street corner.[25] French Symbolism had encouraged wondrous escapist dreaming among the Austrian-German middle classes faced with the threat of the new and Rilke picked up an element of that. The English bourgeois fashion for arts and crafts had encouraged his interest in buildings and interiors, and he loved the great houses and their gardens years before Paris. He loved parks. Yet in the end all these fashionable things were only pegs for his unique mentality, because he was able to transform them.

A satirical columnist for *Jugend*, which was based in the Bavarian capital, somewhat tongue-in-cheek encouraged its readers

> to paint your walls simply white and put in the corner or on the wall one of those wonderful bowls that have a glow of flying humming-birds, sunsets and the foaming sea... put things in your rooms that *you* can love, not as cold, strange things but as your brothers and sisters! That way you will grow rich and never be lonely.[26]

The journal that published Rilke's poetry was not beyond making fun of him in another issue. The sense of those times, which has become clearer a hundred and more years on, is of a flight out of realism, and out of a positivist, scientistic emphasis on facts. So how shall we do those early Rilkean times justice? Unneedy lives sought ever-new cultural diversions, some of which were merely pretty. On the other hand, poetry and *Jugendstil* art, symbiotically bound, were trying to make something aesthetically arresting out of *fin de siècle* decadence, as the power of religion faded and philosophers worried about disenchantment. Rilke himself feared nature was about to disappear under concrete. As a Munich historian put it some time ago: 'The palette of the time shimmered with self-conscious materialism, mystical spiritualism, democratic anarchism and aristocratic individualism.'[27]

When different fashions in painting crossed his path, they enriched Rilke's sense of the object and its place in the world. But still it was the Darwinian revolution that exerted a truly revolutionary pressure on his art. He mentioned the work of the fantastical Swiss-born, sometime Munich-based painter Arnold Böcklin. It may be that Böcklin helped stock his mind with images of tear-stained, pale, upturned faces, faded silk, (Pre Raphaelite) hair, and (*fin de siècle*) gold.[28] But Böcklin's art was also a radical response to Darwin's discovery of the darkest and wildest origins of nature. In a body of work obsessed with 'origins', this artist who would influence the French surrealists famously painted *Triton and Nereide* rising out of the sea. This huge canvas (105.3 cm tall × 194 cm wide) hung in the Schackgalerie at the time of Rilke's visits. It showed the beautiful white-bodied nymph lightly embracing a prehistoric reptile while beside her a Caliban-like figure, half merman, half hominid, blew into a giant seashell like a horn.[29]

Rilke wrote in 1902–3 that Böcklin was part of a move to reinvent the relation of the human person, and the human form, to the natural landscape. This relation would redefine architecture too:

> Art... is the medium in which landscape [nature], the human figure and the world meet and find each other. In reality they live alongside each other, hardly knowing of each other, and in the image, in architecture, in the symphony... they seem to join together in a higher prophetic truth... how seductive it would be to pursue this relation in different works of art... [and show] how a piece of architecture could be half a reflection of ourselves and half of a forest... sometimes the human

being seems to emerge from the landscape and sometimes the landscape from the human person. There are moments when nature seems to come closer, when it gives the cities an appearance of landscape, and with centaurs, mermaids and old men of the sea, Böcklin-style, humanity grows closer to nature. It's always a matter of this relationship, in poetry not least, for poetry has the most to say about the soul when it shows a landscape...

He noted that the human relationship with nature for thousands of years had been 'very one-sided'. The implication was that Darwin (unnamed), with his explanation of the darkness out of which human beings had emerged, had changed the balance. In the wake of Darwin nature for us was now 'cruel and strange':

The landscape is something alien for us, and we are terribly alone among the trees that blossom and the streams that pass. Alone with someone who has died we are nowhere near as exposed as we are alone with trees. For however mysterious death is, life is all the more so, a life that is not our life, a life that takes no part in ours, that celebrates its festivals without seeing us, and which we look upon with a certain discomfort, like guests who have turned up by accident and speak a different language.

Further,

It seems over and over that nature knows nothing of what we make of her and how we anxiously avail ourselves of a little part of her strength. In many ways we intensify her fruitfulness and in other places we stifle her springs with the paving stones of our cities, just as they were about to arise out of the rubble.

We lead the rivers to our factories, but they know nothing of the machines they drive. We play with dark forces that we can't contain with our names for them, as children play with fire, and it seems for a moment as if all the energy was lying unused in things till now, until we came and applied it to our transient life and its needs.[30]

By this token 'the self-conscious materialism' of the Austro-German *fin de siècle*, so apparently superficial and decorative, was in fact deeply agitated about the relation of humanity, and its objects, to nature.

Rilke's monograph on the Worpswede painters, finished in 1902 and published the following year, allowed him to talk about the widest trends in German art as he saw them. Deeper into the text, which astonishingly has never been fully translated into English, Rilke recalled how of a winter evening the first of the half-dozen or so painters to arrive in the little artists' colony, Fritz Mackensen and Otto Modersohn, would sit and talk about Böcklin, 'who drew the deepest and most essential things out of nature and had a blessed gift for expressing them. Memories of Rembrandt surfaced and joined those thoughts.'[31] Rilke found that these local, Nordic artists were itching to join the European mainstream, just as he was.

To canvases by another older German painter, Hans Thoma, Rilke meanwhile dedicated two poems.[32] One was on moonlight. But let me dwell on the second, a short poem about a knight. In 'Ritter' the poet intimates that the man beneath the armour must pulsate with an inner terror of death. Yet outwardly and as we see him as if in uniform the knight is moving boldly through our outside world. This dynamism of the knight in action—the same as belongs to the imagination of 'The Boy'—produces a wonderful procession of things, cultural and natural. The foreshortened lines are intensely rhythmic, alliterative and tightly rhymed. The stream of 'thingliness' is Rilke's measure of how we live in the world.

> Outside is it all: the day and the vale
> the friend and the foe and the feast in the hall
> and May and maids and woods and grail,
> and God many thousand times unveiled
> abounds in the streets.[33]

Rilke's original also has minimal punctuation in its second stanza, only that end stop.

The chance to meet the Worpswede painters came after Rilke took up Vogeler's invitation to visit in August 1901 and stay in one of the richly coloured rooms at the Barkenhoff. Here was the first of Rilke's stays in a house where he enjoyed patronage and hoped to get on with his writing in peace. The exterior of the Barkenhoff was fashionably white. With its rose garden and birches, and its lovely organically curving architecture, it was to its owner and creator what Kelmscott and the Red House were to Morris: places where all the objects were either beautiful or useful, created by the owner's own craftsmanship. Soon after Rilke's arrival, as we know, the publisher Richard Muther, also curious about this artists' colony, followed.

Worpswede is far less well known than the *Rodin*, but, also commissioned by Muther, and with its multiple illustrations, it is indispensable for understanding Rilke. The north-German painters drawn to the flat, sparsely populated countryside beyond Bremen had formed a new kind of artistic community. In England the Cornish painters of St Ives come to mind, and there was in Worpswede the same self-appointed task to understand the local light, and to live next to people whose work bedded them into the landscape. The Worpswede *plein-air* artists, Nordic and German, as Rilke would call them, had had a successful Munich exhibition in 1895. Their subject was a vast moorland long left behind by the North Sea. They painted the canals that silently crossed it and the peasants who scraped a living by digging out the peat and sending it on one of the small flat canal barges to the Bremen market.

In the event, Rilke's essay, with the exception of his celebration of Vogeler, did not lift the painters out of their provincial location. But it gave yet another glimpse of the modernizing journey on which German poetry, painting and drama were embarked in the last twenty years of the Wilhelmine Empire. German art, through heightened realism, was moving towards, eventually, expressionism. Rilke, effectively a German artist of two late empires, was part of that journey too, and I think in his two-track introduction to his monograph, to landscape painting in general, and to its specific role in German painting, he was also once again creating space and context for his own work. Any art historian, he said, 'must be able to see and speak colours'. Any artist must establish his relationship with nature.

It was part of the psychology of the artist—or should we read, autobiographically, of Rilke himself?—that the artist as child struggled to grow up. In his childhood he happily busied himself with nature. But when he reached adolescence, when he really needed nature's sympathy, nature withdrew. Rilke mostly wrote about girls feeling a terrible breaking off of their earlier happiness. Here the moment in the life of the artist generally, when he lost his innocent absorption in things, was what Rilke also had felt, in the course of his girlish inner life. But then again he was talking about landscape, and what he had concluded for himself, that his mature artist should make landscape out of the inner life.

In one guise he wrote *Worpswede* as a historian of the genre of landscape, and described it as a marginal tradition beside portraiture. But then he began to find traits of his own within it.

Landscape painting was people-shy, he said. It loved independent nature 'out there' and saw it as not to be understood in human terms. Nature was, in fact, uncaring; and still we live in it and care deeply for it. As Böcklin showed, it might be a matter of confronting something monstrous. Much ink has been spilt over what Rilke meant by terror, horror, what the angels know, but before he even invented those angels here was the basic fear he shared with Böcklin: a tangled juxtaposition of the prehistoric and the civilized, the feral and the refined, the brutal and the Christian.

The Worpswede painters worked with the genius of locality. The local detail mattered, Rilke said, the uniqueness of every leaf—and he referred his readers to Constable. Cottages submerged in the landscape, 'as if they drew trees in front of them like curtains', and wind-blown trees (which lent their shapes to Vogeler's prints), featured in the Worpswede oeuvre. The scattered, hardly numerous red roofs and the deep-red-brown soil which gave the people their work, took their places too. Worpswede's 'northern colours, colours within', seemed as if waiting for their moment to emerge in the work of these artistic pioneers. The interiors of the cottages, the space shared with cows, were barely furnished with a table and a few chairs, and beds that folded away, and into these cramped interiors the great events of a human life were squeezed. Of passages that seem to be unconscious drafts for the content and/or the form of future Rilke poems, one is the already mentioned meditation on a lonely childhood and melancholy adolescence led in the presence of an unsympathetic nature; another is the way the Umbrian and Tuscan religious painters of the Renaissance added an ideal background of village life; and a third graphically portrayed the rich and the lowly, as they did, as equal features in the landscape.

★

Where are we with Rilke's life? Italy and southern Germany broadened his experience of art and encouraged his questions and, already, his transformations. The two great visits to Russia added vastly to his stock of things-in-the-world and gave him a new exotic vocabulary like those words *boyar* and *gosudar* (Lord).[34] And then he moved to Paris.

I want only to reflect here that the move to Paris directly from Worpswede was really a huge upheaval. From the open-air working life of the north-German peasant Rilke moved to the delicately cultivated life of the Parisian bourgeois strolling through the park. It did jolt him. It did bring confrontations with things that were new inventions, like the electric tram and the telephone and the motor car. Van Gogh coming to Paris from rural Holland had dramatically changed his palette fifteen years earlier. I don't think Rilke's transformation was so fundamental. But the shock was enormously productive.

On a holiday to Sweden and Denmark in the summer of 1904 his art as a painter was a kind of realism shot through with a feeling for personhood—of the perceiver and of the world itself.

> Is that a sky?
>> Light-filled blissful blue
> where the purest of pure clouds drift,
> the ones beneath, white as they lift
> up, the ones above of greyish hue,
> massing warmly as if lined with red
> and over all, sinking to its bed,
> a silent shining sun.[35]

In *Das Buch der Bilder* (*The Book of Images*), where the Skåne poems like this one fit, colours are like garments the world wears. The Russian monk of *The Book of Hours* might have observed that 'Slowly the evening puts on the garments / held for it by a rim of ancient trees'.[36]

But then the poem 'Entrance', by which one enters *The Book of Images*, pays equal attention to the human artist, contributing his work, adding it in to the whole. Here he captures a silhouette.

> Whoever you are: of an evening you come outside,
> from inside your room, which you know so well.
> You know your house is that one there, last on that side;
> wherever you may dwell.
> Your eyes are tired; even so they must try to free
> themselves from the narrow room and lift up a black tree
> against the sky—slowly slowly,
> so it stands there slim and lonely.
> You've made a world, a world immense:
> it's like a word not yet
> emerged from silence. And as your will contains its sense
> your eyes should let
> it go.

The idea is that even to form an image is to impose on the world. It expresses Rilke's passivity in handling the world and its object that Kassner couldn't accept. Yet it is also a wonderful celebration of the active capacity to make images, through enjoying an almost holy contact with things. It is peculiar to Rilke that he has this almost sexual reticence about engaging in his love of the world.

Paris, though, really was an artistic triumph. There Rilke applied to his own art the idea that everything coincided, that everything had its own weight, that every colour and glow mattered, and that when that idea touches things in urban reach the effect is more modern. In this last instance Van Gogh helps him work out what he was after. Van Gogh, with his red of the wine and yellow of the lamp and 'shallow' green of the walls, dwelt in the complete world of *The Night Café*; but there was a sense that what engaged him still more was the relation of colours.

> A park or a municipal path through a park in Arles, with black figures right and left on benches, a blue newspaper reader in the foreground and a violet woman in the background, beneath and between the green of the trees and bushes in the process of being pruned. A man's portrait on what looks like a background woven out of fresh reeds (yellow and greenish-yellow) but which simplifies itself into a unified patch of brightness when you step back. A middle-aged man with a black-and-white moustache trimmed short, hair just as short, sunken cheeks beneath a broad scalp: the whole [done] in a wet dark blue and a layer of bluish-white over it—right up to the huge brown eyes—and finally, one of the landscapes... [with] a setting sun, yellow and reddish-orange, surrounded by a glow of round, yellow fragments: full of rebellion and in complete contrast then blue blue blue the slope of flowing hills, cut off by a strip of soothing dabs of paint (a river?) from the darkness of night which, in the immediate front third of the picture, transparently in antique gold, allows us to see a field and some haystacks.

Rilke sent this magnificent description of five Van Gogh canvases to Clara on 17 October 1907, having seen them in a magazine.

There was some affinity between Rilke and Van Gogh, as I suggested. Both arrived in Paris after being steeped in the country-side; Van Gogh still more. Both were dazzled by the bourgeoisie at leisure. Both felt God still had to have a place somewhere. Both became preoccupied with colour that faded—the subject of Rilke's 'Blue Hydrangea'. Both tried to overcome their existential fears by enjoying the thingliness of things and living in the presence of colour.[37]

In Paris Rilke kept trying to deepen his relationship with colour, noticing how light and surface did their work for Rodin, and then, through the painters, through Cézanne, repatriating the colours in nature. Think, he said, how our colours get their names: ochre from the soil, the blue of shadows, the grey of doves, the white of aluminium, the scant blue of a distant ocean, the sudden flash of bright green in a bed of moss. 'We must in every minute be able to lay a hand on the earth like the first man' (20 October 1907).[38] Coloured things, which are also white and black, and copper and bronze, shiny and shimmering, signal and luxuriate in their strange and haunting splendour. Cézanne works with pigment to capture the spectacle, and the task is to let the colours speak for themselves. 'Let them sort it out among themselves.' Yet the task seems almost impossible. 'Anyone who interposes himself, brings in his own order of things, who brings into play his human superiority, his wit, his advocacy, his intellectual desire to take over, spoils and dims their activity.' Which is why Cézanne works at self-overcoming. He endures 'colossal and humble', leaving the colours to sort themselves out (21 October 1907).

Rilke's encounter with Cézanne, as reflected in his letters to Clara, is among his best-known work. It's only important to note that, definitive as it was, it continued preoccupations that already existed many times over in Rilke's life and practice. One of those deep-rooted responses was fear. Fear that life might be monstrous under the surface, and light a lie. Is Cézanne also afraid of what he sees, he wonders (19 October 1907)? He's relentless, grim, does nothing else but paint, sitting in front of his object, the unknowable world (12 October 1907).

Rilke's alter ego, Malte Laurids Brigge, couldn't survive the feeble gloss of the city barely covering the existential horror. Even for those of us who are happy, could we bear to live 'in a new existence beyond colour, without previous memories' (18 October 1907)? Colour has a vital importance for Rilke, as joy and substance and promise, but he worries there's an element of deep dishonesty. Truer to say we are not very at home in the 'interpreted world', as the first Duino Elegy has it.

The letters to Clara on Cézanne are a treasure. Yet it's possible to exaggerate Cézanne's influence, all the same, for as with Rodin, so with Cézanne, when Rilke talked of the artist's attitude, and his achievement, he talked of himself. Cézanne has the capacity to create presence by tapping into the indwelling presence in things (19 October 1907). He shows 'devotion and [reveals] hidden splendour' (16 October 1907). But these statements are simply what Rilke would like to say of himself. Cézanne is apparently free from judgement and superiority, just the way Rilke has told the young poet any creative artist should be (18 October 1907). With Cézanne one sees that the disciplined artist does not let his emotions overflow. And so on.

Rilke achieved his own finest poem–painting in fact before he saw the Cézannes. From the New Poems, 'The Merry-Go-Round' dated from June 1906 and is actually more like an impressionist painting. It also has elements of an early phonograph recording. An enchanted turntable furnished with teams of wooden horses, under a wooden roof, whirls its child passengers on a gallop through imagined lands. We hear the man-made contraption clunkily turning, and see the horses and other animals painted in bright colours propelled round and round, and with them see and hear the laughing children, also in bright clothes. We can read the poem and hear the actuality of the roundabout in the park.

There's a roof and beneath it shade
and on it turns a slow display—
of colourful horses from lands far away
from here—where the sun never wants to fade.
Most are harnessed. They must not stray
from their carts. But all are brave and sparkle-eyed.
A wicked red lion runs beside—and now and now—
an elephant's whiteness—joins in for the ride.

Over twenty-seven lines the painted wooden animals turn on their way, vanish and return, slowly, creakingly, with here and there a flash of white as the elephant reappears. More animals join the parade: a little girl in blue is sitting on a saddled stag. There's a boy in white on a lion. The elephant comes round again, and blonde girls, their hair flying, seem to outleap the horses. Red, green and grey go past, who knows where, dispatched on their way. Fleetingly a profile or a smile can be discerned. But these images seduce and then disappear as if they are being deployed in a 'breathless' game whose purpose is beyond our grasp. Like the ways of bourgeois children at play, Rilke's composition was formal, yet it hinted at sweet abandon and, again, a mystery that might be painful.

It wasn't all of his talent, and all of his vision, that was on show here. But, just like Van Gogh, he painted this scene as one of his peculiar artistic responses to Paris, as he wandered out one morning.

NINE

The House That Rilke Built

W here Do We Come From? What Are We? Where Are We Going? The title of Gauguin's 1898 painting comes to mind. Rilke lived out a comparable sense of biological, social and historical upheaval. Just like Malte Laurids Brigge he roamed Europe with a suitcase and books, and a sense of unbelonging. Malte remembered the stately homes that sheltered him in his childhood. These days the furniture he inherited was in storage. This was the context in which Rilke liked to toy with his own putative aristocratic heritage.[1] That he took temporary refuge in the properties of other grand families out of favour with the new century symbolized the crisis of the times: the passing of that great sense of continuity that was the nineteenth century.[2]

Rilke's problem of course was also psychological. He and his fictional alter ego were archetypal homeless characters. Malte said he had no ground under his feet. When his childhood was over, 'I was left with just so much beneath me as a lead soldier has, in order to be able to stand.'[3] Neither writer nor character made the transition to adulthood well. Both lacked a place in the real world of business and friendship, prosperity and survival. 'Heavy, massive, desperate time' weighed upon Malte.[4] He became paranoid. The least sound from a neighbour in his cheap lodgings made him frantic. A tin lid spun to the floor. In a letter to Lou, Rilke said his bodily processes kept time for him—a symptom surely of terrible physical isolation and immobility. Malte imagined a clock where the only hand was his own body.

'*Denn Bleiben ist nirgends.*' We have no place to rest. Life is relentless. Nothing stops to wait for us. This tight, four-word sentence in the first Duino Elegy is crafted like a baroque motto. Biologically the moment we're born we're dying. Psychologically we're restless. Socially we're insecure. In the second Elegy, in a more beautiful imagining of our fate, Rilke says we evaporate like dew in the early morning.[5] Similarly in 'Blue Hortensia' the hydrangea is dying, but then its lovely blue, with yellow, violet and grey in it, has just one more surge.

> Washed out like the apron of a child.
> Nothing more happens to it. It goes unworn:
> how one feels unreconciled.
>
> So short a life. But suddenly the blue just seems
> to reappear, in one of the bracts, and look, yes, there's blue,
> alive and stirring, enjoying the green.

So short a life, even so. The ninth Elegy breaks out in rebellion:

> But then because it means so much to be here
> and things, which also fade, seem to need us,
> our concern is vast. We who fade most of all.
> We have one time of it. Just one time each of us.
> And you and I too, just this once. Never again.
> Yet to have been here once, even if only once;
> to have been earthly: who can revoke that?

And so our distress reverses into praise. It's the Duino moment, when the wanderer brings a handful of earth with a flower from the very edge of the mountain. He brings it down into the valley and it's the yellow and blue gentian.

> Are we not here to say: the house,
> the bridge, the gate, the well, the jug; fruit tree, window—
> maybe pillars, even a tower... here to say it, understand me,
> in such a way that the things themselves never
> knew how they were. It's the secret way
> of the sly silent earth to push its lovers
> to be so delighted by everything. Am I right?
> A threshold: what's that for two lovers
> but that they employ their own? Open the door
> and pass over it, they too, like many before
> and many to come... treading softly.

In Rilke *almost* every time despair opens up, home is the antidote. Home as shelter and as *some*where. '*Erde, du liebe, ich will*'—'Earth, dear thing, this is what I want.'

The tenth Duino Elegy is that by-now-familiar catalogue of somewheres: '*Stelle, Siedlung, Lager, Boden, Wohnort*'—the place where we are standing, the place we've settled, the place where we have struck camp, the ground beneath us, our address. There are so many ways of looking at how we live, with whom we settle, in what relation to nature and soil, whether the ground supports us, how we tell people where we live. The context in the poem is the pain life causes us, as if pain were part of any habitat. Pain is our winter foliage. Where we are naturally embedded pain colours itself dark green. Pain has dates and many places on our calendar. This is how we experience the *Weltinnenraum* of space and time.

Nature maps our dispositions, and the poet with his own 'secret, homely' intentions, does the same, using domestic interiors to illustrate our souls.[6] From the monk's cell to the aristocrat's castle, our feelings live in this parlour and that street, in this region and beyond. There we can visit them.

Rilke's 'inside of us' undid the philosophical suspicion of the day that private language was impossible. He convinced his readers he was evoking something real; something we all know; where we live: a tent, a hut, a room with a view. It works, doesn't it? I mean, has there ever been such a spectacular poet of the interior, figured as a familiar place?

When the rain rains in, a woman realizes she is in distress.[7] A young girl looking outside into the night wonders: where is my life's limit and where does night begin?

> This is my window. Moments ago
> my waking was so sweet
> I thought I was flying. O,
> does the edge of my life reach so
> far, I thought. Where does night's heart start to beat?[8]

I quote this poem again because of its window. Rilke's poems contain many windows. He takes us across many thresholds, and there's something sacred for him in that opening onto, or going through to, new experience. We look out from inside ourselves; or we are outside in the world looking in somewhere. Either way the effect is now of permanence, now of shattering change.

> A storm is raging, altering
> forest and trees and time,
> and everything is forever;

> the land is like a psalter. Things
> are grave and heavy there: beyond our tether.[9]

If the landscape is like a Psalm Book as we look out, then the
implication is it encloses us like a church, and so again Rilke
captures the dual effect. We're both inside and outside life itself.
If we're poets that's what makes us want to sing.

> The things we make with, they're so small
> but when they make with us, they're world and all;
> if, more like things, we could give
> way and let the storm, really let it live,
> our way would be nameless and we'd still grow tall.[10]

I suppose this wandering through landscapes as if they were interiors is Rilke at his most 'religious', and perhaps not all readers
will find it easy to share his sentiments. As if anticipating that
difficulty, he seems to say, well, let's start with the fact that we all
know what it is to feel safe and well at home, and then look out
of the window and then step outside into the night.

The line about the landscape as a psalter occurs in a 1901 poem
called 'The Boy Who Watches'. It is clearly autobiographical, and
so similar in substance to the *Elegies* of ten and twenty years later,
that it does not make sense to me to talk of early and late Rilke.

There's no place to rest. But is that necessarily bad? The fourth
Elegy of November 1915 delivers the answer to *'bleiben ist nirgends'*
in just the terms of that boy from fourteen years earlier: *'Ich bleibe
dennoch. Es giebt immer Zuschaun.'* It means: 'I'm staying anyway. I
can always watch the world go by.' There may be nowhere to rest.
Life may be incessant. But, says Rilke, I want to stay and watch.

All his work is a search for home. Home is the perfect balance
of inwardness and landscape, achievable by the right kind of going

about in the world and seeing and bringing home. In our lives we see and are seen. The things see us. Our thingly neighbours also watch. Through all the things the world reaches in, as we try to reach out. The inner life enters by the door and beds down for the night and gazes out of the window in the morning.

Of course, there are echoes of Christian inwardness here. The Bible even talks of God's many mansions. But it is a distant connection, as if vaguely reminding Rilke how he might turn his metaphor. More helpful to our understanding of this most difficult moment in Rilke is once again *The Book of Hours*, where the monk describes the loss he feels when he can't pray:

> I was a house burnt out by fire:
> a place where killers laid their heads
> before pursuers chased them from their beds;
> I was like a seaside land
> hemmed in by plague and torpor:
> too heavy a floating corpse for
> children to lift from the sand.

The incantatory lines expressing fear and disorientation just go on and on in that unparalleled early work. The monk brings God into being in an astonishing welter of house-related imagery, but still he doesn't own up to being in the room.

> And so, dear Lord, it happens every night
> some people wake, overwhelmed by their plight
> and walk back and forth and try to find
> you. Can you hear them walking like the blind
> in the dark, groping?
> Down winding stairs, saying prayers
> and hoping?

Can you hear them falling on the way?
You must have heard their tears,
falling on the dark stone, for they have such fears.

I'm looking for you because they walk past my door.
I can almost see feet pacing the floor.
Who shall I call for?
I summon the one more powerful than night,
he who in darkness walks without light,
and fears not; I summon this deep man
so much better because he needs no lamp.
I know him because he heaves trees
out of the earth with ease;
and wafts a breeze
towards my lowered face.

Rilke keeps summoning up these buildings that we know, at this
address and that, with their thresholds and their rooms with open
windows. This though must be a boarding house, full of strangers
with troubles. It recalls the wretched interiors Malte glimpses in
Paris, where the front wall of a tall building has fallen down.[11]

> One saw the inner side [of those walls]. On the different floors
> there were the walls of rooms, still with wallpaper sticking to
> them, and here and there the spot where the floor or the ceiling
> joined... rottenness.

Here in this famous passage the inner life is exposed to the
gaze from without. Other people's foetid domestic quarters are
revealed to resemble a sick human body, reduced to its functions.
It's already being eaten by maggots. The inside of things is not
always good. But that's also how human beings are.

Rilke conjures sumptuous and occasionally terrifying pictures out of the topography of domesticity. What can we hope for? Whoever has not built a house now will never build one. *Bleiben ist nirgends*. Nothing stays fast.

But Rilke loved his childhood also as a room. The magic and the sweet content and the streak of heroism in his poems comes from the realm of bedtime stories, as in this 'From a Childhood' dating from 1900:

> Darkness fell, and when its realm unfolded
> the boy sat hidden in the room, hardly beholded.
> And when his mother entered as if in a dream
> a glass on a shelf trembled, so quiet it seemed.
> She felt the room give her presence away:
> and kissed her boy: where've you gone? Oh
> where? Both then looked at the piano
> rather scared, for of an evening when she would sing
> he fell deep into the singing's magic ring.
> He sat so very still, his eyes aglow
> at her hand with the ring on the keys
> as if making its way through the snow
> drifts with something other than ease.

Here was sweetness, albeit also faint apprehension.

Ever after it would seem to analysts of Rilke's poems that there was an extraordinary storyteller lingering in a scene like this, perhaps remembering the joy of the picture-filled story-book as part of his childhood happiness. Hugh MacDiarmid was absolutely right with his analysis, that in Rilke metaphors 'turn into autonomous imaginative realities'. From line to line we step inside story after story, and dwell there.

In the second Duino Elegy the Biblical figure of Tobias is

no longer a child. He is an adolescent and a mortal about to be approached by an angel. Prompted by verses in the apocryphal Book of Tobit, Rilke sketches the story of a boy who answers a ring at the door and sees a boy rather like himself. The other too is dressed as if he's about to go on a journey. Tobias is charmed and a little shy, seeing himself as if mirrored.

(A boy facing a boy, he peered out at him curiously.)

And so they set off.

It ought to be an everyday occurrence to meet an angel. A ring at the door. But we get so excited (here an innocent love on first sight, between Tobias and the angel). When we're excited it's as if we're suddenly in a palace, and we're racing and tumbling our way through all the lovely rooms and fixtures:

Doors on hinges exuding light; long long halls,
flights of stairs, thrones, rooms as vast as all our being,
shields of delight; the turbulence of stormy
enchanted ecstasy—then, suddenly,
it all ends in some mirrors: which, each of them,
takes back the beauty it has been streaming forth
and uses it to make its own face.[12]

Mirrors are difficult things for Rilke. They seem to offer us renewed vistas of experience, and yet they close the door on us. We glimpse ourselves there and are left alone again. Frames enclose us and then let us go.

There are of course ways of staying calm and fulfilled. Malte experienced them as a youth:

Almost the whole day I took myself out into the grounds and into the beech woods or up onto the heath; and fortunately there were dogs at Urnekloster who came with me; here and there was a crofter's house or a dairy where I could get milk and bread and fruit, and I believe I enjoyed my leisure almost without a care... I spoke nearly to no one, for it was my joy to be alone; only with the dogs did I have a short conversation now and again; I got on with them excellently.[13]

The still feudal estate of some grand family was always for Rilke one version of paradise. Yet Malte, happy-unhappy in the family home, was already so defenceless. How would he ever deal with the streets of Paris? The Russian monk had a more austere plan for living:

> In circles ever wider is how I'll live: priestly
> is my way. I'll probably not do it completely
> but I'll try; I want, flying widely, so much to know.
> And circles do that: they fly among things below.
>
> Around God, and the ancient tower, I go,
> for a thousand years, I fly on and on;
> am I a falcon? I still don't know.
> Maybe I'm a storm; or a great song.[14]

Like the monk, so close to things that he has become a thing himself, Rilke wants to live *with* things, among them, so long as he can endure the ecstasy:

> Look, trees just are; and we live in houses.
> They endure; only we behave like air meeting air.
> So everything agrees to keep quiet from us,
> half in shame, maybe, half in hope beyond words.[15]

It can't be right that the world we love hides from us. To avoid existing in empty air requires our effort.

Rilke and Malte agree on the joy of living with animals. They also respect their canniness. The poet 'abandoned bare on the heart's mountains…' is a fine poem from 1914, in which he, Rilke, let's say, is cast out to die like a Spartan girl-child. If only this were his natural environment. He contrasts his suffering with 'many a mountain animal liv[ing] secure, / chang[ing] and stay[ing]'. Hear again an echo of *Bleiben ist nirgends*—literally there's nowhere to remain. As for the animals, the original German is much fonder than seemingly any translator can render it. It suggests the way little creatures burrow and nestle close to each other, weathering and enduring.[16]

Animals and other small creatures—ultimately the famous gnat—are movingly celebrated in the eighth Elegy:

> In the warm and wakeful beast there is also
> the weight and care of a great melancholy.
> For he too is touched by what overwhelms us:
> the remembrance of things past,
> as if once, whatever it is we seek,
> that once was nearer; more certain; and to
> approach it was to feel infinite
> tenderness. Now everything is
> distance. Then it was breath. Home then
> was not like it is now: windy and twitchy.
>
> O bliss of the little creature,
> never to leave its birth lap.
> O happy gnat, hopping there within;
> even at her wedding she stays there; for
> the birth lap is everything, and the birds

half know it too, safe in their origins,
as if each was the soul of an Etruscan,
sprung from a dead man, propelled into space,
yet with a resting figure on the lid.
How shocked is one that still must fly
and comes from a single birth lap. What
a shock to itself, as, like a crack in a cup,
it makes its way through the air. It's like a bat
leaving its trace in porcelain one evening.

Rilke was fascinated, as many of us have been ever since, by the work of the zoologist Jakob von Uexküll. One of Rilke's more interesting celebrity-cum-aristocratic acquaintances, Uexküll made new scientific ground in Rilke's lifetime when he described how, just as *humans* have a home and a world, animals have an *Umwelt*— an existential environment or 'Lifeworld', where they follow their instincts for safety, food and shelter.

In his resumé for a new zoology von Uexküll concluded that:

Every animal carries its surrounding world around with it from day to day like an impenetrable dwelling [*Gehäuse*].

And:

The same is true of the observer's world of phenomena, which, in so far as they present him with his surrounding world, shut him fully out of the universal.[17]

The *Umwelt* of the animal is 'like some form of house'. Von Uexküll seems to have invented *Gehäuse* as a collective noun for all types of dwelling, and by doing so to have extended its meaning to include, say, the shell that some creatures carry on their backs;

but that then is only a concrete illustration to help us grasp the metaphor of how all living creatures, ourselves as well, surround themselves, or are by nature surrounded by, what they need to survive. Our human dwelling is more than a house. It is a whole given world where we naturally feel at home. And that, the idea of an *Umwelt* put that way, is exactly what we have in common with the animals. In each case knowledge is limited. We can't know what it is to be a gnat. The given world of the animals limits our knowledge of them, and theirs of us. But we can admire the way they live similarly, and to us mysteriously.

Von Uexküll himself makes special mention of the gnat—a clear Rilke borrowing.

> It is undoubtedly right, when we say that in the gnat's world there are only gnat-things. But as for what gnat-things are like, that requires an exact enquiry.

The gnat does not have knowledge of his own bite. It's just part of his function—his *Umwelt*—like the circle he flies in.

> The difficult problems that arise here must be fully solved before we can reckon on having a real understanding of how animals live.

And the things we don't know about ourselves, as humans? Those are difficult problems too.

In Rilke's day, and ever since, animals began to show sophisticated societies the price of progress: many instinctive skills were going lost. Forty years ago the critic John Berger evidently had Rilke in mind when he wrote that 'Man becomes aware of himself returning the look [of the animal]'. He went on to ask: 'Surely it's true that the animals are magical insofar as they are at once us and not us?'[18] Indeed. Animals keep us company and earn our respect for needs that are in the end quite close to ours.

Continuing the old debate with Kassner, Rilke insisted that animals show up the folly of our obsession with abstract knowledge and meaning. In the first Duino Elegy animals are 'findig'—they can find their way about within their given world, whereas we struggle to orient ourselves:

> maybe some tree
> somewhere, on a slope, stays with us; we
> see it every day; and recall the street
> of yesterday, as if it were just for us,
> and in a tangle of feeling return there.
> They liked it with us, so they didn't leave.

The poetry of the first Elegy is rich and complex. But the human plight it states is simple. We hugely overestimate our power of agency. If we're happy, it's more likely that things are being kind to us.

I don't share Rilke's dislike of critical thought. The scientific achievement is magnificent. We have medicines to heal the sick, and the technology to allow billions of us to live on one planet. In the humanities we have tried to map the vast riches of the human imagination and to conceptualize the achievement, the better to hold on to it. But, yes, also remember the gnat. Don't forget what is simply existing.

Rilke's unclear credentials as a philosopher, or as a poet who speaks to philosophers, emerge from his encounter with animals, and again we can find his fundamental position in *The Book of Hours*. There, in a neat rhyme, he sets '*die Tragenden*'—beasts of burden—against '*die Fragenden*'—those who ask questions.[19] The antithesis was too simple. Kassner thought it faintly barbaric.

But here too was a response to the shock of the times, to which Rilke's difficult psychology and terrible loneliness, in earlier times, always added.

He concludes the eighth Elegy by saying that when we conceptualize our experience we forever take leave of it. It's a view that has itself become banal today, although it was fresh and challenging when it was Rilke's view a century ago. To me it means something when I think about how experience is commercialized. If everything we feel is promptly converted into something to buy or sell then we are hollowing out our own lives. Language is also a threat to the joy of our simply being here. We banalize that joy by using humdrum phrasing supplied to us by others—sold to us, in a way. It's difficult to own the words 'love' and 'friendship'. Most recently it's become difficult to own the word 'own'—because the banter of the world has thrown it back at us as something we ought to do, and perhaps might pay someone, or idolize someone, to learn how to do. All this has a terrible effect on us of estrangement. As a species we wear language out, and it's true animals don't use referential language. That would be another way to read Rilke today: to think of the difficulty of building our own home in language; mindful that if we don't do it soon we'll never have one. Autumn is already here.

I wonder what Rilke would say about anyone starting out on that path to building their own language. Not literally of course, but in the sense I've just set out. We dwell, at the start of the first Elegy, in our 'time and space' or 'cosmic space' and the feeling is 'gently disappointing'—I suppose because there is no God there. It's troubling to feel alone and unable to account for our existence. When we are with our lovers we get the impression that being together will save us. But that would be like hiding behind used-up words like 'love' and 'friendship'. The only way out of our spiritual dilemma is to turn our inner fears out into nature, and to try to see them pictured, out there. To make pictures, not, as philosophers say of sentences, propositions.

In the ninth Elegy:

> This is the time for what is sayable, this is its home.
> Speak it and recognize it for what it is. For now
> more than ever things that could be lived as such
> just fall away. People do things but make no image thereof.

There will be another moment to complain that the contemporary world has lost its sense of wonder. Part of wonder, part of the miracle we live, is having the language to reach that far.

★

Rilke disliked kitchens, just like T. S. Eliot disdained bedsitters. Our poets, not yet fully of the democratic age, were sure too many people were leading banal lives in cramped quarters suffused with a smell of cooking. Perish the thought that in the impoverished life and even in the modest life better choices can't always be made. In Eliot's imagination, some peremptory attempt at sexual intercourse on a narrow bed was made in the same bedsitter, still with the traces of the nasty meal in the air. Eliot doesn't mention them directly in his poem *The Waste Land*, to which I'm referring, but by Rilke bedrooms are not much liked either, after the idylls of childhood.

Bedrooms are for sex, but that conflicts with the way they house our night thoughts. Rilke in his one room finds the need to have the occasional visitor is annoying:

> (What to do with her,
> when those who come and go and like to stay
> the night with you are your big strange thoughts.)

There's humour here, in the first Elegy, though it is often lost in translation.

Otherwise in Rilke the bed is the scene of one of those primeval masturbatory adventures to which the third Elegy devotes great poetry. The girl is at best an onlooker, and a partner for his soul, when convenient. 'Cherish him...' the Elegy says in its last line,[20] and indulge him the rest. It's not a sin but the habit is awkward. 'Alas', he writes in his very first line, and again, addressing the girlfriend in the opening line of the second section of this intensely 'inward' poem:

> It's not you, alas, who has tensed the bow, nor his mother
> who has bent his brow in expectation.

In the third Elegy, between those two 'alases', he copulates with the night:

> Listen, how the night hollows herself and arches.
> You stars, are you not why a lover longs to see
> the face of the loved one?

Looking in on this scene we 'listen' to the way the wind contorts (her)self, somewhere upstairs, in a room with bed and a window open.

Another image of sexual consummation opens the sixth Elegy. But there it is not the lover becomes the wind but the bedroom becomes the fruit garden. D. H. Lawrence, in a comparable age of sexual discovery, saw in the open fig a woman's most intimate flesh. Rilke remains staunchly—perhaps that should be raunchily—phallic. For him the fig tree somehow contorts itself to penetrate its own fruit; the juice leaps out of sleep.[21]

Rilke loved gardens: sometimes sexualized, but also some-times innocent (for 'playing' in the second line here is to be read without innuendo).

> Think of it, gardens once built by a king:
> who played there with his girls hour upon hour,
> girls still quite young, now weaving some flower
> around the sound of their laughter's ring.
> They kept these weary parks awake;
> they filled the bushes with breeze and delight,
> their velvets and furs cast wondrous light,
> and the rustle of silk of a morning bright
> rang hard on the gravel like stream into lake.[22]

I can only imitate it imperfectly, but rhyme in Rilke is like a net that catches us. So much happiness in reading depends upon it.

> Come soon after sunset.
> Notice the evening green of the grass;
> doesn't it seem as if long ago we met
> it and saved it now for last,
> so that out of memory and awareness,
> new hope and half-forgotten pleasure
> mixed with darkness from inside us,
> we can spread it out and consider its measure.
>
> Under trees once Dürer might have drawn
> laden with fruit as heavily born
> as the weight of a hundred days of labour
> —those trees are serving patiently, wondering

How to get a grip on what exceeds
all measure and still to give it away.
So we can if through a life of deeds
we keep growing to will one thing, and otherwise don't say.

'The Apple Orchard', inscribed as from in an old castle in Sweden, Borgeby Gård, was another beautiful poem, written on one of his periodic flights from Paris.

By 1914 he can do the streetwise tone too. But it's such a contrast:

Superb to be here; but then, girls, you knew that,
though you were destitute, and trudged
through the worst, festering streets, rotten with muck
like open wounds. Each of you had an hour,
scant time measurable between two gaps—
each had a life. Had it all. In her veins.

The fate of discarded, abused women always aroused his sympathy, something he shared with Baudelaire. Yet the lives of the poor and the dispossessed he could barely contemplate—because he couldn't transform them.

Read this stanza, for instance, with the accent on 'we':

Even if we know the landscape of love
and in the churchyard recall the names so,
dear, we also know the vile silent trench
where the others end.

In the seventh Duino Elegy the unwanted are cast out on the streets, without a headstone when they die. But then from his early career Rilke made great poetry out of the cruelty, squalor and metaphysical forgetfulness of the city.

Then Lord, see, the cities are maimed;
lost and doomed, place become non-place.
Vast, they seem to run from flame,
and nothing exists could grant a solace,
as their portion of time runs out.

And people there lead lives so wrong.
In dense dim rooms, always fearing,
nervous as a herd of yearlings.
Outside your earth is still breathing.
But they don't know that any longer.

And children grow at windows' side
always shadowed, always cold
and know no call from flowers outside
to live a day that's fresh and bold
and must be children, already old.

The lament for the city is reprised a few pages on:

The great cities are untrue; they lie to
day and night and beast and child and thing;
their silence lies, so too their cry and hue,
things let them lie, somehow willing.
Nothing that is true and real occurs
that would be part of Your becoming.
Not in them. Your wind that stirs hits
the alleyways. They set it humming,
the sound is of a nervous strumming.
The winds blow down avenues and on.

The unrhymed seventh Elegy of February 1922 cannot achieve what these hardly known lines from 'The Book of Poverty and Death' (1903) did early in Rilke's career. But it is a record of the contradictory feelings he experienced in the unbearable 'out there', that he had to declare in the seventh, with renewed passion: *'Hiersein ist herrlich.' 'Die Adern voll Dasein'*—It's magnificent to be here. Our very veins are full of our being-here. We must keep trying to feel that fullness because a truer life, one illuminated by death, is always near.

> How strange it is to live no more on earth;
> to make no further use of customs learnt;
> no longer to attribute to the rose
> or anything of fair especial promise
> a metaphor of human destiny;
> to be no longer that which once we were,
> in over-fearful hands; to throw aside
> even our personal name, a broken toy!
> Strange to desire no more the consummation
> of our desires! How strange to see all things,
> related to this earth, float free in space!

>   .   .   .   .   .

> Yet all the living fall into the error
> of over-sharp distinction. I have heard
> that angels may themselves be unaware
> whether they move amongst the quick or dead.

This magnificent first Elegy needs to be metrically translated to catch the shimmer of awe and unfamiliar joy it projects, the light not unlike the gleam of the Archaic Torso, the promise one of sweetness, but which our senses will never be able to put to the test. This is Vita Sackville-West's translation of a passage where, with a change of metric patterning, the sense of passing over is palpable.

What separates life and death is wafer-thin and almost transparent, and the way Rilke presents it to my ear is like a radical shift of mood in Mahler. With the marvellous and majestic monosyllables of 'How strange it is to live no more on earth' we are feeling our way to what in the first movement of Mahler's Sixth Symphony the musicologist Deryck Cooke describes as 'a vision, as of a mountain summit far above earthly strife'. Mahler's texture changes from restless march rhythms to pianissimo high-tremolo strings and cowbells. Halfway through the Interlude the music moves from its main key of A Minor on a journey which is the furthest possible distance away—from G Major to E Flat Major. This is also how I hear the Rilke.[23]

The crossings-over in Rilke revived old motifs beloved of Virgil and Dante and Goethe of wanderings in the underworld which then enrich the life we have.

Rilke makes another pilgrimage in the tenth Elegy, beyond all familiar feeling. A visitor to a fairground meets a woman who, like Virgil, leads Dante through the underworld, takes this young man to a magical place on the edge of the city. He finds himself in the poignant Never-Never Land where 'the Plaints' live. Their task is forever to lament what has been lost. They are a wounded little group, with a common identity, and memories, and he finds them as if suspended in timelessness:

> She shows him the tall tear-trees and the fields
> Where the flowers of sadness blow (the living
> Only know them as the softest leafage). She points out
> The animals of mourning, as they browse;

And often a bird, in sudden flight, flies straight
Across their upward vision, drawing far
The image of its isolated cry.[24]

Rilke was at his most Dantesque imagining these other realms through which a pilgrim might walk, and yet, far from thinking of them as hellish, he was half in love with easeful death.

★

The first three *Duino Elegies* were complete, and the sixth, ninth and tenth begun, along with fragments originally intended to fit in a fifth, when the First World War broke out.[25] The hostilities meant Rilke could no longer return to Paris, where he had left his belongings, including copies of his own books. He complained of depression and heartache and the poetry took up the horror of conflict. The *Five Cantos* from early August 1914 may make the contemporary reader impatient, for they reach back, in the fashion of Hölderlin, to the idiom of gods and mortals. Yet given that actual hostilities had not yet begun, and Rilke's topic was the thunder of war in the air, the effect was plangent. This is from the first canto:

Finally a god. Often we don't grasp the peaceful god. Now
suddenly the battle god grasps us. He
hurls a torch; and his reddened sky, where he indwells like thunder,
marches over our home-loving hearts.

The third song heightens the drama:

And now he arose; stood tall; taller
than tall towers, towering

over the air we used to breathe on ordinary days.
Towers over us. For how is it with us? A red-hot glowing
is the new creature he brings to life, in us; deadly.
So I am not me any more; out of the heart shared by all
so my heart beats, and the mouth of all of us opens mine.

Rilke recognizes the moment of collective fate. He can't help but
speak for all. But none of the popular patriotic vocabulary of the
day finds its way into these pared-back cantos. Moreover, the third
song becomes intensely moving as he finds his way back into his
own most familiar, and cherished, idiom:

Even so, each night, questions torment me
the way sirens haunt ships: which way? Which way?
Can the god up there see it, the tall one, from over his shoulder?
Is he the light from the lighthouse, showing us the way
to a future in battle that we've long desired? Is he wise?
Can he be wise, this destructive god, destroying all we know?
It had lasted so long, and like a kingdom of love
we believed in it. Depended on it. Now the houses
lie in ruins around his temple.

The third canto, or song, ends then with a compressed allusion to
how the heavy industry that capitalism has brought to his familiar
world has created a new sensibility:

We've become other people: each of us suddenly
changed alike because a heart, a meteor,
no longer our own, has leapt into our chest,
a heart of metal out of a world of metal, burning.

Rilke has been complaining about the effects of industrialization since his first devastating experience of Paris, when he imagined the iron ore longing to return to the mountain whence it came. He resets his task at the end of the fourth canto of 1914:

> Don't be ashamed to protest. Do it. You'll only know
> the unknowable, the destiny no one grasps,
> when you protest without end and at the same time see
> this immeasurable, least desirable thing and think
> it's what we wished for.

It's spiritual protest, of course, but Rilke the last inward man is on the edge of a vast shift in Western behaviour, and values, whereby the protests will become civic, and political, not just private anger and mourning. He's on the cusp of that change, yet because human fate is impenetrable, still he can't become a poet of political change, and so, at the end of the fifth song, he falls back on the familiar need to make existential terror palpable:

> For to understand,
> learn and hold in high esteem, inside yourself, so much,
> alien things too: that was always the task where your feelings led.
> Now you are once more stuck with yourself. Only
> that self is more. It may not be the world, oh no,
> but take it as such! And use it as a mirror
> which catches the sun and from within
> turns the sun against the mistaken fools. (Burn up
> your own foolishness in your heart's pain and terror.)

In a letter written to Lou from 9 September 1914, enclosing the Five Cantos, he noted that the war caused him 'daily horror' and he couldn't just retreat into nature because 'of being simply aware, along with everyone else, of the nameless human fate that is playing out incessantly day and night'.

A relationship of autumn 1914 failed almost as soon as it had begun, with Rilke 'taking back almost all that had been given by way of joy and hope'.[26] It meant that into the new year of 1915 he was living in a Munich apartment on the Finkenstrasse in painful tension with Loulou Albert-Lasard.[27] 'I read into myself, and I think it must be like that when someone takes to drink, in order not to be there.'[28] Amidst the emotional chaos and the misery he was feeling over the state of the world, his mother pressed to come and stay, and despite his protests arrived on 9 February, bringing wafer biscuits from Prague and a hungry maternal love. Life itself is surreal.

The son fled to the countryside and avoided answering the door. Meanwhile he begged Lou Salomé to come and stay with him and help show Loulou the door. Lou, who arrived in mid-March and stayed to the end of May, brought her puppy Druzhok with her from Berlin, filled Rilke's diary with cultural appointments, and the other Lou(lou) was soon relieved to escape. No sooner was she gone, however, than the Finkenstrasse flat was requisitioned for war use. Rilke, who now narrowly escaped military call-up, turned to yet another woman to help him find a new address.[29] Jealous and angry, Princess Marie von Thurn und Taxis, who had lent him her castle at Duino, wrote that he was something between a big booby and an incorrigible Don Juan.[30]

He was, but he had to take his opportunities, just as he had once accepted the Rodin commission in Paris. Now what came about was the chance to live with a Picasso, and, because of it, draft another Elegy.

Hertha König was a thirty-one-year-old art collector and salon host, and would become known as a prolific writer of poetry, fiction and memoirs. They first met in January 1910 and, when, three years later, a fabulous Picasso was for sale in a Munich gallery he got the idea of alerting her to it.[31] The painting was *La famille des saltimbanques*, or *Die Gaukler* in German. Hertha bought it, and installed it in her luxury Munich flat beside the river. Rilke then offered himself as its 'guardian'.[32]

Rilke and Hertha sat for hours, as if in religious contemplation of the painting. *Les saltimbanques* is a static, quasi-late-medieval tableau, its six figures painted flat and stylized against a vague landscape. All the characters have a kind of homelessness and mystery about them. They reminded Rilke of a group of jugglers he admired in real life, when he was in Paris, and so began what became the fifth Duino Elegy, with himself as an invisible member of the group.[33] This little group of homeless outsiders, like characters in search of an author, touched Rilke's imagination, as the Plaints did in an already existing draft for the tenth.[34] The acrobats also drew his attention because they performed like puppets. Puppets already featured in the fourth Elegy in Rilke's tribute to leading a passive existence, not making individual and active demands on the world.

But then the metaphor grew and grew.

The acrobats, as he remembered similar characters from Paris years ago, lived by bending and weaving their own bodies. It reminded him of how he wrote poetry. He and they wove a tapestry, an artistic form which 'praise[s] everything and expose[s] nothing' and which excludes 'what we are not allowed to know'.[35]

Just as words are manipulated by the poet, the implication goes, so the acrobats are woven by 'a will that is never satisfied':

> he upends them,
> bends them, sends them looping, sends them hurtling;
> throws them up and catches them back; as if
> the air is oiled and smooth, so he brings them down...

It's a pattern for the embroidery needle to follow, but also for the poet's phrases and rhymes. Another pattern forms as the spectators come and go around the performers.[36]

Someone else in the poem is also sewing, and her name is Madame Lamort. This 'Madame Death' is a fashionable Paris seamstress who

> Twists and ties earth's non-stop antics
> loops them and winds them with reams of ribbon
> making frills and ruffles, faking fruit with
> untrue colours—for the cheap winter hats
> of fate.

And so the entire fifth Elegy becomes a tapestry of acrobats and a dressmaker and a poet weaving their respective materials. Meanwhile carpets proliferate, for they are essential to the world that clothes and houses us. A thin carpet on which the acrobats perform is wearing ever thinner from their constant departures and landings upon it. This carpet, 'lost in the totality of things', functions as a sticking plaster laid on the ground.[37] It covers the place where the suburban sky has done harm to the earth.

Another 'indescribable' kind of carpet is, Rilke imagines, one on which lovers might display their acrobatics.

Finally there is an actual carpet, in the very last word of the poem, that in its arabesques immobilizes and eternalizes the lovers' smiles. Here, says Rilke, against Madame Lamort's meretricious weavings, is a true poetry of death. The lovers are dead, but their feelings are eternalized in those patterns.

> On this carpet beyond expression
> where the lovers have never yet grasped the art
> to leap the heights of their heartfelt longings

and make a tower of their desire, the
trembling ladder they form never
touching the ground—well if they could do it...

Rilke, it is true, is obsessed with death. But in his preoccupations he reminds us of a past culture in which death played a far richer part than today, as we passed from one dwelling to the next. He didn't believe in another life in the beyond, but we can't understand his poetry if we can't grasp how important it was for him for life and death to be woven together and how, in a fundamental Christian sense, that thought did help him confront the rottenness inherent in human ways, and the futility of so many ill-housed lives.

TEN

The Last Inward Man

Rilke had hoped that the end of war would release his creative powers. But early in 1919, between Western and Russian Christmas, a time of year he regularly picked up his slowed correspondence with Lou, he despaired. He wrote from yet another address in Munich:

> Dear, dear Lou, I'm so out of sorts. My inner life has retreated and taken cover and offers me nothing, and my desire-not-to-take-anything-in-from-out-there has gone so far that not only the war, but the most uncontrived, pure things of nature don't reach me and have no effect. It's never happened that I am not touched by the wind, by trees, by the stars at night, but since I had to stare blankly out of that piece of evil dressing-up called an infantry uniform, a change has set in, that complete unwillingness to engage, which I needed at the time to stop it ruining me. With that in mind I spent the summer of '18 nowhere, that is, my flat here was new, I was looking forward to making it mine, but that was just a pretext for being inwardly condemned to inertia.

In fact Munich had witnessed one of several socialist revolutions that broke out in Germany with the end of the Wilhelmine Empire, and some writers, keen to extract from Rilke any interest in current affairs at all, have stressed his sympathy for the Bavarian Workers' State declared on 7 November 1918. But seven months before the fate of that remarkable uprising and distant echo of the Soviet takeover in Russia played out, Rilke decided it had almost immediately lost momentum, and fell back on thoughts about his personal, rather than the communal, future.

> So here I am again sitting here, giving priority to my own existence and reflecting and planning and setting it against the grim background. And everything that I was, if I try to put a figure on it, belongs to six years ago, and more. A bad fate has played havoc with us.[1]

It's hard to think Rilke, aged forty-three, in radically changed political and social circumstances, might have had the time, and capacity, to become an *engagé* poet more in line with the twentieth century. He was neither Georg Heym, whose dramatic, unstable temperament had exploded onto the scene of German poetry with a barrage of violent, modern urban imagery; nor Ernst Toller, the expressionist playwright who through most of April 1919 was head of that Bavarian Soviet State and in command of a small army. Rilke's inwardness was a preference for experiences drawn from art and nature, reinvested in objects in a shared world. He put his feelings into objects in the hope of making them general. That's what you need, said Lou: to get your feelings out there. Through the exquisite artistic or natural objects he wrote about he was trying to hold on to a value for individual experience as such, something threatened by the times.

On the other hand, what was 'individual', and 'an individual'? The huge expansion of psychology as a science was opening up new cultural perspectives. One model was psycho-mechanical. To exist as an individual was to amass psychic energy, and memories that pressed for outward expression. Essentially it was to be a subject, but the emphasis on expression made both Lou and Rilke think there was not necessarily a great difference between artists and madmen. Both creative and insane individuals felt this expressive need intensely and resorted to strange devices to make it happen.[2] So individuals were vehicles for expression. Yet that way of seeing hugely diminished them, as if personality and presence and experience no longer counted in their own terms. It was the scream that mattered, not the screamer.

Faced with this kind of model, human beings will always rebel, it seems to me, and say, this is who *I* am; and one way to find themselves as more rounded, less abstracted people will always be to retake their place in nature. Although then it was part of the aftermath of war, around 1922 there was very much a German fashion for retreating into nature and a life of manual labour, somehow to preserve authentic feeling. German writers and poets overwhelmingly associated their war with the malevolent influence of technology. Ruth Rilke, a teenager during the war, after it ended briefly worked for a farmer, to feel the elementary satisfactions of a life of manual toil. She took inspiration from the Norwegian writer Knut Hamsun and her father was impressed.[3]

Hamsun was another artist, like Rilke and like Rodin, poised on the cusp of modernism, but otherwise anchored in the nineteenth century, in Hamsun's case in realism. Rilke, meanwhile, read Oswald Spengler on *The Decline of the West* and wondered whether that vision of Russia in the new cultural vanguard—the old religious Russia as Rilke remembered it, despite his and Lou's dismayed awareness of the Bolshevik Revolution—was the way forward. But who could know? Who was wise?

The crisis over his petrified inner life dragged on. But then he began to travel again. Venice was no comfort because it gave the false impression the world had not changed. But then Paris revived him and propelled him on to Switzerland. He took up residence in a borrowed castle in the rural area of Berg am Irchel, near Zurich. Needing to vacate it then led him to his last refuge, Château Muzot, in the Valais. He was still a wanderer, but the accommodation was now bespoke. The Swiss years, six of them, were initially marvellous, until he fell ill, and it was in Muzot he finished the *Duino Elegies* and wrote the *Sonnets to Orpheus*.

Those years showed greatness. But they revealed a limitation: Rilke could not bear too much negativity.[4]

In this respect the comparison with Eliot's *The Waste Land*, also published in 1922, is hugely instructive. For to read the Eliot after the *Duino Elegies* is to be struck by Eliot's worldly sophistication and by his erudition. Rilke was childlike by comparison. It is also to feel a negativity—Eliot's scepticism—that Rilke couldn't have borne. Rilke by comparison with Eliot was neither bored nor detached from existence. He loved the words he used and the pictures into which they formed themselves, first in Paris and then back in Switzerland:

> The prospect of healing arose… and from then on a stream of hundreds of thousands of transformations poured forth, new and old, outrageous and unnameable, as the blood circulated around my consciousness and restored it at last. Those days! It was autumn, with all the grandeur that the sky and the light have in Paris, which intensifies this season in nature so that it turns into a season in a city—but one that long ago became nature; what excesses of light, what transparency in things,

such that the atmosphere flowed through them, vibrated, and that vibration went on making itself felt, what a unity there was between the object here and now and all that it is not in this moment, between the nearness and depth of the world...[5]

It's why we love Rilke, that he was *not* alienated from the world. A few years later, not long before his death, Lou would tell him how much solace her patients drew from reading his *Elegies*.[6]

Eliot's problem was the world's incoherence. He was a highly educated critical intellectual and yet he needed faith if his world was not to fall apart. As he observed in that magnificent but disconcerting five-part poem of 1922, complete with notes, to be so clever with words threatened his spiritual ruin.

The Waste Land had a powerful impact on literary modernism because it was multi-voiced and spoke simultaneously out of different places and times. It juxtaposed different languages and played with what generations of students would be taught to call intertextuality, by setting Dante and Virgil and Richard Wagner, and the sound of the English publican calling closing time, and common chatter and high literary style, side by side. But it also revealed the man for whom poetry was 'severed from all beliefs', as the critic I. A. Richards put it.[7] Eliot's philosophical training in that most unlikely of schools, British idealism, bound him unhappily to the authority of concepts in the search for truth. But then *The Waste Land*, written by the poet in him and not the philosopher, jeered at those damnable concepts' pretensions. It jigged and mocked and pulled faces. How dare some rigid mental apparatus presume to capture the truth of the world? 'Twit twit twit / Jug jug jug jug jug jug'. 'Shantih shantih shantih'. It must have been a liberation to set those potentially meaningless syllables down on the page, unpunctuated and potentially endless. But it was an uncertain liberation.

★

In what follows I am going to treat Rilke as a poet who now enters the English twentieth-century canon. The Eliot comparison is the foundation for how Rilke also in English would become modern, modernist, and not.

There were some crossover points between the Rilke and the Eliot of 1922. Eliot's Madame Sosostris and Rilke's Madame Lamort were vivid soul-sisters, and both evoked a world out of joint after the war. Eliot was just as inclined to believe in the wisdom of the Tarot cards as any other pretension to truth. Rilke, meanwhile, worried about a world becoming infinitely tawdry under urban industrial pressure; a world no longer capable of 'resonating'. Yet all the while Rilke had this anchor: that he believed in death and death was not a negative feature of our lives but their consummation. Death betokened another way of existing in our imagination, in a constant house next door, beyond the wall. Death was, one might say, what gave birth to our imagination.

On the very issue of negativity, German readers will most readily remember Goethe's Mephistopheles as the one who taunts the spiritually wavering Dr Faust: 'I am the spirit that always negates.' No, No! Impossible! Rilke needed to praise human existence. Eliot, more grounded in society, less psychologically and physically fragile, had Mephistophelian troubles.

Eventually Eliot needed a church, whereas Rilke had a kind of belief. It was not a faith in a benevolent God. In terrible pain during his last months he asked Lou: 'I'm terrified, you see, for the past two years I've been living more and more in the midst of terror... It's a fearful circle, a circle of black magic, which shuts me in like in one of Breughel's paintings of Hell... Do you know anyone in your circle who could help me?'[8] But it was faith in what he felt, in the art I have described and illustrated in this book, and the life that went with it.

In his loneliest, most alienated years Rilke felt disdain towards 'ordinary people'.[9] He had no ground to stand on, and the poor and destitute threatened to drag him down. He was fragile in the city at large and yet hated being shut up in a room. He quickly withdrew from intimate relationships out of abject fear. The early confession 'I never quite knew what to do. I actually ran away several times' applied as much to women as to Paris.[10] His soul, easily frightened, was as delicate as his body. In Lou's diagnosis his personality was so disturbed as to jeopardize all truly intimate relationships. Meanwhile as a writer he was wary of success, because success was an institution where he also didn't fit. 'The system' made him hostile, without that meaning anything political. Like Malte, his was 'an individual heart'.[11] But in an almost Nietzschean fashion he overcame all these obstacles, and found his art, and his own way of being. By the end of the war he was offering a performance of himself to the outside world, as brilliant and vulnerable. He was an example of an individual who couldn't adjust.

It was on a reading tour in Switzerland in 1919, which saw him in Bern on 24 November. He stood there on stage, reciting, a diminutive, hollow-cheeked figure in his dark suit and white gloves. He read well and the performance was redeemed by his sonorous German baritone. But in the next breath he was asking his latest potential patron: 'Could you grant me protection and shelter?'[12] A poem written thirteen years earlier spelt out the perpetual terror:

> You take yourself from me, friendly hour.
> Your wings flap and it hurts.
> I'm alone: what's the point of my mouth?
> And my night? And my day?

I have no love, no house.
What do I stand on and where do I dwell?
All things to which I give myself
grow rich; I grow unwell.

The fact that 'Der Dichter' was written in Meudon, during the relatively happy months with Rodin of 1905–6, makes it all the more astonishing.

The poem is shot through with raw emotion. *'Allein: was soll ich mit meinem Munde?'* 'Well, what do you expect me to do with my mouth now?' is a question that resonates with impudent—or should that be impotent—fury, as the muse departs. Given Rilke's obsession with how, through the mouth, the outer world enters and the inner voice responds in creative consummation, it is angrily erotic.[13] On and on.

Over the decades, we have barely heard of Rilke in despair, close to the suicide Lou always felt he might be capable of. For the twentieth-century critics who built a canonical modern Western culture with Rilke as part of it, Rilke's losing the will to go on was just not acceptable.[14] And so for instance the English poet of the 1940s Sidney Keyes insisted 'All things to which I give myself / Grow rich; I grow unwell' actually announced the triumph of the poet's spirit.[15] Keyes misread the closing line to mean Rilke transcended his bleak state of mind, whereas in truth he very nearly succumbed to it.

Such a reading was not exactly an error. More likely it bore out Eliot's truth that we cannot bear too much reality. A hundred years ago, when Rilke entered the canon of English literature, great works were expected to deliver if not a Christian, then a life-affirming message close to it.[16] Here was a reason, if hardly the only one, why the great novels of Tolstoy, and particularly Dostoevsky, whose work was actually full of negativity, cynicism and perversion, became beacons of hope in early twentieth-century England. In those days works of culture either enhanced or corrupted the quality of life, according to the Cambridge critic F. R. Leavis, whose values were essentially Christian.[17]

According to the Bible a Christian writer should praise all the good things in the world:

> Finally, brethren, whatsoever things are true, whatsoever things are honest, whatsoever things are just, whatsoever things are pure, whatsoever things are lovely, whatsoever things are of good report; if there be any virtue, and if there be any praise, think on these things.[18]

But Rilke inwardly lived much of his life 'in weakness and in fear and much trembling'—a state which St Paul told the Corinthians was by contrast with faith miserable and godless.[19]

The shock of Rilke was to make public this faithlessness. Malte watched an old man who was dying:

> He sat there in a thick black winter coat and his strained grey face was buried deep in a woollen scarf around his neck... He knew he was leaving everything familiar now; not only people. A minute more and everything will have lost its sense, and this table and this cup and this chair, which he's holding on to so fiercely, everything everyday and familiar will become incomprehensible, heavy and alien. Like that he sat there and waited for it to happen. And didn't resist any longer.
>
> But I'm still resisting. I'm resisting although I know that my heart is away somewhere and that I can't live any longer...[20]

The Christian imperative was not to accept defeat: to be bolstered, in life and death, because the Saviour had died on the cross to redeem human turmoil. But Malte's misery expunged the value of a consoling inner life. Even as he tried to attach value to the bundle of impressions he called his 'self', he failed. 'You spurt out of yourself like a beetle someone has stepped on and your little bit of outer hardness and adaptation is meaningless.'[21]

German culture was on the edge after the First World War. The Leavisite English interwar years seem conservative and spiritually evasive by comparison. The great German writers, or, better said, writers in German, openly despaired of the 'bad mood of God'. The critic Walter Benjamin, in his youth an admirer of Rilke, coined the term. Benjamin asked his readers to imagine 'an ellipse with foci that lie far apart and are determined on the one hand by mystical experience... and on the other by the experience of the modern city-dweller'.[22] The spiritual coherence of the world had fallen apart. Later Hannah Arendt would describe how Benjamin witnessed 'an irreparable break in tradition and loss of authority'. Authority of course included religious authority.[23] The sense to one great German mind after another was of two vastly differing perspectives on life, the spiritual and the political, pulling steadily away from each other, with Rilke at an extreme that might soon become unintelligible.

Rilke and his Malte lacked the guiding inwardness and centredness that the Bible once taught. That raised the question, if there is no power within us to cherish and transform a human life with modesty, grace and forbearance, then what are we to do about sex and death other than confront their crudeness and cruelty head-on? Throughout his life Rilke saw the conventional religious reassurances as particularly cruelly parodied in the Catholic faith of his mother.

She, meanwhile, must have been shocked by his 1906 poem 'Pietà'. It was collected in volume one of the *New Poems*. But it had nothing of the thingly and objective sobriety for which that collection is praised. This was a poem about subjective fury, as the Virgin Mary's jealousy—*she* should be his only lover—turned to ferocious desire for her son:

> But look, loved man, your hands are shredded
> not from me, but from my bites—
> your boundless heart lets in the crowd;
> but I alone should be allowed.
>
> Now you are tired, and your tired kiss
> does not lust for my anguished kissing.
> Oh Jesus, was there once a time to be alloyed?
> Now we're both startlingly destroyed.

The urge to penetrate the body of the other, fluctuating between the sexes, ignoring the prohibition of incest, becomes in this poem any woman's desire uniquely to be allowed into Christ's heart. The carnality, fierce and devious, echoes that of the 'Leda' poem, where the god is twice fulfilled, seduced by the beauty of the swan he becomes and the girl he penetrates with his pulsing white neck.

Raw sex was one of the tools of Rilke's honesty about the age he lived in. He wrote a number of longer studies of the unmortified flesh, as if avenging himself on Christian teaching. 'A Nun's Lament' (1909) expressed a woman's intense erotic torment after a life of disappointed faith. She despaired of finding any satisfaction, and Christ was to blame:

> My life has departed—Herr Jesus.
> Tell me, Herr Jesus, do you know for where?
> Did you see it coming?
> Am I inside you, within?
> Am I inside you, Herr Jesus?

Just think, that's how the boisterous
daily round can end.
In the end everyone denies it,
no one has seen it.
Was it mine at all, Herr Jesus?

Was it really mine, Herr Jesus?
Are you sure?
Is not one woman just like another
if a bite, say,
doesn't leave a scratch behind, Herr Jesus?

Isn't it possible that my life
hasn't been part of things at all?
That it's lying somewhere in bits,
and the rain is raining inside,
and standing inside and freezing inside, Herr Jesus?[24]

Translating this and other of the poems I am quoting here, Michael Hamburger in 1982 urged a new generation of English-language readers to confront those 'complex and uncomfortable realities' that he felt a quasi-official version of Rilke downplayed or ignored.[25] Leishman agreed that in Rilke's submerged work were to be found 'many... among the most memorable of German poems'.[26] One might add that they are also the cruellest and most erotic.

The collapse of faith, coupled with his own temptations and frustrations, drove Rilke to apocryphal extremes. His version of the harrowing of Christ, in 'Christ's Journey into Hell'—a poem written for Easter 1913—hideously prolonged the suffering. The original is written in twenty-nine mostly very long lines. This is a prose poem version:

In the end, tortured out of existence, whatever was him slipped away from the terrible suffering of the flesh. Up there. Left the flesh. And the darkness was afraid to be alone and hurled bats against the pallor—fear of colliding with stone-cold torment still flutters in their wings, of an evening. Dark, unstill air lost its purpose when it met the corpse; and in the strong attentive creatures of the night there was mute unwillingness. His former self had the thought perhaps to hold on, in nature, without further deed. For what he had been through was still an event. He could take the measure of how things are in themselves at night, and he groped around him as if in a melancholy room. But the earth was dry, had a thirst for his wounds, ripped itself open, and the abyss called him. He, connoisseur of martyrs, heard hell screaming for him, lusting to learn of his final hour; so that by way of his (infinite) torment, it might take terrifying stock of its own. And he tumbled, this consciousness, down, down, with the full weight of his exhaustion; strode like a man hurrying past the alien gaze of grazing shadows, looked up to Adam, hurried on, down, vanished, appeared and went to his last, falling through ever wilder depths. Suddenly (higher higher), above the foamy sea of cries, right in their midst, on the tall tower of endurance he stepped forwards: not breathing, he stood, no guardrail, pain his estate. Silent.

Rilke seems to have had a Nietzschean loathing of the Church, even while he borrowed scriptural motifs. Thus he wrote of another apocryphal suffering figure, Simon the Stylite:

> People crowded in on him from every side,
> those he damned and those he let abide;
> and guessing there was no way out,

he escaped the people's stinking rout
and handily climbed a tower.

Here again in 1908 Rilke had been struggling with disdain for
the crowd. He finally wreaked a grisly revenge when the isolated
saint's entrails fell on to the heads of the rabble below.

Sometimes he saw himself as a Christ figure with needs that
no one recognized, except a few women, as in this fragment of
autobiography:

The rumour went abroad
that there was a man, one who could see,
and it touched women, for they are more
inclined to doubt the visible.

A seer. For how long had he been looking?
How long was he so inwardly deprived,
begging from the depths of his gaze?

'Turning Point' (1914) contained these lines.

The quality of Rilke's poetry has made him, I think, the great
poet of Christian vanishing. He didn't only describe the tide
as receding. He wrote on behalf of individuals who were left
feeling spiritually abandoned. If he could invent a language on
their behalf, expressing the inner life as it teetered on the edge of
meaninglessness, he had his task.

As the monk put it in *The Book of Hours*, it was still a sweet duty:

because you were once wanted by someone
I know we can want you too.
We may reject all depths, but even if we do
when gold lies deep, buried in some mountain,

and when no one bothers to bring it to light
yet the river brings it into sight,
silently reaching into the shingled ore,
full of something.

Even when we don't want it:
God is more.[27]

The Book of Hours is a foundational pilgrimage to nowhere.[28] The monk longs for God's hands to reach out towards him. Elsewhere the image is of the two hands holding a little darkness between them. The intensity is extraordinary, and Rilke's whole incantation a study of devotion and receptivity. It is as if a vast spiritual energy in humanity threatens to go to waste. Once we were able to muster it. There was a point to crying out, even though the monk knows 'you are not there'.

Throughout this book I have felt that Rilke's undeclared opponent in nearly all he wrote—and this in the face of that famous donation from a wealthy patron to a poor writer—was Wittgenstein. Wittgenstein told his generation that it is with the help of words in common currency that we communicate with others and so lead the right kind of life. The alarming feature of this pragmatic dedication to the present day was, historically, the threat to experiences no longer shared. They risked dying out because no one had words for them. Religious experience might be one of those sets of once-meaningful feeling faced with extinction. Like other life forms, cultural habits also habitually lose out to stronger rival forces. Rilke's response to this post-Darwinian vision was to picture the layers of human consciousness remaining. They would endure, sedimented like the geology of the earth. Crumbled past civilizations return to the natural landscape. So too do beliefs, and the words of poets reach back down to them.

Ruins are prevalent in the *Duino Elegies*, and elsewhere in Rilke. Judith Ryan, among the finest Rilke scholars, makes the connection with the eighteenth-century Italian painter Piranesi. Piranesi is famous for his glorious fictive ruins. He depicted in minute details the remnants and traces of an imagined antique past. Rilke likewise sang of absences and gaps. An archaeologist, the way Piranesi and also Sigmund Freud were, Rilke dug down into the layers of spiritual memory, and pictured the journey.

The myth of Orpheus and Eurydice inspired him. The poem 'Orpheus. Eurydike. Hermes' began with the line:

It was at that wondrous mine of the soul, in the mountains

And added:

There were rocks
and ghostly forests. Bridges over emptiness
and that great grey blind lake
that clung to the farthest lay of the land
like rain clouds over a landscape.

Here, on this not-yet-human earth, 'there arose a world out of sorrow' ('*daß eine Welt aus Klage ward*'). *That* was the beginning of our culture: the dream of a second existence arising on the far side of grief:

Dear, he so much loved her, such that the lute
sang more than the wailing women ever could;
that to pine for her became a world where
everything happened a second time: valley and woods
and homely path and field and stream and beast;
and that there circled this lamenting world,

just like the other earth, a sun and stars which
kept the heavens quiet above,
a sky so fully in lament its stars mis-shone—
he so much loved her.

The first Duino Elegy repeated the theme of a kind of resurrection. Perhaps everything can happen a second time, without the pain, though to go through it won't be easy.

> Und das Totsein is mühsam
> Und voller Nachholn, daß man allmählich ein wenig
> Ewigkeit spurt...

'Nachholen' is what you do at school, if you need to stay down a year and catch up. We may not make it for all sorts of humdrum reasons. And even when we do, we'll still be confused. We'll cross the bridge—like the Gods in Wagner's *Rhinegold*—and stand there baffled.[29]

> And it's difficult to be dead.
> There's all that catching up to do before one feels
> just a little eternity...[30]

If we turn from Eurydice back to Linos, music suggests a kind of rebirth beyond suffering:

> The legend has a point, that mourning Linos
> a daring new music broke through the air;
> that in the shattered space which a most godly boy
> left empty, the emptiness put forth feelings
> that now harrow our heartstrings, and deliver us from pain.

The Linos song, mentioned by Homer, was a dirge for the departing summer. Rilke infused it with his feelings for Orpheus. The great recent prose landmark announcing modern culture's dependence on music was Nietzsche's *The Birth of Tragedy out of the Spirit of Music*, whether or not Rilke had read it.

Rilke did have a terrible flaw: his inability to love other human beings in the moment. Yet it seems to me that to remove intense experience from the sphere of *living* emotion was the only way Rilke could deal with people at all, to imagine them effectively dead, turned into things. He loved faces. Angels, puppets and lovers all had beloved faces. See what happens in the 1913 poem 'Once I took your face in my hands'. The face of the beloved becomes 'like something docile that quietly endures / it felt almost the way a thing feels.'[31] It is a truth about Rilke that he strained to reduce everything living to what was impersonal and inanimate. It might be stone, or plant. It might be poem or painting. Just not something living and breathing, unless it was the universe itself.

Once you are primed to watch out for it, the trope of living people and living emotions becoming solid objects is everywhere. People become silk or wool or stone or a carpet. Amid the leaping and twirling of the fifth Elegy the acrobats' smiles stand bottled and labelled on an apothecary's shelf. It is not so unusual: many artists have tried to write or paint or sculpt or otherwise create art out of emotional pressures they can't otherwise surmount. They 'nail' life as an event. They pin it like a butterfly to the board.

Still Rilke created an inwardness that the times of fading religious faith could bear, and that was an unparalleled achievement.

Eliot wrote: 'With the Duinese Elegies, I admit, I... could be content to enjoy the verbal beauty, to be moved by the music of the verse; and I have to force myself to try to enter into thought which is for me both difficult and uncongenial.'[32] Here is not the place to pursue why Eliot found Rilke uncongenial. Eliot was somehow confused. He thought poets should 'feel their thought as immediately as the odour of a rose', but did not see that Rilke was a model for that very gift.[33] Most interesting is that Eliot knew the same crisis moment in history:

> The trouble of the modern age is not merely the inability to believe certain things about God and man, which our fore-fathers believed, but the inability to *feel* towards God and man as they did. A belief in which you no longer believe is to some extent a belief you can continue to understand; but when religious feeling disappears, the words in which men have struggled to express it become meaningless. It is true that religious feeling varies naturally from country to country, and from age to age, just as poetic feeling does; the feeling varies even when the belief, the doctrine, remains the same. But this is a condition of human life, and what I am apprehensive of is [its?] death. It is equally possible that the feeling for poetry, and the feelings that are the material of poetry, may disappear everywhere; which might perhaps facilitate the unification of the world which some people consider desirable for its own sake.[34]

Poets, and poetry in the long future, would lead public protests in pursuit of that more unified world. But Rilke was no more political than Eliot and would never be of their kind.

We might think of Rilke dying in 1913, when the old world was still breaking up, rather than in 1926, as he actually did. He wrote great poetry in those interim nine years, but against their grain. In 1899 in Florence, when he tried to incorporate the rising power of the politics of the people, signified by the red flag, into his own poems, he was still trying to bend the will of the day to his own. But the passing of the years overran him. Musil hinted at the end of Christian bourgeois life in Rilke's day, and knew it was not in his compass.

★

The rest of my story is how others discovered Rilke was, and was not modern, in the ten to fifteen tumultuous years after his actual death. For many in a new German generation, Rilke's concerns were too spiritual and lofty, and his poems politically inadequate. 'These poems [of Rilke and others] tell ordinary people nothing, sometimes comprehensibly, sometimes incomprehensibly,' Brecht wrote in his youth. Rilke 'developed taste at the expense of appetite'.[35] Brecht's own poems of the 1930s were floodlit with political engagement, a far cry from Rilke's mystical baying at the night. Likewise, the critic Theodor Adorno sought an antidote to Rilke in Kafka, as he too tried to understand modernity.[36] Kafka wrote in parables, but those parables about authority and identity were modern, with a political meaning.

England was a different case. Contra to the progressive mood in Germany, Auden when he reviewed Leishman's translation of the *Duino Elegies* in 1939, positively celebrated a poet *not* caught up in present times:

> It is, I believe, no accident that as the international crisis becomes more and more acute, the poet to whom writers are becoming increasingly drawn should be one who felt that it was pride and presumption to interfere with the lives of others (for each is unique and the apparent misfortunes of each may be his very way of salvation); one who occupied himself consistently and exclusively with his own inner life.[37]

Evidently Auden was using Rilke to justify his own reluctance to engage with politics. Having fled to the United States to avoid the Second World War, Auden persuaded himself that inwardness, construed as standing outside or above politics, might be more needed than ever. Valuing the revolution Rilke had brought about in lyric poetry, he continued:

> Rilke thinks of the human in terms of the non-human, of what he calls Things (Dinge), a way of thought which, as he himself pointed out, is more characteristic of the child than of the adult. To the former, tables, dolls, houses, trees, dogs, etc., have a life which is just as real as their own or that of their parents. Indeed, as a rule children think of life in terms of things and animals rather than in terms of people: a conscious interest in people does not commonly begin until adolescence.[38]

And:

> Rilke's most immediate and obvious influence has been upon diction and imagery. One of the constant problems of the poet is how to express abstract ideas in concrete terms.[39]

But then Auden flipped in the space of less than a year, and defined Rilke as 'the Santa Claus of loneliness'.

> And RILKE whom die Dinge bless,
> The Santa Claus of loneliness.
> And many others, many times,
> For I relapse into my crimes,
> Time and again have slubbered through
> With slip and slapdash what I do,
> Adopted what I would disown,
> The preacher's loose immodest tone.[40]

It was an odd confession, for it used Rilke's abrupt juxtaposition of registers to condemn Auden's own past failings as a social poet. The phrase 'Santa Claus of loneliness' has much in common, to my mind, with a spiritual world 'sanitized and shut and disappointing like the post office on Sunday'. As it seems, Auden found Rilke both a comfort—'for I relapse into my crimes'—and a curse, for what was a modern poet doing coveting loneliness, when civilization was on the brink? Rilke was a crisis for Auden: the same crisis he evoked later that same year, in 'Musée des Beaux-Arts'. Happy in Paris, in circumstances that would just as readily have etched themselves on the mind of Malte Laurids Brigge, the poet visiting beautiful works of art realized the irresolvable conflict with life outside.

Although Auden wrote nothing more about his feelings for and against Rilke after 1940, he found it hard to give up the diction and the imagery that had impressed him. They were something new born even of something out of date. And so, I would suggest, Rilke's *Elegies* became Auden's 'Funeral Blues'.

Auden's poem, beginning 'Stop all the clocks, cut off the telephone', had first appeared in 1936, in a play—*The Ascent of F6*, written with Christopher Isherwood—that was sharply satirical of the hypocritical politics of British society. The poem gave thanks for the life of a thoroughly nasty member of the establishment. The play had a powerfully discordant score by Benjamin Britten, further jazzing up the classical idea of an elegy as a poem of praise and mourning.

But then, in 1940, that crucial year in which Auden tried to sort out his Rilkean legacy, he reworked 'Funeral Blues'. The shortened 1940 version became an elegy and a love poem:[41]

Stop all the clocks, cut off the telephone,
Prevent the dog from barking with a juicy bone,

Silence the pianos and with muffled drum
Bring out the coffin, let the mourners come.

Let aeroplanes circle moaning overhead
Scribbling on the sky the message He Is Dead,
Put crêpe bows round the white necks of the public doves,
Let the traffic policemen wear black cotton gloves.

He was my North, my South, my East and West,
My working week and my Sunday rest,
My noon, my midnight, my talk, my song;
I thought that love would last for ever: I was wrong.

The stars are not wanted now: put out every one;
Pack up the moon and dismantle the sun;
Pour away the ocean and sweep up the wood;
For nothing now can ever come to any good.

Auden had learnt from Rilke to find the intensity of inner feeling in *things* in common experience, so that now his traffic policemen and aeroplanes and pianos could take over from Rilke's 'the bridge, the gate, the well, the jug; fruit tree, window—' even while both lists retained the power to become chants for the dead.

The imperatives are the most memorable feature of 'Funeral Blues': nine in the first eight lines. Their grammatical force testifies to the intensity of feeling which the next three lines amplify. *This* is what that love was like. *This* is why the clocks must be stopped. Life ahead is unbearable.

Rilke's own most famous love poem, 'Tear out my eyes; I still can see you', was also a wondrous assemblage of imperatives:

Tear out my eyes; it's you I can see.
stop up my ears: it's you I can hear.
And I can walk to you without feet.
And I can talk to you without lips.
Break off my arms: I'll hold you
using my heart just like using my fingers,
seize my heart and my brain still lingers,
and if you set my brain on fire,
I will carry you on my bloody pyre.

The imperatives in Rilke's poem are grammatical imperatives but they function as conditionals. 'If you were to tear my eyes out I still could see you.' The power of the speech act comes from their devastating directness, from one person deep inside himself, as the world threatens to take his love away.

Could Auden have read it, in the original, or in an American translation? I don't think we can ever know. I only feel about number IX of the cycle of 'Twelve Songs' that its concluding 'The stars are not wanted now: put out every one' is also a way of leaving a great love for Rilke behind.

*

Another measure of Rilke's being modern, but not quite, is visible in yet another European literature. The young Jean-Paul Sartre, who knew German and read Rilke, and was of the same generation as Auden, had the same sense that politically Rilke was left behind. And yet Rilke was a poet of genius, of infinite value. So what was to be done?

It was in 1928, as a twenty-three-year-old student, that Sartre first read *Malte Laurids Brigge* in the French translation Maurice Betz had published the previous year. Sartre was the most brilliant student of his year and yet full of self-hatred. He had had a cosseted, highly cultivated upper-middle-class upbringing that, he later felt, had forced a terrible sexual and psychological dishonesty upon him. Feminized by his mother (just like Rilke), he was declared a child prodigy. His grandfather, a distinguished professor of German literature, and a great influence after his father died, importantly shaped his childhood fate as a cultivated idealistic bourgeois (I'm using Sartre's own terms for his family history here). In early adulthood Sartre set about sanitizing this terrible inwardness he felt he had been burdened with—and the irony was Rilke helped him do it.

His first novel, *Nausea*, published in 1938, had in an earlier version been called *The Notebooks of Antoine Roquentin*, an evident echo of *The Notebooks of Malte Laurids Brigge*.

> Existence is not something which allows itself to be thought of from a distance; it has to invade you suddenly, pounce upon you, weigh heavily on your heart like a huge motionless animal—or else there is nothing left at all.[42]

And:

> Why so many existences, since they all resemble one another? What was the use of so many trees that were all identical? So many existences failed and stubbornly began again and once more failed—like the clumsy efforts of an insect which had fallen on its back. (I was one of those efforts.)[43]

The aim of Roquentin, Sartre's version of Malte, was to paint as absurd the very fecundity of imagination that had saved Rilke from himself:

Every existent is born without reason, prolongs itself out of weakness and dies by chance. I leaned back and I closed my eyes. But pictures, promptly informed, sprang forward and filled my closed eyes with existences: existence is a repletion which man can never abandon.[44]

In search of a solution to what consciousness is *for*, the philosopher-protagonist would willingly give up this imaginative capacity. He sees the thingly world as a trap.

I am all alone in this white street lined with gardens. Alone and free. But this freedom is rather like death.[45]

And this is the gist of the modern Roquentin's sally against the not-quite-modern Malte: if it is true that imagination is our one asset, and that without it nothing would be left of experience but black bile, well then that's absurd, the world is absurd, and we have to get out of this inward/outward way of giving our experience value.

In fact, Wittgenstein said something similar. But surely this great shift in our sensibility cannot just be stated. It needs to be felt. We need the testimony of imaginative writers of the highest order who felt it.

In his autobiography, a supreme work of literature, Sartre later described how it was impossible for him to be 'an inward man':

I had tried to take refuge... in the loneliness of my true self; but I had no true self; I found nothing inside me except a surprised insipidity. Before my eyes a jellyfish was striking against the glass of the aquarium, feebly gathering its ruffle and fraying into the shadows... The mirror had told me what I had always known: I was horribly ordinary. I've never got over it.[46]

And so Sartre exchanged Rilke's solitary inwardness, finally at home in the windowless Château Muzot, for the constant comings and goings of the public cafe. Inwardness was perverse, even sexually perverse, he suggested. To reject a humanist belief in God's aftermath, as inwardness, to abandon it entirely, was the greatest choice of Sartre's life.[47] Sartre went on to prefer the public spaces Rilke couldn't bear. He chose the place where friends and strangers loved, hated and competed with each other, dominated and were dominated. When he made his anti-Rilkean turn Sartre turned his back—he admitted as much himself—on anything that might resemble an 'intelligible heaven'.[48]

Yet Sartre was nothing if not the most subtle and inventive of writers, and even as he devoted his life to suppressing and diverting the Rilkean gift he wrote a play that might well be rooted in a fantastic counter-reading of the first Duino Elegy.[49] In *Les jeux sont faits* (1947), 'The Die Is Cast', the moment that mattered was that awe-inspiring, angelic crossing-over into an unnamed heaven:

> How strange it is to live no more on earth;
> to make no further use of customs learnt;
> no longer to attribute to the rose
> or anything of fair especial promise
> a metaphor of human destiny;
> to be no longer that which once we were,
> in over-fearful hands; to throw aside
> even our personal name, a broken toy!
> Strange to desire no more the consummation
> of our desires! How strange to see all things,
> related to this earth, float free in space![50]

In Sartre's play, which also became a hugely successful film, Rilke's delicate musing became a philosophical comedy of manners in which Pierre and Eve, after their separate violent deaths, meet in heaven and believe they are made for each other. Reversing Rilke's trajectory, they ask to go back to live as only undead lovers can. Their wish is granted, on condition they trust each other for twenty-four hours. They don't manage it, so back to disembodied, 'ideal', heaven they go.[51] Sartre created this witty, touching farewell to the Christian idea of the afterlife, the eternal commitment of love between two people, and the beautiful idea of death, out of which Rilke had squeezed a final sweet libation.

A few readers have imagined that there was after all something profoundly anti-bourgeois about Rilke himself. Remember Hugh MacDiarmid's comparison with Lenin. Less dramatically, but still making an unusual point, the critic Martin Seymour-Smith wrote almost fifty years ago that

> Rilke's attitude towards death may have something to teach his readers, inasmuch as it can help them (Christian or not) to overcome the disastrous complacency of official Christianity, with its promise of an earth-like heaven.

And:

> repudiat[ing] bourgeois pseudo-certainty [Rilke] showed as much courage... as other more politically oriented writers who exposed other failings of the bourgeois life.[52]

On the other hand, this is a very different assessment of Rilke's legacy, and much conditioned by reading Rilke in a country, Britain, where Church and state are one, and indeed there is, or was, an official Christianity.

What all the critics and creative admirers did see was how, not being *quite* modern, Rilke was nevertheless at the end of something desperately important. The critic mistook the Church for God, and therefore could not name what Rilke was. The writers were too caught up in their own imaginings. But we can see what Rilke was now. He was a pagan modernist poet responding to Christian memories. He was a materialist, but not in any trivial sense. He was a materialist because the matter of the world is everything of value to us. Human lives are led in the weighty and dazzling presence of things.

Where is God? Is he in stone, as well as in poetry? The sculptor Barbara Hepworth was profoundly aware and no little in love with 'this [Rilkean] consciousness of the *in betweenness* of things'.[53] Her 1953 work *Monolith (Empyrean)* stands beside Kenwood House in north London, where, on a break from writing this book, I found it all the more ravishing for having Rilke as my guide. It is a breathtaking tribute.

A terrifying answer to Rilke, meanwhile, but not a repudiation, can be found, back in the German sphere, in the poetry of Paul Celan.[54] Celan's poetry is a response to the Holocaust in terms of the thingliness of all things. A number of his collections have Rilkean titles, such as *Von Schwelle zu Schwelle* (From threshold to threshold), *Atemwende* (A change in the direction of breath) and *Die Niemandsrose* (The rose that is or belongs to no one).[55] But what Celan does is to turn the worldly equivalent that Rilke found for his inwardness into a challenge to an eternity shattered by evil. His poetry suggests that because we live our material existence amid the contingency of all other material things there is always a trace of us; we can't be destroyed. The poems are themselves 'matter', as in the masterpiece 'Sprachgitter', a 'Mesh of Language'. A mesh is something which can hold fast a trace.

★

Was Rilke really so blameworthy for not being a committed social-ist and a good parent? A life well lived takes many forms, and moral goodness is not the only good we admire. How extraordinary it is even to have to say it.

Here is Rilke once more describing his own plight: what he had to escape in order to achieve anything at all:

> What should a man do who has so little grasp of life that he must just let it happen to him and who learns that his own volition is always something less than some other great will in whose current he sometimes gets caught up like an object on a receding tide? What should a man do, Lou, when the books he wants to consult open to him as none other than heavy doors, which the next gust of wind will slam shut? What should a man do, when to him human beings are just as difficult as books, equally superfluous and strange, because he can't take what he needs from them, because he can't choose among them and takes what is important and what is merely incidental and they become a burden? What should he do, Lou? Should he remain entirely solitary and get used to living with things, which are more like him and don't put any pressure on him?[56]

All readers of this book can probably sympathize with these ruminations. Finding our place in life is not easy, and an inner life may be our most precious resource: an inner life that forms around an 'I' that is an elaborately evolved, thought-out self and not just a linguistic device; an 'I' that can resist the pressures of all the external authorities and forces that prey on individuals, from markets to states, regulations, rules, and all forms of out-ward conformity.

Deep conviction or preference can seldom
Find direct terms in which to express itself.
Today on this shingle shelf
I understand this pensive reluctance so well,
This not discommendable obstinacy,
These contrivances of an inexpressive critical feeling,
These stones with their resolve that Creation shall not be
Injured by iconoclasts and quacks.

This is Hugh MacDiarmid in 'On a Raised Beach', paying tribute to Rilke in 1934.[57]

In a country where regulation and conformity did take over for half a century, in a dictatorial modern era that tried to obliterate the personal and the private, and of which Rilke had no inkling, the Polish poet Zbigniew Herbert once declared that almost the only poetry that would remain of 'our mad [twentieth] century will be Eliot and Rilke'. So much of Herbert's own work 'had to keep the quest for aesthetic perfection secondary because of the more urgent necessity of articulating the dreadful contemporary moment'.[58]

Rilke developed an 'I' not in conflict with political circumstances, nor with markets, but certainly 'far in excess of the needs of practical life'.[59] He built his own castle and invited no one in.

Many contemporary readers will find this hard to imagine. But the key to the inwardness he proposed might lie in another question. Is there some way of holding together our cosmic feelings, our sexuality, our self-understanding, our childhood, our temperament and our existential discontent? Rilke is one of those few writers who, because of the profusion of the imagery, and the unparalleled music in which the questions are embedded, can still remind us how it can be done.

Notes and Further Reading

Many notes in the text are references to frequently cited sources. They are highlighted here.

The standard seven-volume edition of Rilke's works in German is *Sämtliche Werke*, ed. Ruth Sieber-Rilke and Ernst Sinn (Frankfurt am Main, 1965–98), hereafter *SW*. An e-edition is virtually free online. Every poem is meanwhile available also online, and more conveniently, at http://rainer-maria-rilke.de/, together with notes on its genesis and where it is to be found in that print edition. For any reader with German it is an unrivalled instant resource. Unless otherwise stated, translations of the poetry and prose cited in this book are my own, but any reader without German will want to consult several translations to get the feel of the original.

Stephen Mitchell's *Ahead of All Parting: The Selected Poetry and Prose of Rainer Maria Rilke* (New York, 1995), hereafter **Mitchell**, is widely regarded as the best overall translation to date, although for many years J. B. Leishman's translations of the *New Poems* (London, 1964), hereafter **Leishman, *New Poems***, the *Duino Elegies*, translated with Stephen Spender (1939; 4th edn, London, 1963), hereafter **Leishman+Spender**, and *Poems 1906–26* (London, 1957), hereafter **Leishman, *Poems 1906–26***, were regarded as standard and are still often to be recommended. Edward Snow also rivals

Mitchell in his translations of *The Book of Images* (New York, 1994), hereafter **Snow,** Book of Images, *Diaries of a Young Poet* (New York, 1998), with Michael Winkler, hereafter **Snow+Winkler**, and *Uncollected Poems: Bilingual Edition* (New York, 2014), hereafter **Snow, Uncollected Poems**.

Other references are to William H. **Gass**, *Reading Rilke: Reflections on the Problems of Translation* (New York, 2000); *The Rilke of Ruth Speirs: New Poems, Duino Elegies, Sonnets to Orpheus, and Others*, ed. John Pilling and Peter Robinson (Reading, 2015); *Duino Elegies*, tr. Edward and Vita **Sackville-West** (1931; reprinted with an introduction by Lesley Chamberlain, London, 2022); *An Unofficial Rilke: Poems 1912–1926*, tr. Michael **Hamburger** (London, 1982); *Letters to a Young Poet*, tr. Reginald **Snell** (New York, 1929); and *Die Aufzeichnungen des Malte Laurids Brigge* (*The Notebooks of Malte Laurids Brigge*) (Frankfurt am Main, 1963). I have also referred to the translation by Jessie Lemont and Hans Trausil of Rilke's essay *Auguste Rodin* (1919; London, 2006), hereafter **Lemont+Trausil**, which can also be found at https://www.gutenberg.org/files/45605/45605-h/45605-h.htm.

Of the early collection *Das Stundenbuch* (*The Book of Hours*) there are now two translations to supplement judicious early versions by Babette Deutsch (*Poems from the Book of Hours: 'Das Stundenbuch'* (1940; New York, 2016)): *Rilke's Book of Hours: Love Poems to God*, tr. Anita Barrows and Joanna Macy (New York, 1995), still somewhat abridged, hereafter **Barrows+Macy**, and *The Book of Hours: Prayers to a Lowly God*, tr. Annemarie S. **Kidder** (Evanston, IL, 2001). References in the notes to *Das Stundenbuch* alone are to the illustrated Insel Verlag edition: *Das Stundenbuch enthaltend die drei Bücher: Vom Menschlichen Leben, Von der Pilgerschaft, Von der Armut und vom Tode* (Leipzig, 1918).

It's perfectly possible to read Rilke's poetry without regard to the events of his life. But since my approach has been to situate that poetry historically, I see some aspects of his biography as indispensable to the fullest experience of Rilke. The reader will want at least to dip into Ralph **Freedman**, *Life of a Poet: Rainer Maria Rilke* (Evanston, IL, 1996). I also have a fondness for Wolfgang Leppmann, *Rilke: A Life*, tr. Russell M. Stockman (New York, 1984). I have not drawn on Donald A. Prater, *A Ringing Glass: The Life of Rainer Maria Rilke* (Oxford, 1986; rev. edn, 1994), but Pater's approach to Rilke's personality is much admired.

In German, the standard two-volume edition of the letters, Rainer Maria Rilke, *Briefe* (Wiesbaden, 1950), and *Rainer Maria Rilke, Lou Andreas-Salomé: Briefwechscl*, ed. Ernst Pfeiffer (Wiesbaden, 1952; rev. edn, 1976) are indispensable—hereafter *Briefe* and *Briefwechsel*, respectively. All translations from the letters are mine but the reader is also referred to *Rainer Maria Rilke and Lou Andreas-Salomé: The Correspondence*, tr. and annotated by Edward Snow and Michael Winkler (New York, 2006).

There are a number of biographies of Lou Andreas-Salomé in English but my preference has been for Stéphane **Michaud**, *Lou Andreas-Salomé: L'alliée de la vie* (Lou Andreas-Salomé: an ally in life) (Paris, 2000). I also refer to her memoir, *Lebensrückblick*, ed. Ernst Pfeiffer (Frankfurt am Main, 1977), and her work *The Erotic*, ed. Gary Winship, tr. John Crisp (London, 2012).

References to all other sources will be found in full in the following notes.

I. HOW TO READ RILKE TODAY

1 Rilke 'is seen as a force counteracting those aspects of American society and culture of which he himself was so critical'. See Steven Kaplan, 'Modern American Poets on Rilke's "Things" and Robert Bly as a Translator of Rilke's Images and Objects', *Translation Review* 38/39 (1992), pp. 66–71.

2 Rilke's famous term is '*Weltinnenraum*', which would be the space we make within ourselves. How feasible such a concept might be is also the subject of this book.

3 Ingeborg Schnack, *Rainer Maria Rilke: Chronik seines Lebens und seines Werkes 1875–1926*, 2 vols (1975; Frankfurt am Main, 2009), vol. i, p. 51. Rilke attended a class in 'Darwinian theory with Professor Pauly'. My thanks to the fine translator of Rilke, and chronicler of Rilke in Paris, Will Stone, for this reference. Margareta Ingrid Christian, *Objects in Air: Artworks and Their Outside around 1900* (Chicago, IL, 2021), pp. 79–80, draws together the sources.

4 Theodor W. Adorno, 'Cultural Criticism and Society' [1951], in Theodor W. Adorno, *Prisms*, tr. Samuel and Shierrey Weber (Cambridge, MA, 1967), p. 34. See Detlev Claussen, *Theodor W. Adorno: One Last Genius* (Cambridge, MA, 2008), p. 330, for how this remark was widely misunderstood to mean there could be no poetry after Auschwitz. Adorno clarified elsewhere that he meant 'no further poems are possible except on the foundations of Auschwitz itself'.

5 Celan was also the prompt for Adorno's Auschwitz remark.

6 Michael André Bernstein, *Five Portraits: Modernity and the Imagination in Twentieth-Century German Writing* (Evanston, IL, 2000) includes essays on both poets.

7 F. A. Flowers and Ian Ground, eds, *Portraits of Wittgenstein* (London, 2015), p. 1015.

8 Louis Sass, 'Deep Disquietudes: Reflections on Wittgenstein as Anti-philosopher', in James C. Klagge, ed., *Wittgenstein Biography and Philosophy* (Cambridge, 2001), pp. 98–155 (102–3, 114, 132).

See also Bryan Magee, *Confessions of a Philosopher* (London, 1997), pp. 122–3.

9   See Rilke's 'Florence Diary' (1898), with a strangely appropriated red flag in the poem 'Renaissance I' and its attacks on 'the people' and defence of aristocracy, individual exceptionalism and eternity, in Snow+Winkler, e.g. pp. 5, 21, 24, 26.

10   Eric Santner, for instance, in *On Creaturely Life: Rilke, Benjamin, Sebald* (Chicago, IL, 2006), p. xvii and ch. 1 (passim).

11   There were nevertheless versions in Italian and Polish and English (from mostly American translators) in his lifetime, and he corresponded with his Polish translator.

12   'The history of the German lyric culminates in a Rilke who [nevertheless] stands as if he were the author of himself and knew no other kin'—S. S. Prawer, *German Lyric Poetry* (London, 1952), p. 229.

13   'An Hölderlin' (September 1914). Alternatively, Mitchell (p. 135) always produces finely worked versions, though it seems to me that if his diction relaxed the reader would have a much more immediate grasp of Rilke's meaning. Hamburger (p. 57) is disappointingly awkward, an unexpected outcome in such a distinguished German-born poet and translator.

14   Edmund Jephcott, *Proust and Rilke: The Literature of Expanded Consciousness* (London, 1972).

15   Mitchell; Gass; Sackville-West.

16   Mitchell. Although Rilke mentions music, the idea of harmony is not there in the original.

17   Set to a poem by Stefan George, a poet well known to Rilke.

18   In the introduction to *Uncollected Poems*, Snow writes about the significance of Rilke standing 'opposite'—*gegenüber*—something to orient himself creatively.

19   In German literature, compare Walter Benjamin's *Einbahnstraße* (*One-Way Street*) and Brecht's technique of alienation in the theatre.

20   The equivalent, which so affected Ruskin, had happened fifty years earlier in England, but because British philosophy was predominantly empirical, concerned since Bacon and Locke and Hume with impressions

impacting on the senses, rather than the mind understanding the world by imposing concepts upon it, it did not produce the same innovation in philosophy.

2. THE RESTLESS DOMAIN

1   Robert Musil, 'Rede zur Rilke-Feier in Berlin' [Speech on the occasion of the Rilke celebrations in Berlin, 16 January 1927], repr. in *Insel-Almanach auf das Jahr 1997. Rainer Maria Rilke: 1926 bis 1996. Erinnerungen an den Dichter. Begegnungen mit dem Werk. Eine Dokumentation* [The Insel almanac for 1997 documents regarding memories of the poet and encounters with his work] (Frankfurt am Main, 1996), pp. 68–9. Musil writes in the first part of this passage: '*Man könnte sagen, hier handelt es sich, wenn auch nur in einem Teil, um das Gefühl als Ganzes, auf dem die Welt wie eine Insel ruht.*' In my translation I have preferred to turn these abstract nouns into transitive English verbs and verbal phrases. The hope is the reader will see that Musil makes profound sense and not Germanic unsense.

2   '*Der Sturz*' in the third line of the penultimate verse in the original is not 'fall' as in high German but a contraction of the Austrian *Lampensturz*, the name for those milky round or oval glass globes that covered the gas lamps on street lights. The 1842 catalogue of the Austrian glass manufacturer Glasfabrik J. B. Vivat zu Benedictthal lists them for sale as item 49. See https://www.pressglas-korrespondenz. de/archiv/pdf/pk-2005-2w-08-parlow-gamilschegg-vivat.pdf.

3   It may make readers think of W. H. Auden's poem 'Musée des Beaux-Arts', for which see Chapter 10.

4   For an alternative see 'Almost all things beckon us to feeling' in *Rainer Maria Rilke: Selected Poems*, tr. Robert Vilain, Susan Ranson and Marielle Sutherland (Oxford, 2011), p. 117.

5   Quoted in Karl E. Webb, 'Rainer Maria Rilke and the Art of *Jugendstil*', *Centennial Review* 16/2 (1972), p. 134, translation amended. Originally *SW*, vol. v, p. 561.

6 For the standard translation see Leishman, *Poems 1906–26*, p. 193.

7 Lines 113–22.

8 For a reading that complements mine without identifying the theme of prehistory, see William Waters, 'Answerable Aesthetics: Reading "You" in Rilke', *Comparative Literature* 48/2 (1996), pp. 128–49.

9 I talk about this at length in Lesley Chamberlain, *A Shoe Story: Van Gogh, the Philosophers and the West* (Chelmsford, 2014). See especially ch. 2.

10 Bölsche reached out to Goethe. See Nicholas Saul, 'Darwin in German Literary Culture 1890–1914', in Thomas F. Glick and Elinor Shaffer, eds, *The Literary and Cultural Reception of Charles Darwin in Europe*, 2 vols (London, 2014), vol. i, p. 42. As I see it, if Goethe's poetry could somehow contain Darwin, then the great ebbing away of meaning that Matthew Arnold feared in England, and Max Weber in Germany, might not come to pass. Possibly Rilke is offering the twentieth century something similar, though this is not a matter of influence.

11 Quoted in Suzanne Lilar, *Aspects of Love in Western Society* (London, 1965), pp. 107, 244. Lilar (1901–92) was a Belgian writer who found in Rilke support for her Neoplatonic vision of love. The book was originally called *Le Couple* [The Couple] in French.

3. SEXUALITY, CHILDHOOD AND THE BEGINNING OF THINGS

1 Lou Andreas-Salomé described her friendship with Rainer Maria Rilke in *Lebensrückblick*, pp. 91–122. The basis for understanding their relationship is otherwise their correspondence, *Briefwechsel*.

2 Rilke first signed himself 'Rainer' in his letter of 5 September 1897 (*Lebensrückblick*, p. 91). But he explained to his mother (29 August 1897) that this was for signing his books and essays, and continued throughout his life in correspondence with her to sign himself René. See Rainer Maria Rilke, *Briefe an die Mutter*, 2 vols, ed. Hella Sieber-Rilke (Frankfurt am Main, 2009).

3 *Lebensrückblick*, p. 112.

4   Michaud, p. 360. *Briefwechsel*, e.g. pp. 199 and 240, show where Lou blacked out words referring to 'love'.

5   *The Erotic*, pp. 1, 6.

6   Ibid., p. 106.

7   The monograph belonged in a series called 'Gesellschaft' [Society].

8   Quoted in Suzanne Lilar, *Aspects of Love in Western Society* (London, 1965), p. 146.

9   Sigmund Freud to Wilhelm Fließ, letters of 25 March 1898 and 7 August 1901. See also David M. Carr, *The Erotic Word: Sexuality, Spirituality and the Bible* (Oxford, 2005), p. 148. Rilke is quoted on p. 206.

10   Of the first, Kidder's translation reads: 'Extinguish my sight and I can still see you; plug up my ears, and I can still hear.' Of the second, Leishman's translation, 'How shall I hold my soul, that it may not be touching yours?' (Leishman, *New Poems*, p. 49) is superior, though somewhat forced. Mitchell lapses here, losing the crucial stress on 'hold' or 'contain', introduces an extraneous 'in me' and misses the delicacy of Rilke's original with his common-sense diction. The repetition of 'soul' is also clumsy. 'How can I keep my soul in me, so that / it doesn't touch your soul?' (Mitchell, p. 29).

11   *Briefwechsel*, p. 23 (9 June 1897), and p. 26 (July), when the finished poem is sent.

12   Ironically, it was Lou who reclaimed it. See *Lebensrückblick*, p. 113.

13   *Briefe*, vol. i, pp. 249–50 (to Clara Rilke, 4 September 1908).

14   This observation first made by Edmund Jephcott, in *Proust and Rilke: The Literature of Expanded Consciousness* (London, 1972).

15   D. H. Lawrence, 'Foreword', in D. H. Lawrence, *Fantasia of the Unconscious* (New York, 1922).

16   Mitchell.

17   *Briefwechsel*, p. 14.

18   *The Erotic*, pp. 61, 54–5.

19   Ibid., p. 72.

20   Ibid., pp. 67, 72, 70.

21   Biddy Martin, *Woman and Modernity: The (Life)Styles of Lou Andreas-Salomé* (Ithaca, NY, 1991), p. 44.

22   *The Erotic*, p. 65.

23   See Lou's essay 'Narzissmus als Doppelrichtung' [Narcissism as a dual-orientation], *Imago* 7/4 (1921).

24   *The Erotic*, pp. 64–6.

25   Their conversations often focused on gender. See Dorothee Ostmeier, 'Gender Debates between Rainer Maria Rilke and Lou Andreas-Salomé', *German Quarterly* 73/3 (summer 2000), pp. 237–52.

26   *The Erotic*, pp. 91, 92, 106.

27   Rainer Maria Rilke, *Poems to Night*, ed. and tr. Will Stone (London, 2020), p. 51.

28   Ostmeier, 'Gender Debates'.

29   Her own experience with Rilke was of their 'mutually interpenetrating lives', 'something ungraspable shared between us', and that 'calmness and all that we could take for granted, which bound us together, as if we had always been like that'. It was for her a matter of 'co-living the rarity and extraordinary nature of one person's inner destiny'—*Lebensrückblick*, pp. 138–42, 151 (my translation).

30   Darwin addressed the issue of gender in *The Descent of Man*. Chapter 1 referred to humanity's hermaphrodite heritage. Chapter 2 stressed the malleable nature of all life. Chapter 6 spoke of historical plasticity and androgyny. For the importance of the nineteenth-century Darwinian heritage to theories of bisexuality in the twentieth century, see Steven Angelides, *A History of Bisexuality* (Chicago, IL, 2001).

31   Her review is discussed in Martin, *Woman and Modernity*, p. 138.

32   That said, Rilke would have agreed with his future mentor Rodin that something about the 1882 *Kiss* was old-fashioned and unadventurous, given the changing times.

33   See Judith Ryan, *Rilke, Modernism and Poetic Tradition* (Cambridge, 1999), pp. 35–6 and 112–14.

34   In 'Requiem for a Friend'. See Chapter 7.

35   Ryan, *Rilke, Modernism and Poetic Tradition*, pp. 100–10.

36   Rilke's 'Judith's Return', translated by Justin E. H. Smith, available at https://www.jehsmith.com/1/2011/02/a-translation.html.

37   *The Erotic*, p. 94. Rilke is writing this poem just as Lou's book on *The Erotic* appears, with such sentences as: we have 'a sacred right to stoop: the right to stoop, in a constant return, towards the most primitive states'.

38   An exception is Kidder (p. 205): 'O where is one who outgrew possessions and time'.

39   Snow, *Book of Images*, p. 23.

40   Ibid., p. 17. Translation revised (for, tempting as it may seem, there is no mention of angels in this poem).

41   Part of the cycle piously called *Das Marienleben* (*The Life of Mary*).

42   'Das fühlgewaltige Vorrecht der weiblichen Natur'—Hans Egon Holthusen, quoted in Elizabeth Boa, 'Rilke's "Marienleben"', *Modern Language Review* 79/4 (1984), p. 848. Boa speaks of 'the horrific force of Pietà' and 'of the suffering the powerful inflict on the weak'.

43   Snow, *Book of Images*, p. 41.

44   'Musik' ('Music').

45   Though *The Lay of Cornet Christoph Rilke* was not published until 1912, Rilke first wrote it in 1899.

46   Snow, *Book of Images*, p. 47.

47   'Ich bin nur einer deiner Ganzgeringen', in *The Book of Hours*. *Gering* belongs to the Biblical phrase in German for all things great and small. For other translations, see Speirs, p. 130 ('I'm merely one of your most humble servants'), and Kidder, p. 113.

48   Nicholas Saul, 'Darwin in German Literary Culture 1890–1914', in Thomas F. Glick and Elinor Shaffer, eds, *The Literary and Cultural Reception of Charles Darwin in Europe*, 2 vols (London, 2014), vol. i, pp. 46–77.

49   '[E]in reines, verhaltenes, schmales / Menschliches, einen unseren Streifen Fruchtlands / zwischen Strom und Gestein'. On the meaning of the verb *verhalten*, expressed here as 'cherishable', and of the idea in English of restraint, which recurs in Rilke, variously expressed, see Chapter 7, n. 6.

4. SHALL WE STILL TRY TO BELIEVE IN GOD?

1 'Gebet für die Irren und Sträflinge', *SW*, vol. ii, p. 35 ; 'The Last Judgement', *The Book of Images*, pp. 126, 128. See also 'The Florence Diary', *Diaries of a Young Poet*, p. 27.

2 Perceived early in Rilke studies by Reginald Snell in his often-reprinted edition of *Letters to a Young Poet*: 'Rilke was a natural worshipper' (Snell, n. 17).

3 Robert Musil, 'Rede zur Rilke-Feier in Berlin' [Speech on the occasion of the Rilke celebrations in Berlin, 16 January 1927], repr. in *Insel-Almanach auf das Jahr 1997. Rainer Maria Rilke: 1926 bis 1996. Erinnerungen an den Dichter. Begegnungen mit dem Werk. Eine Dokumentation* [The Insel almanac for 1997 documents regarding memories of the poet and encounters with his work] (Frankfurt am Main, 1996), p. 70.

4 Saul Bellow, *Herzog* (Harmondsworth, 1965), p. 139.

5 *Briefwechsel*, p. 54 (23 June 1903).

6 I agree with Heimo Schwilp, *Rilke und die Frauen: Biographie eines Liebenden* [Rilke and the women: the biography of a man in love] (Munich/Berlin, 2015), p. 23: 'She is a woman who made demands on herself and the people around her. She wants love, passion and fun' (my translation).

7 *Phia Rilke: Gedanken für den Tag*, ed. Hella Sieber-Rilke (Frankfurt am Main, 2002), p. 67.

8 *Briefwechsel*, p. 143 (15 April 1904).

9 Rainer Maria Rilke, *Briefe an die Mutter*, 2 vols, ed. Hella Sieber-Rilke (Frankfurt am Main, 2009), vol. i, pp. 99–100 (22 April 1899). The article about his mother's religious experience was entitled 'Erinnerung an Ostern 1899 in Arco'.

10 Michaud, p. 171.

11 Robert J. Clements, 'Rilke, Michelangelo and the *Geschichten vom Lieben Gott*', *Comparative Literature* 6/3 (summer 1954), pp. 218–31.

12 He had far too idealized a view of pre-revolutionary Russia. Even the Russians he met in 1899 and 1900 were aware of that. See Konstantin Asadowski, *Rilke und Russland* (Berlin, 1986).

13 Collected in *SW*, vol. i. Although translations from *Das Stundenbuch* are my own, page references are to the illustrated Insel Verlag edition *Das Stundenbuch enthaltend die drei Bücher: Vom Menschlichen Leben, Von der Pilgerschaft, Von der Armut und vom Tode* (Leipzig, 1918).

14 It was Rilke himself who denigrated *The Book of Hours* as too easy. See Leishman, *Poems 1906–26*, p. 19. I agree with Lou Salomé that their existence almost makes nonsense of critical divisions between early and late Rilke. See *Lebensrückblick*, p. 101: 'I quote from *The Books of Hours* especially because they contain early and late thoughts, which is why Rainer often referred to them in conversation as the undateable books, just like *Malte* and the *Elegies*' (my translation).

15 Babette Deutsch and Avram Yarmolinsky have a very serviceable translation at https://poets.org/poem/what-will-you-do.

16 *Das Stundenbuch*, p. 9.

17 Ibid., p. 12.

18 Ibid., p. 10.

19 Ibid., p. 22.

20 Quoted in Asadowski, *Rilke und Russland*, p. 24 (to Emil Faktor, 20 May 1899).

21 *Das Stundenbuch*, pp. 13, 21, 60.

22 Ibid., p. 20.

23 In E. M. Puknat and S. B. Puknat, 'American Literary Encounters with Rilke', *Monatshefte* 60/3 (fall 1968), p. 247, the poet Wallace Stevens seems to take this view.

24 This is the thesis of a magnificent study by Walter Rehm, *Griechentum under Goethezeit Geschichte eines Glaubens* (1936; Berne, 1952), many times reprinted.

25 Rilke's contemporary Hugo von Hofmannsthal also continued this line, while preferring the magical to the spiritual.

26 See also Mitchell, p. 135. Leishman, *Poems 1906–26*, p. 194, on this occasion is even better.

27 A professor of lyrical philosophy, says an admirer online.

28 *Das Stundenbuch*, pp. 16–17.

29 'Hier ist des Lebens stille Opferstelle'. See 'Here is life's quiet place of sacrifice', Snow+Winkler, p. 4.

30 *Das Stundenbuch*, p. 9.

31 'Die Hand' (1921); 'Handinneres' (1924). Leishman, *Poems 1906–26*, p. 328, and Mitchell, p. 181, both have this mystical late poem as 'Palm'. The latter translation is fine.

32 *Das Stundenbuch*, pp. 17, 29, 30.

33 Ibid., p. 16.

34 'The Last Judgment' (July 1899), in Snow, *Book of Images*, p. 121 ff.

35 *Das Stundenbuch*, p. 15.

36 Ibid., p. 57.

37 Ibid., p. 58.

38 Ibid., pp. 71. Compare Barrows+Macy, p. 79.

5. PARIS (1)

1 *Ein Jahrhundert französischer Malerei* [A century of French painting] (Berlin, 1901). Apart from commissioning Rilke, Muther's other achievement as a sponsor of the burgeoning German artistic scene was to publish Julius Meier-Graefe, soon to become Germany's foremost authority on contemporary French art.

2 Gatherings which could nevertheless leave him alienated. See 'Menschen bei Nacht' (November 1899).

3 *Briefwechsel*, p. 42 (26 February 1901) and pp. 521–2.

4 Ibid., p. 41.

5 The Barrows+Macy translation of *Das Stundenbuch* using this term is available at https://archive.org/details/rilkesbookofhouroorilk.

6 Quoted in Eric Torgersen, *Dear Friend: Rainer Maria Rilke and Paula Modersohn-Becker* (Evanston, IL, 2000), p. 139.

7 *Briefwechsel*, p. 46 ('Tuesday', end of June 1903).

8 Snell, Letter 4 (16 July 1903).

9 *Baudelaire*, vol. ii, *The Poems in Prose*, tr. Francis Scarfe (London, 1989), p. 53.

10   *Briefwechsel*, pp. 54–5.

11   See also Snow, *Book of Images*, p. 87.

12   Quoted in B. J. Morse, 'Contemporary English Poets and Rilke', *German Life and Letters*, new ser., 1/4 (1948), p. 274.

13   See the poem 'I am, you frightened one. Can't you hear me'. Mitchell has a translation, p. 7. See also *Poems: Rainer Maria Rilke*, tr. Jessie Lemont with an introduction by H.T. (New York, 1918), available at https://www.gutenberg.org/files/38594/38594-h/38594-h.htm#Thou_Anxious_One. Lemont's is a translation that benefits from a more natural opening line and the tight rhyming which holds so many of Rilke's shorter poems together and gives them their unique incantatory character. It loses in the present context an all-important reference to the city in the last line. Rilke has to escape it by becoming a star.

14   *Briefe*, vol. i, p. 207 (to Clara Rilke, 19 October 1907).

15   'Human Beings at Night', Snow, *Book of Images*, p. 61.

16   Babette Deutsch, 'Preface', in Rainer Maria Rilke, *Poems from the Book of Hours: 'Das Stundenbuch'*, tr. Babette Deutsch (1940; New York, 2016).

17   *Das Stundenbuch*, p. 86. See also Barrows+Macy, p. 142: 'For we are only the rind and the leaf.'

18   *Das Stundenbuch*, p. 85. See also Barrows+Macy, pp. 128–9.

19   Ibid., pp. 90, 98.

20   I pursue this theme among others in my book *Street Life and Morals: German Philosophy in Hitler's Lifetime* (London, 2021).

21   Snow, *Book of Images*, p. 258.

22   Morse, 'Contemporary English Poets and Rilke', n. 14.

23   Mitchell's selection is powerful, and to be recommended. Snow offers the whole cycle.

24   Erich Heller, 'Notes on Language and Its Deconstruction, on Translating and Stephen Mitchell's Translation of Rilke', *Poetry* 145/4 (January 1985), pp. 238–9.

25   Also on biographical grounds, for Rilke wrote it in Paris on 21 September 1902, at a time when his dependence on staying in great houses had not yet materialized.

26 'Winterliche Stanzen'. See Leishman, *Poems 1906–26*, p. 156, for a translation.

27 'Narzissmus als Doppelrichtung' [Narcissism as a dual-orientation], *Imago* 7/4 (1921), n. 5.

28 See also Leishman, *Poems 1906–26*, p. 145.

6. PARIS (2)

1 This sentiment can never be expressed in a German context without reference to Goethe's 'Talent nurtures itself in silent retreat, but character develops in the stream of life'.

2 Snell, Letter 4 (16 July 1903).

3 The opening sentiment of Rilke's essay on Rodin, as translated by Jessie Lemont and Hans Trausil. See Lemont+Trausil.

4 'The Panther' is the earliest of the *New Poems*, according to Leishman, *New Poems*, p. 89.

5 Lemont+Trausil, p. 39 (translation modified). Note that Lemont+Trausil contains only the 1903 essay, and not that of 1907, which was more critical. The 1907 text in German—*Auguste Rodin: Zweiter Teil: Ein Vortrag* (Auguste Rodin: part two: a lecture)—can be found in *SW*, vol. v, pp. 203–42, and is available at https://www.projekt-gutenberg.org/rilke/rodin2/rodin2.html. *SW*, vol. v, has the standard texts as of that 1955–66 edition of Rilke's work. Readers wishing to consult a critically annotated text in German should see Brigid Doherty, 'Rilke's Magic Lantern: Figural Language and the "Projection of Interior Action" in the Rodin Lecture', in Ewa Lajer-Burcharth, Beate Söntgen, eds, *Interiors and Interiority* (Berlin, 2015), p. 313, for a note on variants. Those differences need not concern us here.

6 *Briefe*, vol. i, pp. 32–3 (to Clara Rilke, 2 September 1902). Quotations from Rilke in the following passage, relating to the Meudon visit, are also from this letter.

7 Recollections of a private visit in September 2016.

8 Also in a reference to a photograph of Rodin taken around 1880: 'an image... which seems to reach back like a river god and to look forward like a prophet. It is not made by our times... it makes one think of those who built the great cathedrals'—from the 'Dinge' chapter of the 1907 lecture (*Auguste Rodin: Zweiter Teil: Ein Vortrag*), available at https://www.projekt-gutenberg.org/rilke/rodin2/rodin2.html. All translations from the 1907 lecture are my own. The image of the river god, which combines rampant male sexuality with artistic creativity, also occurs in the first essay, in English in Lemont+Trausil, p. 22, and recurs in Rilke's own Dionysian third Duino Elegy.

9 Lemont+Trausil, p. 22.

10 From the 'Dinge' chapter of the 1907 lecture (*Auguste Rodin: Zweiter Teil: Ein Vortrag*), available at https://www.projekt-gutenberg.org/rilke/rodin2/rodin2.html.

11 Leishman, *New Poems*, p. 77. See also Wolfgang Leppmann, *Rilke: A Life*, tr. Russell M. Stockman (New York, 1984), pp. 210–11.

12 In the United States the pioneer of this discipline would be the art critic and historian Meyer Schapiro (1904–96), who in 1927 was visiting the French Romanesque cathedrals with Rilke in his pocket. See Lesley Chamberlain, *A Shoe Story: Van Gogh, the Philosophers and the West* (Chelmsford, Essex, 2014).

13 *Briefe*, vol. i, pp. 119, 120 (to Clara Rilke, Thursday, 12.30 p.m., 25 January 1906, Chartres; early Friday, 26 January 1906, Meudon-Val-Fleury).

14 Ibid., vol. i, pp. 125–6 (to Karl von der Heydt, the Wednesday after Easter 1906, Meudon-Val-Fleury).

15 Ibid., vol. i, p. 171 (24 June 1907).

16 From the first part of Rilke's Rodin essay (my translation). See also Lemont+Trausil, p. 23.

17 Ibid., pp. 28, 27.

18 Ibid., p. 70.

19 Ibid., p. 45.

20 Ibid., p. 29.

21 Rilke writes of the swan becoming '*mündiger*', which, given the poet's fixation on '*Munde*' (mouths), I think requires a translation closer to the word's bodily derivation than Leishman's 'more mature'. *Mündig* means mature in the sense of having a vote, and a vote in German is a voice, *eine Stimme*.

22 'Memory', from Snow, *Book of Images*, p. 80.

23 Leishman, *Poems 1906–26* has a translation beginning 'Seek no more than what the Attic stela / and its gently-chiselled image know.' To convey both Rilke's literal words and his meaning is so difficult, although the themes that present themselves are simple and recur.

24 In the 1960s Michel Foucault's idea of 'epistemological breaks' radically challenged any surviving idea of a continuum. The idea was also espoused by the Marxist theorist Louis Althusser.

25 Snow, *Book of Images*, p. 121. See *Briefe*, vol. i, p. 36 (2 September 1902).

26 These of course were the two great scientific enterprises of the nineteenth century which, with Darwin, had changed the Western idea of the past.

27 Compare the opening of the fourth and the substance of the eighth letter to Kappus in Snell.

28 *Briefe*, vol. i, p. 209 (to Clara Rilke, 20 October, 1907).

29 Ibid., vol. i, p. 202 (to Clara Rilke, 17 October 1907).

30 The letters ran from February 1903 to November 1904, and a final exchange in 1908. See in English Snell. Eight of the ten letters are also in *Briefe*, vol. i.

31 *Briefe*, vol. i, pp. 49–50. Rilke's German is almost as elliptical here as in some of the poems. In Snell, Letter 4.

32 *Briefe*, vol. i, p. 76. In Snell, Letter 7.

33 *Briefe*, vol. i, p. 101 (12 August 1904, Borgeby Gård). Snell, Letter 8.

34 *Briefe*, vol i, p. 136 (3 May 1906). He was lodging in rue Cassette.

7. CASTLE-DWELLING AND HUMAN TIES

1 *Briefe*, vol. i, p. 341 (4 January 1912).

2 *Sonnets to Orpheus*, 2.16.

3 Ibid., 2.20.

4 *Briefe*, vol. i, pp. 373, 376 (1 March 1912). The three factors to be mourned were '*Gezwungenheit, Unaufrichtigkeit und Verlegenheit*'.

5 *Briefwechsel*, pp. 253–6. Leishman+Spender, p. 113.

6 *Zurückhaltung* (restraint) is the word Rilke uses in the letter to Lou, which is then echoed by *Vorsicht* (prudence, caution, foresight) in the first Elegy. Some 'caution of human gestures', says Mitchell in the second Elegy, followed by 'contain[ment]' and 'repose'. But discretion, which the Sackville-Wests choose, followed by 'restraint' and 'moderation' seem the subtler, more consistent choice—just like resolutions we might make for ourselves, to improve our relations with others.

7 Sackville-West.

8 'Studious as Rilke was of a difficult simplicity...'—Speirs, p. 5.

9 Here there is a section break in the original which Mitchell respects (p. 343) but Leishman and Spender overlook (see Leishman+Spender, p. 37). Rilke delivers the peroration as a plaint, *eine Plage*, but not a com-plaint, *eine Anklage*.

10 *Andrang*, leading to *Maßlosigkeit*. *Briefe*, vol. i, p. 343 (14 January 1912).

11 Ibid., p. 336 (10 January 1912).

12 Ibid., p. 342 (14 January 1912).

13 Ibid., p. 350 (24 January 1912).

14 Ibid., p. 343 (14 January 1912).

15 Ibid., p. 357 (7 February 1912).

16 The eighth Elegy is dated [Château] Muzot, 7–8 February 1922.

17 Leishman+Spender, pp. 134–5.

18 See also the separate poem 'Wendung', translated as 'Turning Point' in Hamburger and in Mitchell, p. 127. Snow, *Uncollected Poems* has 'Turning' (p. 91), and notes that Kassner was nominated 13 times for the Nobel Prize.

19 The full letter of 19 February 1912 is in *Briefwechsel*, p. 271.

20 'Ach wehe, meine Mutter reißt mich ein'. Translations in Hamburger (p. 65) and, better, Leishman, *Poems 1906–26* (p. 213): 'Alas my mother will demolish me!' For Rilke's relationship with his mother, see Heimo Schwilp, *Rilke und die Frauen: Biographie eines Liebenden* [Rilke and the women: the biography of a man in love] (Munich/ Berlin, 2015); also the two volumes of *Briefe an die Mutter* (Frankfurt am Main, 2009). This publication, edited within the Rilke family, has been criticized for sanitizing the relationship and presenting Rilke as a dutiful and affectionate son. See Ursula Krechel, 'Der treue Sohn', *Die Zeit* (14 January 2010), available at https://www.zeit.de/2010/03/L-B-Rilke-Briefe. Yet the text is sometimes revelatory, as my references suggest here. See also Chapter 4.

21 *Briefe*, vol. i, p. 363 (11 February 1912). The readers are Artur Hospelt and a girl Rilke writes to as 'N.N.'

22 See the notes in Leishman+Spender, pp. 107–8.

23 *Briefe*, vol. i, p. 344 (14 February 1912).

24 Mitchell: 'For there is no place where we can remain' is best. 'Staying is nowhere', in Leishman+Spender, copied by Speirs, is incomprehensible, while Sackville-West: 'Nothing, which is, is static' seems to depart for the wrong spiritual country. Interestingly, the same sentiment can be found in Lemont+Trausil, p. 38, in quite a different, though complementary spirit. Rodin found as he sculpted that 'nothing possessed rest, not even death', and this feeling for movement in all things was what made his style so distinctive compared with the ancient and the Renaissance.

25 Admittedly, had they not by mutual agreement destroyed the sexually charged letters they exchanged over their first four years, the imbalance would be less extreme, but it would still be great. See *Briefwechsel*, pp. 644–5, for the exact quantity of letters involved.

26 Pfeiffer notes instances of where Lou retrospectively crossed or scratched out words of love in the extant early letters, though she could hardly interfere with a poem.

27 For Mitchell's translation of these sections, see Mitchell, p. 97. Also Leishman, *Poems 1906–26*, p. 127. Both are to be recommended.

28 Leishman, *Poems 1906–26*, p. 59.

29 'Abend-Lied', ibid., p. 128. For his relations with both Clara and Ruth see Heimo Schwilp, *Rilke und die Frauen: Biographie eines Liebenden*

[Rilke and the women: the biography of a man in love] (Munich/Berlin, 2015).

30 Freedman, p. 263.

31 Rainer Maria Rilke, *Briefe an die Mutter*, 2 vols, ed. Hella Sieber-Rilke (Frankfurt am Main, 2009), vol. 2, pp. 445–6 (Locarno, the first day of Christmas (25 December), 1919).

32 *Washington Post* (31 March 1996).

33 Speirs, p. 4.

34 Nicole Krauss, 'Reading Rilke', *Boston Review* (summer 2000), available at http://bostonreview.net/archives/BR25.3/krauss.html.

35 Denis de Rougemont, *L'Amour et l'Occident* (Paris, 1939); tr. Montgomery Belgion as *Love in the Western World* (Princeton, NJ, 1940). De Rougemont had quoted Rilke in his previous book, *Penser avec les mains* [To think with one's hands] (Paris, 1936).

36 Suzanne Lilar, *Le Couple* (Paris, 1963), tr. Jonathan Griffin as *Aspects of Love in Western Society* (London, 1965) in several passages quoted Rilke.

37 See José Ortega y Gasset, *On Love: Aspects of a Single Theme* (1940); Erich Fromm, *The Art of Loving* (1956); C. S. Lewis, *The Four Loves* (1960).

38 'Everything beckons to us to perceive it', Leishman, *Poems 1906–26*, p. 193.

39 Freedman, p. 295.

40 James Elkins, *Pictures and Tears* (New York, 2004), p. 72.

41 Leishman, *Poems 1906–26*, p. 300. See also *Selected Poems*, tr. Susan Ranson and Marielle Sutherland (Oxford, 2011), p. 248: 'Masks! Bring Masks! For we must shade his gaze.' Available at https://duino-elegies.tumblr.com/post/121740734383/masks-bring-masks-for-we-must-shade-his-gaze.

42 The problem of this exceptionalism, qua moral philosophy, was used by the philosopher Bernard Williams to generate the concept of moral luck, i.e. if the art succeeded (as it did in the case of Gauguin, and in our case with Rilke) then twentieth-century Western society was inclined to take a more lenient view. I'm afraid times have moved on from his particular kind of social liberalism.

43 I take the title from http://rainer-maria-rilke.de/070079requiem. html and *SW*, vol. i. Variations in the precise title derive from its appearing separately in the book *Requiem* (Leipzig, 1909), where it appears in the full title as *Requiem. Für eine Freundin. Für Wolf Graf von Kalckreuth. Für einen Knaben.* Mitchell (p. 78 ff.) calls it 'Requiem for a Friend'. The text is abbreviated. His version of the full text can be found in *Paris Review* 82 (winter 1981), available at https://www.theparisreview.org/poetry/3205/requiem-for-a-friend-rainer-maria-rilke. A. S. Kline's 'Requiem for a Friend (Paula Modersohn Becker 1896–1907)' is available at https://www.poetryintranslation.com/PITBR/German/MoreRilke.php#anchor_Toc527606968.

44 Freedman, p. 289.

45 Erich Heller, *The Artist's Journey into the Interior, and Other Essays* (London, 1965).

46 'Requiem for a Friend', tr. Stephen Mitchell, *Paris Review* 82 (winter 1981).

47 Hugh MacDiarmid, 'To Circumjack Cencrastus or the Curly Snake', in *The Complete Poems of Hugh MacDiarmid*, ed. Michael Grieve and William R. Aitken (London, 1978), vol. i, pp. 197–203. Thanks to Andrew McNeillie for drawing my attention to these lines.

8. THREE ADVENTURES IN ART

1 And still hymned the mirror in his last work. See *Sonnets to Orpheus* 2.3.

2 Ibid.

3 *Briefe*, vol. i, p. 263 (19 August 1909).

4 In a poem of autumn 1900, Rilke was looking through the book *For You* (1899), written and illustrated by his friend, the artist Heinrich Vogeler. 'My feelings... started up through the May blossom / and became now great now small / in the space the rhyme allowed'— Rainer Maria Rilke, *In und nach Worpswede Gedichte* (Frankfurt am Main, 2000), p. 48 ('Meine Hände gingen voran').

5 Snow+Winkler, p. 27.

6 Ibid., p. 37.

7 *Das Florenzer Tagebuch* (Frankfurt am Main, 1994), p. 70.

8 'The Last Judgment', in Snow, *Book of Images*, p. 127.

9 *Das Florenzer Tagebuch*, p. 68: 'That's what it comes down to in the end: to see everything in life as of equal value to everything else; the mystical, and dead, included. No one thing should tower over another, everything should be as a neighbour and domesticate everything else. For everything has its meaning, and, what is the main thing, their sum is a harmonious whole full of harmony and certainty; everything in balance.' See also Snow+Winkler, p. 46. The passage follows immediately upon an anecdote about an old family dachshund being killed by a kick from a horse. It suggests that treating everything equally will also be responsible for some of Rilke's comic effects.

10 'The Cathedral' (1906), Leishman, *New Poems*, p. 77 (translation slightly amended). See also in *Worpswede* where Rilke says poetry can best speak of the human soul through landscape and must despair of being able to speak if it is plunged with Goya 'into boundless empty spaces'. *SW*, vol. v, pp. 20–1.

11 Snow+Winkler, p. 18. The medieval pilgrimage ('Ein Pilgermorgen') in the second book of *Das Stundenbuch*, p. 74 ff. (translated in Kidder, p. 148 ff.), was another spectacular example. For this interweaving of decorative and religious themes, nourished by looking at many paintings and beautiful objects, and by fashion, see further Judith Ryan, *Rilke, Modernism and Poetic Tradition* (Cambridge, 1999), pp. 13–15. It is the story of the making of Rilke's visual imagination.

12 George C. Schoolfield, *Young Rilke and His Time* (Rochester, NY, 2009), p. 103.

13 'The Florence Diary', Snow+Winkler, p. 8 (translation slightly amended).

14 Ibid., p. 4. The poem is dated 15 April 1898.

15 See Twombly's *Ferragosto* series (Rome, August 1961).

16 *Das Florenzer Tagebuch*, pp. 14, 30. Snow+Winkler, pp. 7, 19. The sense in the latter passage of 'what he has liberated' is given in the

preceding paragraph, where he writes of experiences that increase the clarity of his life. It might be thought of as a psychical but not Freudian searching to bring significant moments of experience to the surface of consciousness.

17 Compare 'The Boy' in Snow, *Book of Images*, p. 47.

18 Rilke mentions the influence of Beardsley on Vogeler in his 1903 *Worpswede* monograph (*SW*, vol. v). Astonishingly, this introduction to north-German art and five essays on contemporary artists has never been wholly translated into English, though Edward Neather, 'Rainer Maria Rilke: Concerning Landscape Painting', *Art in Translation* 3/1 (2011), pp. 9–25, offers an extract. The German is available at https://archive. org/details/worpswedefritzmaoorilkuoft?ref=ol&view=theater.

19 I'm mindful of Alexandra Harris's admirable *Romantic Moderns: English Writers, Artists and the Imagination* (London, 2010) as I place Rilke and Vogeler in a context I hope is immediately intelligible to English readers. They are modern, but not quite modernist, in a way that most of Britain remained for more than half a century.

20 Karl E. Webb, 'Rainer Maria Rilke and the Art of *Jugendstil*', *Centennial Review* 16/2 (1972), p. 131. For a fuller treatment see the same author's *Rainer Maria Rilke und Jugendstil* (Chapel Hill, NC, 1978).

21 The painter, typographer, graphic artist and poet Emil Rudolf Weiss (1875–1942) did the illustrations for Rainer Maria Rilke, *Geschichten vom lieben Gott* [Stories about the Dear Lord] (Frankfurt am Main, 1900). In fact only the second edition bore the subsequently definitive title. It was originally entitled 'About the Dear Lord and Other Things as Told to Adults for Children by Rainer Maria Rilke'.

22 *Sonnets to Orpheus* 1.22.

23 Ibid., 2.29.

24 The difference was Behrens and Vogeler changed their art radically. Behrens became a modernist architect, while Vogeler, after a period as an expressionist, was so stricken by experience of combat that he imagined a new humanity and left Germany for Soviet Russia to help as he could. He died in a labour camp. See Lesley Chamberlain, 'A German William Morris', *Twenty Minutes*, BBC Radio 3 (5 October

2012), available at https://www.bbc.co.uk/sounds/play/b01n3h7x
and at lesleychamberlain.wordpress.com. See also Lesley Chamberlain,
'From Art as Life to Blood and Soil', *Standpoint* (29 May 2012), available
at https://standpointmag.co.uk/dispatches-june-12-from-art-as-life-
to-blood-and-soil-lesley-chamberlain/.

25 'The Florence Diary', of all documents, is shot through with
references to equality and justice and the red flag.

26 Quoted in Linda Koreska-Hartmann, *Jugendstil—Stil der Jugend*
[Jugendstil—the style of youth] (Munich, 1969), p. 88.

27 Hannsludwig Geiger, *Es war um die Jahrhundertwende* [It happened
round the turn of the century] (Munich, 1953), p. 14, quoted in Linda
Koreska-Hartmann, *Jugendstil—Stil der Jugend* [Jugendstil—the style
of youth] (Munich, 1969), p. 19.

28 Schoolfield, *Young Rilke and His Time*, p. 103.

29 Pamela Kort, 'Arnold Böcklin, Max Ernst und die Debatten um
Ursprünge und Überleben in Deutschland und Frankreich' [Arnold
Böcklin, Max Ernst and the debates over origins and survival in Germany
and France], in Pamela Kort and Max Hollein, eds, *Darwin: Kunst und
die Suche nach den Ursprüngen* (Frankfurt am Main, 2009), pp. 24–91.
Rilke refers to this painting in *Worpswede*.

30 *Worpswede*, SW, vol. v, p. 16.

31 Ibid., p. 48.

32 Schoolfield, *Young Rilke and His Time*, p. 103.

33 See also Snow, *Uncollected Poems*, pp. 8, 255.

34 Lesley Chamberlain, *Motherland: A Philosophical History of Russia*
(London, 2004), pp. 263–7, reflects upon Rilke's encounter with Russia.

35 'Abend in Skåne'. See also Snow, *Book of Images*, p. 97.

36 'Abend', Snow, *Book of Images*, p. 99.

37 Lesley Chamberlain, *A Shoe Story: Van Gogh, the Philosophers and
the West* (Chelmsford, 2014).

38 Rilke's letters on Cézanne (*Briefe über Cézanne*), often regarded
as a separate work, can be found in several editions.

9. THE HOUSE THAT RILKE BUILT

1   Phia Rilke came from a wealthy family. Her father was managing director of the Bohemia Savings Bank and owned a chemical factory. She and her siblings grew up in a large baroque villa, in the central Prague street known today as Panská. In Austrian times the family address was Herrengasse 8. See *Phia Rilke: Gedanken für den Tag*, ed. Hella Sieber-Rilke (Frankfurt am Main, 2002), p. 65.

2   One was the Bohemian aristocrat Sidonie von Nádherná, her estate near Prague severely hit by land taxes under Czechoslovakia's first government. See Lesley Chamberlain, 'Letter from Janovice', *TLS* (30 July 1999).

3   *Malte Laurids Brigge*, p. 175.

4   Ibid. p. 197.

5   See James 4:14—that man is like a vapour that disperses.

6   The word *heimlich* means both 'secret' and 'homely'.

7   See 'A Nun's Lament', discussed in Chapter 10.

8   My free translation of 'Die Liebende' ('A Girl in Love') (1908).

9   '[D]ie Landschaft, wie ein Vers im Psalter / ist Ernst und Wucht und Ewigkeit', from 'Der Schauende' ('The Boy Who Watches') (1901).

10   Ibid.

11   *Malte Laurids Brigge*, pp. 43–6; *SW*, vol. vi.

12   My translation, combined with two lines from Sackville-West.

13   *Malte Laurids Brigge*, pp. 29–30.

14   *Das Stundenbuch*, p. 7.

15   Second Elegy.

16   The translation here is by Michael Hamburger, a surprisingly disappointing translator of Rilke.

17   See the section headed 'Der Beobachter' [the Observer], in Jakob von Uexküll, *Umwelt und Innenwelt der Tiere* (2nd edn, Berlin, 1921), pp. 215–19.

18   John Berger, *Why Look at Animals* (1980; London, 2009), pp. 13–14.

19   *Das Stundenbuch*, p. 63.

20 Not, alas, in all translations. 'Restrain him' is in my view far too harsh.

21 Ruth Speirs has a fine translation of all this—Speirs, p. 76.

22 *Das Stundenbuch*, p. 91.

23 Thanks to the composer David Matthews for providing a precise reference for this affinity which struck me.

24 Tenth Duino Elegy, ll. 8–91, tr. Edward Sackville-West.

25 The fragments became known as the 'Antistrophen'. See Leishman, *Poems 1906–26*, pp. 270–1.

26 *Briefwechsel*, p. 385 (9 March 1915).

27 Freedman, pp. 393–5.

28 *Briefwechsel*, p. 381 (last day of January 1915).

29 In May 1915 he escaped military call-up. But a revised decision later led to a painful month of training, illness and finally service in the wartime press office in Vienna, where in April 1916 Lou Andreas-Salomé noted him at work from eight to three—*Briefwechsel*, p. 391. M. Allen Cunningham dramatized the moment in his novel *Lost Son* (2007). While Rilke's colleagues were simply in awe of him, his professional inner life became suspended.

30 *Briefe*, vol. ii, p. 542 (note to letter 231).

31 His Munich doctor, Stauffenberg, had told him Frau König already owned several Picassos—*Briefwechsel*, p. 368 (9 September 1914).

32 His patron departed, he moved in on 14 June, and stayed until the end of October.

33 There is also an essay by Rilke, unpublished, 'Les saltimbanques'.

34 Luigi Pirandello's play of 1921 is itself one of the key works of modernism, like Rilke's *Duino Elegies* published a year later.

35 *Malte Laurids Brigge*, p. 118.

36 They fall away like the petals of a rose around its pistil. The extended metaphor is so complicated, involving Rilke's minding about the boredom and fake smiles of both onlookers and performers, that I can only defer to Leishman for his patient explanation. See Leishman+Spender, p. 126.

37 *Pflaster* could be a sticking plaster or a paving stone. As the first it's a modern convenience, like the street lamps and post offices and the man in his kitchen that jar so when Rilke smuggles them into his existential wanderings. It's a kind of humour, and a comment on the disjunctiveness of the modern world.

10. THE LAST INWARD MAN

1   *Briefwechsel*, pp. 397–8 (13 January 1919).

2   Ibid., p. 449 ff. (10 September 1921).

3   Ibid., p. 408 (7 February 1919).

4   Ibid., pp. 445–72 (5 January 1921–24 February 1922).

5   Ibid., p. 439 (end of December 1920). In my translation I've amplified certain points for clarity.

6   Ibid., p. 504 (12 December 1925).

7   Quoted in Peter Ackroyd, *T. S. Eliot* (London, 1984), p. 161.

8   *Briefwechsel*, pp. 498–50 (On the Last Day of October 1925). The first ellipsis refers to words excluded by the editor (see his commentary, p. 651).

9   Which I infer from his advice in *Letters to a Young Poet* to avoid such an attitude.

10   *Briefe*, vol. i, pp. 364–5 (to Norbert von Hellingrath, 13 February 1912).

11   *Malte Laurids Brigge*, p. 141.

12   Jean Rodolphe de Salis, *Rainer Maria Rilke: The Years in Switzerland* (Berkeley, CA, 1964), p. 55; Freedman, pp. 442–4.

13   The poem is a typical translator's challenge, because it's impossible to capture Rilke's tight rhyme scheme along with his sonorous, incantatory repetitions, his elliptical syntax, the challenge of the German present tense and the familiar '*Du*' form of address in the original opening line. This last topic is explored in William Waters, 'Answerable Aesthetics: Reading "You" in Rilke', *Comparative Literature* 48/2 (1996), pp. 128–49.

14   Harold Bloom, *The Western Canon* (San Diego, 1994), p. 555. It's surely a fault of this impressive but too American work that Rilke gets

no mention of his own in the text, only a minute part in the story of Emily Dickinson and inclusion in a list of suitable reading for 'The Chaotic Age'.

15 See B. J. Morse, 'Contemporary English Poets and Rilke', *German Life and Letters*, new ser., 1/4 (1948), p. 282, and Karen Leeder, 'Rilke's Legacy in the English-Speaking World', in Karen Leeder and Robert Vilain, eds, *The Cambridge Companion to Rilke* (Cambridge, 2010). Keyes did, in fact, lose his life in combat.

16 Matthew 10:39.

17 Michael Bell, *F. R. Leavis (Critics of the Twentieth Century)* (London, 1988), p. 18.

18 Philippians 4:8.

19 1 Corinthians.

20 *Malte Laurids Brigge*, p. 49.

21 Ibid., p. 70. This is the translation by Barton Pike; see Rainer Maria Rilke, *The Notebooks of Malte Laurids Brigge*, tr. Barton Pike (London, 2008), p. 55.

22 Momme Brodersen, *Walter Benjamin: A Biography*, tr. Malcolm R. Green and Ingrida Ligers, ed. Martina Derviş (London, 1996), pp. 83, 219. In 1913 Benjamin declared himself a great admirer of Rilke, whom he briefly met, and it was only more than twenty years later that in correspondence with Adorno he retreated into finding him old-fashioned.

23 Hannah Arendt, 'Introduction', in Walter Benjamin, *Illuminations*, tr. Harry Zohn (London, 1970), p. 41.

24 See also Leishman, *Poems 1906–26*, p. 108.

25 Hamburger, p. 9. The uncollected poems 'now seem no more private, slight or occasional than a good deal of the work he did choose to collect' (p. 10). Michael Hanke, reviewing Hamburger with discomfort in *PN Review* 28 9/2 (1982), took Hamburger to be saying the opposite.

26 Leishman, *Poems 1906–26*, p. 2.

27 *Das Stundenbuch*, p. 15. I offer the reader two translations of this poem. For the earlier one see Chapter 4.

28 Judith Ryan, *Rilke, Modernism and Poetic Tradition* (Cambridge, 1999), pp. 11–121; Mitchell, pp. 549–75.

29 *Seltsam*, the word Rilke repeatedly uses for 'strange' here, points to disorientation. It is a relative of *unheimlich*, 'not like home', and which usually gets translated as 'uncanny'.

30 Gass, pp. 191–2.

31 Snow, *Uncollected Poems*, p. 81.

32 T. S. Eliot, 'Goethe as the Sage' [1955], in T. S. Eliot, *On Poetry and Poets* (London, 1957), p. 225.

33 Eliot felt abstraction threatened poetry; his poetry and English poetry in general, unless it could be written with the panache of the seventeenth-century metaphysical poets. See T.S. Eliot, 'The Metaphysical Poets', in *Selected Prose of T. S. Eliot*, ed. Frank Kermode (New York, 1975), p. 64.

34 Eliot, *On Poetry and Poets*, pp. 24–5.

35 Bertolt Brecht, *Arbeitsjournal 1938–1955* (Berlin, 1977), p. 191. See also Michael Hofmann, 'Singing about the Dark Times: The Poetry of Bertolt Brecht', *The Liberal* 9 (2007), available at http://www.theliberal.co.uk/issue_9/poetry/hofmann_9.html: 'Other German poets of the times—Rilke, George, Benn—were anathema: [Brecht] hated the hallowedness of poetry, its claim to other-worldliness and spirituality, its immateriality, its complacent separateness.'

36 *Theodor W. Adorno and Walter Benjamin: Briefwechsel 1928–1940*, ed. Jean Howard, Alan Sinfield and Lindsay Smith (Frankfurt am Main, 1994), p. 172.

37 W. H. Auden, 'Rilke in English', *The New Republic* (6 September 1939), available at https://newrepublic.com/article/102274/rilke-in-english.

38 Ibid., n. 37.

39 Ibid.

40 W. H. Auden, 'New Year Letter' [1 January 1940], in W. H. Auden, *Collected Longer Poems* (London, 1974), p. 85.

41 Seamus Perry, 'An Introduction to "Stop All the Clocks"', British Library [website] (2016), available at https://www.bl.uk/20th-century-literature/articles/an-introduction-to-stop-all-the-clocks.

42 Jean-Paul Sartre, *Nausea*, tr. Robert Baldick (Harmondsworth, 1963; repr., London, 2000), p. 189.

43 Ibid., p. 190.

44 Ibid., p. 191.

45 Ibid., p. 223.

46 Jean-Paul Sartre, *Words: Reminiscences of a Precocious Childhood Spent within the Confines of French Provincialism before the First World War*, tr. Irene Clephane (Harmondsworth, 1967), p. 69.

47 Bernard-Henri Lévy, *Sartre: The Philosopher of the Twentieth Century*, tr. Andrew Brown (Cambridge, 2003), pp. 72–3. Lévy doesn't mention Rilke by name in his massive, diffuse, brilliant and impossible 500-page meditation on the master, but the context for his overcoming Rilke is clear. See for example Janet Lungstrum, 'Deflecting from the Imaginary: Existential Creativity in Rilke's *Aufzeichnungen des Malte Laurids Brigge* and Sartre's *La Nausée*', *Comparatist* 15 (May 1991), pp. 41–63. Lévy also only mentions 'God' once, but that is a travesty of the childhood struggles described by Sartre in his autobiography.

48 Lévy, *Sartre*, pp. 72–3. For a stimulating commentary on this moment in European literature, which demands a getting beyond of the inside / outside metaphor of language and meaning, see Paul de Man, *Allegories of Reading: Figural Language in Rousseau, Nietzsche, Rilke, and Proust* (New Haven, CT, 1982), esp. pp. 48–51 on Rilke.

49 Lévy, *Sartre*, p. 98, sees the 'diversionary' trick as trickery, betrayal, robbery, even an act of war, against the many writers, philosophers and poets Sartre worked through to create himself.

50 Sackville-West.

51 Lesley Chamberlain, 'Through a Cocktail Glass Darkly', *Modern Drama* 31 / 4 (December 1988), pp. 512–19.

52 Martin Seymour-Smith, *A Guide to World Literature* (3rd edn, London, 1985), p. 559.

53 She learnt of it through her friendship with the art critic E. H. Ramsden, to whom this paraphrase of a reference to the *Duino Elegies* belongs. See Rachel Smith, 'Figure and Landscape: Barbara

Hepworth's Phenomenology of Perception', *Tate Papers* 20 (autumn 2013), available at https://www.tate.org.uk/research/publications/tate-papers/20/figure-and-landscape-barbara-hepworths-phenomenology-of-perception.

54 Paul Celan, *Selected Poems*, tr. Michael Hamburger and Christopher Middleton, with an introduction by Michael Hamburger (Harmondsworth, 1972), p. 18; *Poems of Paul Celan*, tr. Michael Hamburger (London 1988), p. 24. Rilke and Celan used German to form compound words in a similar way. '*Atemwende*' and '*Sprachgitter*' would be examples from Celan.

55 These are my fresh translations of Celan's titles, to convey their Rilkean content to the reader.

56 *Briefwechsel*, p. 72 (25 July 1903).

57 Hugh MacDiarmid, *Selected Poetry*, ed. A. Riach and M. Grieve (Manchester, 2004), also available at http://www.writingthenorth.com/wp-content/uploads/2013/09/on-a-raised-beach1.pdf.

58 Neil Corcoran, *Poetry and Responsibility* (Oxford, 2014), p. 51. The words 'our mad [twentieth] century...' are Herbert's. See also pp. 137–8 for *Duino Elegies*.

59 Edmund Jephcott, *Proust and Rilke: The Literature of Expanded Consciousness* (London, 1972), p. 21.